JESUS: THE
EVIDENCE

JESUS: THE EVIDENCE

THE LATEST RESEARCH AND
DISCOVERIES INVESTIGATED BY

IAN WILSON

Weidenfeld & Nicolson
London

Weidenfeld & Nicolson Ltd
The Orion Publishing Group
Orion House 5 Upper St Martin's Lane
London WC2H 9EA

ISBN 0 297 83529 7

A catalogue record for this book is available
from the British Library

Book design by The Design Revolution
Printed in Italy

CONTENTS

AUTHOR'S PREFACE *6*

INTRODUCTION *8*

1 GETTING BACK TO BASICS *10*

2 HOW MUCH CAN THE
GOSPELS BE TRUSTED? *24*

3 CAN WE BE SURE OF ANYTHING ABOUT
JESUS' BIRTH? *40*

4 WHAT OF JESUS' UPBRINGING? *50*

5 HOW DID HE ACQUIRE
HIS SENSE OF MISSION? *64*

6 FISHER OF MEN AND WOMEN *76*

7 MAN OF MAGIC *90*

8 THE ROAD TO JERUSALEM *102*

9 THE ROAD TO THE CROSS *118*

10 DID JESUS REALLY RISE FROM
THE DEAD? *136*

11 A FAITH IS BORN *154*

12 THE REAL JESUS *170*

NOTES AND REFERENCES *180*

BIBLIOGRAPHY *196*

INDEX *202*

AUTHOR'S PREFACE

When the first edition of this book was written back in 1984, it was as an accompaniment to London Weekend Television's subsequently notorious three-part television series of the same name. In the course of my working together with the series' makers it became apparent that they had some quite different ideas from my own regarding what constituted a properly objective approach to the historical Jesus. Although we agreed to differ in a variety of ways, even so it was necessary for me partly at least to incorporate elements which they regarded as necessary and topical, but which I would have preferred to omit.

Happily the book has remained continuously in print, and it has been a particular delight to be asked by Michael Dover of Weidenfeld to write a major update of its text, now free of any of the constraints of the former television partnership. One of the benefits of this update, besides the release from such fetters, has been the chance to incorporate the considerable number of discoveries relating to Jesus that there have been since 1984, such as the discovery of a fishing boat of his time; of the bones of the high priest Caiaphas; and of what may be the oldest known fragments of a gospel text. Another of the benefits has been to give the book a whole new look with totally fresh, high-quality photographs specially chosen to bring life, and equally importantly colour, to the world in which Jesus moved.

For much of this fresh material, both textual and visual, I am indebted to an invaluable re-visit to Israel with my wife in 1994, and to one very special publication, *Biblical Archaeology Review* of Washington DC. It was BAR's founding editor, Hershel Shanks, who campaigned relentlessly and ultimately successfully for the recent opening up of the Dead Dea Scrolls to general scholarship. In his superbly illustrated journal, which appears six times a year, Shanks manages that rare feat of providing authoritative up-to-the-minute articles in which both Jews and Christians can find common interest, and his publication deserves much greater acceptance by the world's university libraries than it currently receives. Many of the fine photographs and reconstructions included in this new edition are ones that I first came across in the pages of *Biblical Archaeology Review*, and I am particularly grateful to BAR for introducing them to me.

Overall, this new edition has been designed as a careful meld of both the old and the new, with the joins made as invisibly as possible. As in the first edition, I have almost invariably used the Jerusalem Bible translation of the Old and New Testaments for its clear, modern English. While much of the old framework has been retained, the original book's chapter on the time of Constantine the Great is one that has been dropped on the grounds that it unnecessarily highlighted the divisions between Christians, when the emphasis should be on what they have in common. In several other ways my pro-Christian bias may be rather more to the fore in this than in the earlier edition, but wherever possible I have tried to maintain historical objectivity – even if some purists may frown at my continued usage of the traditional 'BC' and 'AD' rather than the now more politically correct 'BCE' and 'CE'.

For coping admirably with an author now living ten thousand miles distant from them in Australia, my warmest congratulations and thanks to Anthony Cheetham, Michael Dover, Clare Currie and Ariane Bankes of Weidenfeld/Orion of London, together with picture researcher Joanne King, designer Mark Roberts and proofreader Antony Wood. Also, as ever, my thanks go to my wife, Judith, who was by my side throughout our 1994 tour of the land of Jesus, and who, amidst all the chores of moving continents, single-handedly scanned the original *Jesus: The Evidence* text onto my word-processor, saving me much unnecessary re-typing.

Ian Wilson,
Bellbowrie,
Queensland,
November 1995

INTRODUCTION

Short of some unforeseen catastrophe, the great majority of the umpteen million people alive today will live to experience the year 2000 AD, theoretically the two-thousandth birthday of a Galilean Jew named Jesus of Nazareth. For many of those millions, many who even without thinking about it count their years from his birthday, Jesus is a figure of supreme irrelevance. A mere name to use for abuse. Just some Jew who died two millennia ago and who has absolutely no place in today's scientific, material-minded world. For others, however, Jesus is someone very special, a seemingly flesh-and-blood man whose life was preordained and whose death, the most public and degrading imaginable, demonstrated that death is *not* the end.

The issues could therefore not be more clearcut. Have those who believed that Jesus was special wasted the last two thousand years on worthless make-believe? Have they been victims of the biggest hoax in history? Or could those who have consistently chosen to ignore Jesus and his message be the ultimate, very long-term losers?

At the heart of these questions are what should *anyone*, of whatever background, religious or non-religious, believe about Jesus? That he was born of a virgin? That his birthday was on 25 December, 0 AD? That he could heal the sick and walk on water? That he married Mary Magdalen? That he died on a cross, and then resuscitated two days later? That he wanted his followers to dress up in funny clothes and call themselves popes and cardinals, archbishops and bishops, priests and nuns? That he is the second person of a divine Trinity?

The need for straight answers to these questions, reverent and irreverent, has become all the more necessary in recent years with the decline of formal Christian religious instruction in schools, as a result of which a generation is growing up, certainly in the UK, who have never been taught what my own preceding generation learned as basics.

Accordingly, the object of this book is to weed out all that is unworthy, of which there has been a great deal in recent years, and to look at what may be considered truly valid of the human Jesus of Nazareth as deducible from every possible source: the oldest surviving scraps of the gospels; extracts from early historical documents; comments from early opponents of Christianity; the most recent Israeli archaeological finds; the latest insights of theologians; and much more.

Fascinatingly, even in the decade since the first edition of this book was published some significant new discoveries have been made, particularly on the part of Israeli archaeologists, belonging as they do to a people who for twenty centuries have so firmly rejected Jesus. Although this author would be failing the reader if he did not make clear that he has been a practising Christian for more than two decades, and can therefore hardly avoid some bias, he is also a trained historian, and there will be absolutely no attempt to fudge the issues where doctrine and a fair-minded approach to the evidence part company.

For, as even the most hardened sceptic must be bound to admit, the still obscure Galilean Jew who forms the subject of this book, who died a seeming failure, executed as a criminal and abandoned by his followers, is probably the most influential individual there has ever been in all history. And this is not least of the reasons why whatever is written about him should be honest and true to the best of each individual writer's ability, whether that writer is the author of an original gospel, or anyone approaching him afresh at the present time.

1
GETTING BACK TO THE BASICS

I n an ideal world we would obviously want to examine the original manuscripts of the gospels as first written by Matthew, Mark, Luke and John. We might want those authors to have signed and dated them. We might even feel that they should have been accompanied by some sort of curriculum vitae setting out how well each author knew Jesus and/or his disciples. All this should be some form of assurance for us that what they related about Jesus was based on hard fact.

Now, given that there has come down to us no original manuscript even of a single one of William Shakespeare's thirty-seven plays – despite the fact that they were mostly written less than four hundred years ago – it might seem even more unlikely that there should survive the originals of four gospels written about Jesus after a span of two thousand years. Yet in some ways Jesus is better documented than Shakespeare. And as few realize, much of the oldest documentation about him has only come to light within the last century, and is continuing to do so.

The urge to find such early documentation is nothing new. When at the beginning of the sixteenth century the great Dutch scholar Erasmus compiled the first-ever printed edition of the New Testament in its original Greek, he was well aware that the biblical manuscripts he was using derived

Opposite *St Catherine's Monastery, Sinai, seen from the north-east, set at the base of the Jebel Musa, the mountain on which Moses reputedly received the Ten Commandments. Because of its remoteness, St Catherine's has never been pillaged throughout fourteen centuries. As a result, some of its earliest manuscripts have survived to modern times, among these the famous Codex Sinaiticus discovered by the German scholar Constantin Tischendorf in 1844. Reaching this monastery once required an arduous journey by camel, but now there is a proper road, and it has been opened to regular tourism.*

from successions of copyists over many centuries. Inevitably errors and mis-readings had crept in, discrepancies that logically had to be less the further back in time the manuscript had originated.

Erasmus therefore did his best to use only the earliest available manu-scripts, but as a pioneer he had little to guide him on how to date such material. Only after his time did it become realized that the minuscule, or upper and lower case Greek lettering of the manuscripts he had mostly consulted meant that they could not have been written before the ninth century AD. Before then handwriting was in uncials, that is all in capitals, or upper case Greek letters only.

As this became recognized, so better-informed travellers began to look for manuscripts with such writing, particularly when visiting remote monasteries where there was the chance that such documents might have lain undisturbed over the centuries. The ignorance and lack of historical concern of many of those in charge of such treasures quickly became apparent. In 1677, after visiting Mount Athos in Greece, British Ambassador Dr John Covel reported seeing there 'vast heaps … all covered with dust and dirt, many of them rotted and spoiled'. In the 1830s, also at Athos, British aristocrat Robert Curzon came across a page in uncial hand-writing lying discarded in an obviously neglected room, and asked if he might take it. When the abbot, momentarily suspicious that the page might be valuable, asked Curzon the reason for his request, he quick-wittedly concocted the excuse: 'My servant suggested that it might be useful to cover some jampots or vases or preserves which I have at home'. His suspicions allayed, the abbot not only handed the page over, but also generously cut off an inch-think wad of some other early manuscript pages as a gift to his honoured guest.

However it was to be a German specialist in ancient languages, Constantin Tischendorf, a contemporary of Curzon's, who would pioneer an altogether more professional approach to seeking out the very earliest documents attesting to Jesus. As had already become recognized in Tischendorf's time, mediaeval scribes had sometimes re-used the expensive vellum on which ancient manuscripts had been written. They would scrape away the ink of the original writing, then copy some other text on top of this – creating what manuscript specialists call a palimpsest. Sometimes the earlier writing could still be read, but a fifth-century uncial scriptural text beneath one such palimpsest, the *Codex Ephraemi* in Paris, had long been thought irretrievable until the arrival of Tischendorf. He managed the task in two years, using such methods as holding the pages up to the light. In order to familiarize himself further with materials written in uncials, he also travelled to Rome in the hope of examining there the Vatican's *Codex Vaticanus*, dating back to the fourth century. However, although Pope Gregory XVI received him kindly, the cardinal directly in charge of the manuscript was less forthcoming, denying him access for any longer than six hours.

Undaunted, in 1844 Tischendorf set off on what would be his most famous quest: to the monastery of St Catherine in the scorching wilderness of the Sinai Desert. There he hoped that he might find as yet unknown New Testament manuscripts that had been protected from the outside world by the monastery's remoteness. Dating from the sixth century, St Catherine's is spectacularly set at the foot of the granite cliffs on which Moses reputedly received the Ten Commandments, and while today the tourist can arrive there in the comfort of an air-conditioned coach, Tischendorf's only option was a gruelling twelve-day trek by camel.

Furthermore, even when he and his party arrived at the monastery's four-storey-high walls, which seemed to have no gate, their shouts were at first met only by a stony silence, as if the monastery had been abandoned. Then from some internal hoist a rope basket was lowered for Tischendorf's letters of introduction. This was whirled aloft, to be followed, after an unnerving delay obviously for the scrutinizing of the credentials, by the lowering of a second basket for Tischendorf himself. Bumped unceremoniously upwards and over the walls (later he would learn that there was a secret door for true VIPs), he found himself in a world that time seemed to have abandoned long before.

In fact the black-robed Orthodox monks of St Catherine's received their German visitor with characteristic warmth and hospitality, and in the course of the ensuing days they allowed him unrestricted access to their three libraries. Initially he found these somewhat disappointing, suggesting his long journeying might have been for nothing. But then, in his own words:

> I perceived in the middle of the great hall a large and wide basket full of old parchments; and the librarian, who was a man of information, told me that two heaps of papers like these, mouldered by time, had already been committed to the flames. What was my surprise to find amid this heap of papers a considerable number of sheets of a copy of the Old Testament in Greek, which seemed to me to be one of the most ancient that I had ever seen. The authorities of the monastery allowed me to possess myself of a third of these parchments, or about forty-three sheets, all the more readily as they were destined for the fire. But I could not get them to yield up possession of the remainder. The too lively satisfaction I displayed aroused their suspicions as to the value of this manuscript.

Directly as a result of Tischendorf insufficiently concealing his interest in the material, the monks denied the very existence of the parchments on his next visit to St Catherine's, and it was to take another fifteen years, and only then with the leverage of credentials provided by Tsar Alexander II of Russia, before he was allowed to visit the monastery again. This time the monks received him with renewed warmth, their steward even inviting the visitor to his cell to enjoy a glass of home-brewed date liqueur. And it was on this particular occasion that, with the words 'And I too have read a Septuagint' (a Greek translation of the Old Testament), the steward suddenly took down a cloth-wrapped bundle from a shelf, and laid it before Tischendorf. As Tischendorf subsequently related, upon the cloth's removal, he instantly recognized:

> … not only those very leaves which, fifteen years before, I had taken out of the basket, but also other parts of the Old Testament, the New Testament complete, and in addition the 'Epistle of Barnabas', and a part of the 'Shepherd of Hermas'. Full of joy, which this time I had self-commanded to conceal from the steward and the rest of the community, I asked, as if in a careless way, for permission to take the manuscript into my sleeping chamber to look over it more at leisure. There by myself I could give way to the transport of joy which I felt. I knew that I held in my hand the most precious biblical treasure in existence – a document whose age and importance exceeded that of all the manuscripts which I had ever examined during twenty years' study of the subject.

The manuscript which Tischendorf so emotionally leafed through that night, there and then transcribing the 'Epistle of Barnabas' and 'Shepherd of Hermas', is today known throughout the world as the *Codex Sinaiticus*. The monks allowed Tischendorf to borrow it, and although he is often unfairly accused of having stolen it from them, the truth seems to be that he simply acted as intermediary for Tsar Alexander to buy it for the Russian imperial collection. In 1933, by which time ownership had passed to the then impecunious Soviet revolutionaries, it was purchased by London's British Museum for £100,000, at that time by far the largest amount ever paid for any ancient manuscript.

Today the *Codex Sinaiticus* is displayed with little science and even less art in an old-fashioned showcase on the British Museum's ground floor. But as recognized by a consensus of modern scholarship it is a sister manuscript to the much-prized *Codex Vaticanus* that the Vatican cardinal had so obdurately prevented Tischendorf from properly studying. Exemplifying the discrepancies that have occurred as a result of scribal copying, both *Sinaiticus* and *Vaticanus* lack the last eleven verses of the Mark gospel, suggesting this may have been a late addition. They also do not have the John gospel story of the woman taken in adultery. Both have been reliably dated to approximately the mid-fourth century, and they remain the oldest near-complete texts of the Old and New Testaments in existence. Written on expensive vellum – *Sinaiticus* alone required the skins of 360 young sheep and goats – they were most likely created as a result of Christianity winning official status in the Roman Empire following the conversion of the Roman Emperor Constantine the Great.

A page of the Codex Sinaiticus. From characteristics of the uncial handwriting, scholars date the composition of Sinaiticus to the mid-fourth century and, with the Codex Vaticanus, it remains the earliest near-complete biblical text. Most importantly, its New Testament text is virtually entire. All the 346 pages of the manuscript as found by Tischendorf are today housed in London's British Museum, but more came to light as recently as 1975, when workmen at St Catherine's, Sinai opened up a hitherto unknown room in the monastery's north wall, revealing a cache of more than 3,000 manuscripts, icons and other items. The page reproduced, among the latest finds, is part of the 'Shepherd of Hermas', an early Christian apocalyptic work which the compilers of Sinaiticus clearly considered should be included in the Bible.

Thanks both to modern archaeology and to the enterprise of some sharp-eyed Moslem peasants, since Tischendorf's time significant quantities of other even earlier documentation relating to Jesus have been found – albeit in often very fragmentary form. How such material can be accurately dated is a fascinating topic in its own right, for contrary to popular supposition, radiocarbon dating, as used so famously for the Turin Shroud, is rarely the best method. Altogether more reliable are the guidelines set by the changes in fashion in handwriting, punctuation and spacing that have occurred century by century, changes sufficiently well catalogued to have become developed into a near-science (see table, pp.16-17). By noting such variations as they appear on documents that can be internally dated, i.e. by their references to the year of an emperor's reign, etc., scholars can with quite reasonable reliability date documents that do not have such clues.

Unfortunately, the fact that most early Christian documentation seems to have been written on cheap papyrus paper – somewhat inevitable in the years when Christianity was the religion of the poor and oppressed – has reduced the chances of such material's survival virtually to zero in most European countries. However Egypt, with its dry climate, is a happy exception, although many examples probably perished even there beneath workmen's picks during the years when archaeologists' main ambition was to find pharaonic gold. It was only in 1883, when the great Egyptologist Flinders Petrie, tripping over some rubbish, fleetingly recognized a fragment of what he called the 'finest Greek writing' that it became realized

HOW A CHRISTIAN SCRIPTURAL MANUSCRIPT CAN BE DATED

AD	HANDWRITING		OTHER CHARACTERISTIC FEATURES		
1600 –	ERA OF PRINTING				
1500 –				1557 division into numbered verses by Robert Stephanus	ERA OF PAPER
1400 –					
1300 –	irregular, variegated lettering	PERIOD OF MINUSCULE * WRITING			
1200 –				c. 1200 division into present-day chapters by Stephen Langton	
1100 –					
1000 –	precise, upright lettering		breathing marks more regularly used		PERIOD OF VELLUM (animal skin) CODICES
900 –		upright exaggerated lettering	introduction of the comma		
800 –		marked slope to right			
700 –					
600 –		letters ЄΘОС upright ovals			
500 –	PERIOD OF UNCIAL † WRITING	vertical strokes thicken	5th c. introduction of dated colophons †† (initially in Syriac mss)		
400 –					PERIOD OF PAPYRUS CODICES ** (bound books)
300 –		Simple, dignified lettering	c. 300 nut-gall and iron sulphate inks replace soot-based variety	early 4th c. New Testament books consistently titled and divided into sections; Eusebian cross-reference system introduced	
200 –					
100 –		letters ЄΘОС circular			PERIOD OF PAPYRUS ROLLS ** ✧

*   Greek upper and lower case letters, eg. Πυρίοισ

†   Greek capital letters, eg. ΤΑCΕ

†† a colophon is a paragraph, usually found at the end of a manuscript, giving information about authorship, sources, etc.

SURVIVING CHRISTIAN MANUSCRIPTS AND WHEN THEY WERE WRITTEN				
CANONICAL			NON-CANONICAL	AD
LATIN	GREEK	OTHER		
	1516 Erasmus' first printed edition			– 1600
				– 1500
1445 Gutenberg's first printed Vulgate				
	c. 4000 SURVIVING MINUSCULE MSS (but few of complete Bible)			– 1400
				– 1300
				– 1200
ERA OF THE LATIN VULGATE				– 1100
				– 1000
			COPYING OF NUMEROUS APOCRYPHAL MSS (begun at very early date)	– 900
		897 earliest Georgian mss of gospels **887** earliest Armenian mss of gospels		
	835 first surviving dated minuscule of gospels			– 800
716 earliest extant Vulgate of complete Bible	c. 270 SURVIVING UNCIAL MSS (but few complete)			– 700
				– 600
541-6 Codex Fuldensis **late 5th c.** Codex Sangallensis of gospels		**5th/6th c.** earliest Gothic mss of gospels **5th c.** Coptic gospels of Mark & Luke (Barcelona)		– 500
	early 5th c. Codex Ephraemi **4th c.** Codex Vaticanus; Codex Sinaiticus	**4th c.** Coptic Deuteronomy, Jonah & Acts	**4th c.** Achmim 'Gospel of Peter': Nag Hammadi Gnostic hoard and 'Thomas' gospel	– 400
3rd c. Chester Beatty papyri of most New Testament books; Bodmer papyrus fragments from Luke and John gospels			**3rd c.** Dura fragment of Tatian harmony of canonical gospels	– 300
early 2nd c. Rylands fragment of John gospel			**mid-2nd c.** Egerton papyrus of unknown gospel; Oxyrhynchus fragment of 'Thomas' gospel	– 200
late 1st c.(?) Magdalen College fragment of Matthew gospel				– 100

** vellum was in use at this period, but is unknown for surviving Christian documents, no doubt because of expense (although 3rd-c. epistle of Hebrews is written on the back of a vellum roll)

✧ the period of papyrus rolls lasted until the sixth century for literary works, as distinct from scriptural material that such material could sometimes be preserved.

As a result, Egyptian workmen, suitably alerted with promises of reward, soon began turning up odd papyrus fragments, prompting Britain's Egypt Exploration Fund in 1895 to send a young Oxford graduate, Bernard Pyne Grenfell, and his friend Arthur Surridge Hunt specifically to look for such material in a proper scientific manner. Although this partnership's first season in the Fayum was unrewarding, the next year they decided to investigate the apparently totally unprepossessing Futuh el Bahnasa, site of the former Hellenistic settlement of Oxyrhynchus, where in antiquity there had been a long-abandoned complex of early Christian monasteries and churches. Since no papyrus finds had ever been heard of from Oxyrhynchus, Grenfell suspected that it might have escaped the plundering that occurred elsewhere.

Deciding against excavating Oxyrhynchus' early church buildings, which he anticipated would long since have been cleared of anything of interest, Grenfell opted instead for the seventy-foot-high ancient rubbish heaps that lay on the site's outskirts. Recognizing that to investigate these properly demanded using local labour, who would need the most eagle-eyed supervision, he hired a seventy-strong workforce to cut into the most promising looking mound. As he subsequently recalled of the task's more unpleasant aspects, it meant:

> …standing all day to be half-choked and blinded by the peculiarly pungent dust of ancient rubbish, blended most days with the not less irritating sand of the desert; probably drinking water which not even the East London waterworks would have ventured to supply to its consumers, and keeping incessant watch over men who, however much you may flatter yourself to the contrary, will steal if they get the chance and think it worth their while doing so.

In the event, the work soon began to produce encouraging results, as papyrus scraps of considerable variety and quantity began to emerge. Many were private letters, contracts and other legal or official documents, most helpfully illuminating the everyday life of antiquity, though of no special relevance to Christian origins. Also represented, however, were occasional fragments in the characteristic handwriting styles of early religious and literary texts. And it was Hunt who would make the first significant find among these.

Only two days after he had begun preliminary sorting, as he was carefully smoothing out a scrap that seemed to have come from a numbered, paged book (quite different, therefore, from the long scrolls on which early Jewish and pagan religious literature was written), Hunt's eye fell on the word *karphos*. This he recognized as the Greek word which is translated as 'mote' in the familiar King James Bible text:

And why beholdest thou the mote that is in thy brother's eye, but considerest not the beam that is in thine own eye? (Matthew 7: 3; also Luke 6: 41)

As he deciphered further, Hunt recognized the fragment in his hand as being a version of the same well-known saying:

… then you will clearly see to cast the mote from your brother's eye.

The oddity, however, was that the form of words was significantly different from those in the known gospels. From this he quickly realized that the scrap could not be from one of them. Yet it included no less than seven sayings, each clearly preceded by the words 'Says Jesus'. Although three had no obvious counterpart in the known gospels, they still sounded as if they could well have come from the mouth of the gospel Jesus. What is more, the style of uncials in which the sayings were written dated them to about 200 AD. So could this be from a gospel written before what we now know as the canonical gospels?

As Grenfell and Hunt continued their excavations, other fragments of this same unknown gospel came to light. But it was not until nearly fifty years later that its full text was found – totally unexpectedly. Four hundred miles south of Oxyrhynchus, in a cave-dotted mountainside near the Upper Egyptian town of Nag Hammadi, a group of Arab peasants were digging for natural fertilizer beneath a boulder when they came across a large, sealed earthenware jar. Hoping for gold, one of the group eagerly smashed this open with his mattock, but to their disappointment, all that tumbled out was a collection of thirteen leather-bound papyrus books and some loose papyri, mostly written in Coptic, the language of Egypt after that spoken during the time of the pharaohs. When, following various adventures, these reached scholarly scrutiny, they turned out to be mostly apocryphal works of the fourth century – an 'Apocalypse of Paul', a 'Letter of Peter to Philip', an 'Apocalypse of Peter', a 'Secret Book of James', etc. – thought to have been part of the library of one of the fringe Gnostic groups which proliferated during Christianity's earliest centuries.

However, one work beginning 'These are the secret sayings which the living Jesus spoke, and which Didymos Judas Thomas wrote down', was qualitatively different. It seemed nothing spectacular, simply comprising some 114 sayings attributed to Jesus, and without any account of his crucifixion and resurrection. But several of these sayings were so similar to those that Grenfell and Hunt had found at Oxyrhynchus that there could be no doubt that the Nag Hammadi text was a later and altogether more complete Coptic version of the earlier Greek text as found at Oxyrhynchus. This 'Gospel of Thomas', as it became labelled, could therefore be dated as a whole back to the late second century AD, bringing it to within a century and a half of the lifetime of Jesus.

Fragments of the Egerton Papyrus 2, the handwriting of which suggests a date around 150 AD. Part of the text reads: '[...they urged] the crowd to [pick up] stones and stone him. And the leading men would have arrested him to [hand him over] to the crowd, but no-one could take him because the time of his betrayal had not yet come. So he, the Lord, that is, slipped away through their midst. A leper now came up and said "Master Jesus, through travelling with lepers and eating with them at the inn I myself likewise became a leper. If you want to, you can cure me." The Lord then said to him, "Of course I want to: be cured!" And his leprosy was cured at once...' Elements are clearly familiar from the canonical gospels, as for example the attempt to stone Jesus (John 7 and 8) and the healing of the leper (Matthew 8: 2-3; Mark 1: 40-2; Luke 5: 12-13). But differences in wording and sequence show that this cannot be from any canonical gospel, and it is probably the oldest non-canonical text yet discovered.

Now we should not be surprised at the turning up of gospels previously unknown to us, for the canonical gospel writer Luke mentions (1: 1, 2) 'many' other gospels in existence in his time, most of which have clearly been lost. The writings of the early Church fathers provide clues to the existence of a few: a 'Gospel of the Hebrews', evidently of a strongly Jewish character, mentioned by Origen and Jerome; a 'Gospel according to the Egyptians', apparently somewhat ascetic and favoured by Gentile Christians in Egypt, mentioned by Origen and Clement of Alexandria; and a 'Gospel of the Ebionites', apparently strongly opposed to the writings of the apostle Paul, mentioned in a condemnation of heresies by the fourth-century writer Epiphanius. Of the non-canonical material of this kind actually found, besides the 'Gospel of Thomas', the British Museum has two imperfect leaves and a scrap of papyrus, known by scholars as Egerton Papyrus 2, that appear to derive from a narrative work unlike the canonical gospels but with material closely based on theirs. Recognizable from these fragments are a near-identical version of the Matthew, Mark and Luke accounts of the healing of a leper (Matthew 8: 2-3; Mark 1: 40-2; Luke 5: 12-13) together with a description of Jesus escaping stoning, similar to that in John 8: 59. Originally part of a papyrus book, the Egerton fragments, like the Oxyrhynchus and Nag Hammadi materials, had again been found in Egypt, the handwriting identifying them as certainly not later than 150 AD.

Now it might be unsettling if non-canonical, though scarcely heretical, gospels such as 'Thomas' and 'Egerton' were the earliest to have come down to us. But in fact other similarly early-dated canonical discoveries have redressed the balance. Thus in the 1920s and 1930s the American mining millionaire Alfred Chester Beatty managed to acquire, via Egypt's still notorious antiquities black market, fragmentary papyrus texts of most of the recognized books of the New Testament, datable, like the Oxyrhynchus Thomas, to around the late second century. Mostly now in the Chester Beatty Collection in Dublin (though some are in Michigan and Princeton

University libraries and in the Austrian National Library, Vienna), these include parts of the Matthew and John gospels, a little more of the Mark and Luke gospels, half of Acts, a third of Revelation, and some 86 pages from what had once been a 104-page booklet of Paul's epistles. Likewise, a Swiss collector, Martin Bodmer, managed during the 1950s to acquire substantial portions of a late second-century papyrus codex of the John and Luke gospels, again via the sort of semi-shady under-cover deals employed by Chester Beatty.

From such material it is possible to deduce that written copies of gospels as carried among Jesus' earliest followers mostly took the form of codices or booklets, with relatively small, numbered pages. As such they would have been much cheaper and easier to carry around than any scroll. The extent to which each example contains variations compared to others as a result of copying has also enabled specialist scholars to trace back whole families of texts, to which they have given labels such as Caesarean, Byzantine, Western, Alexandrian, etc. The texts can thus also mutually support each other's authority – the Bodmer papyri, *Vaticanus* and *Sinaiticus*, all, for instance, were found to belong to the same Alexandrian text family.

But from the point of view of our aim to get back to the real basics, exactly how old is the oldest scrap of a gospel yet found? Until recently the essentially undisputed claimant to this title was an ostensibly insignificant-looking two-and-a-half inch by three-and-a-half inch papyrus fragment preserved in the John Rylands Library of Manchester University. Consisting simply of verses from the 18th chapter of the John gospel, this was purchased by Bernard Grenfell back in the early 1920s via the same sort of Egyptian antiquities traders that Chester Beatty and Martin Bodmer had cultivated. However, ill-health prevented Grenfell from ever studying it thoroughly, as a result of which no-one appreciated its full significance until 1934, when it was examined by a young Oxford University graduate called Colin Roberts. From Roberts' careful study of the handwriting, he was able to date it to between 100 and 125 AD, i.e. well within a century of Jesus' lifetime. As Princeton University manuscript specialist Bruce Metzger has remarked of it:

Although the extent of the verses preserved is so slight, in one respect this tiny scrap of papyrus possesses as much evidential value as would the complete codex. As Robinson Crusoe, seeing but a single footprint in the sand, concluded that another human being, with two feet, was present on the island with him, so $\mathfrak{p}^{52}$ [the Rylands fragment's international code name] proves the existence and use of the Fourth Gospel in a little provincial town along the Nile far from its traditional place of composition (Ephesus in Asia Minor), during the first half of the Second Century.

But if this Rylands Library find might seem important enough in getting

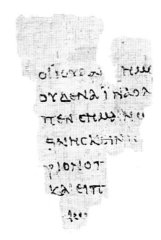

Papyrus fragment of the gospel of John, preserved in Manchester University's John Rylands Library. Analysis of the handwriting indicates that it was written between 100 and 125 AD, i.e. within a century of Jesus' death. On the front (above) is the Greek text of John 18: 31-4; on its back is John 18: 37-8. Because parts of the margins have been preserved, the original page can be calculated to have measured 21.5 x 20 cm and would have formed part of a 130-page codex, or primitive book. Found in Egypt, hundreds of miles from Ephesus in Turkey, where the John gospel is believed to have been composed, this is the earliest known surviving fragment of any gospel, canonical or non-canonical - with the possible exception of the still-contested Matthew gospel fragments at Magdalen College, Oxford.

us back to the earliest documentation for Jesus, it has been potentially eclipsed by claims recently made for another possibly even earlier example preserved at Magdalen College, Oxford. Between 1893 and 1901, and therefore at much the same time that Grenfell and Hunt were working at Oxyrhynchus, the Reverend Charles Bousfield Huleatt spent each winter at Luxor, Egypt, working as missionary chaplain of the English church there on behalf of the Colonial and Continental Church Society. In 1901 he and his family were transferred from Egypt to continue their work in Messina, Sicily, and there they perished during the great Sicilian earthquake of 28 December 1908.

However, just after Huleatt left Egypt, he bequeathed a souvenir of his sojourn there to his old college, Magdalen, Oxford, where he had studied classics. This souvenir, subsequently catalogued as Magdalen's MS.Gr.17,

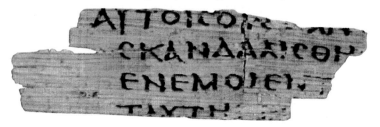

simply consisted of three tiny papyrus fragments that Huleatt had presumably acquired from some antiquities trader. Although the fragments bear on their front and reverse sides just a few words in Greek uncial characters, these are quite sufficient to identify them as belonging to the 26th chapter of the gospel of Matthew, essentially just as we have it today. On one side is part of the story of a woman anointing Jesus' head with costly ointment while he was eating at the house of Simon the leper. On the other are extracts from Jesus' words during the Last Supper. From the fall of the words it is again possible to reconstruct the front and back of the whole page on which they would have appeared, and thereby the whole original papyrus booklet.

But when was this booklet written? When the fragments were first examined at Magdalen back in 1901, they were tentatively assigned to between the third and fourth centuries AD. In 1953 Colin Roberts suggested the late second century and became supported by other acknowledged experts, such as T.C. Skeat and Sir Harold Bell. Although this dating became that of orthodoxy, it still made the fragments comparatively late compared to the Rylands, so much so that they were inconspicuously stored in a college library display cabinet along with Magdalen alumni trifles such as Oscar Wilde's ring and Addison's shoebuckle. Even though an undergraduate at Magdalen between 1960 and 1963, I for one remained unaware even of their existence.

But then in February 1994 the papyrologist Dr Carsten Thiede, Director of the Institute for Basic Epistemological Research, Paderborn, Germany, happened to visit Oxford for a family celebration, and decided to use the opportunity to make a routine call at Magdalen just to make a first-hand assessment of Huleatt's fragments. When courteously shown them by the college's assistant librarian, Sally Speirs, Thiede was astonished to note that the writing was strikingly similar to that of texts from Pompeii, Herculaneum and Qumran, ones with which he had already gained a specialist familiarity, and which had not been available to those who had last examined the Magdalen fragments back in 1953. Crucially, these dated to no later than the third quarter of the first century AD, Pompeii and Herculaneum having been destroyed in 79 AD and Qumran – the site of the Dead Sea Scrolls – closed down in 70 AD.

His interest thoroughly roused, Thiede has subjected the Magdalen fragments to the most intensive scrutiny and concluded that they are in a handwriting that had been common back in the first century BC but which was already petering out as early as the mid-first century AD.

He would date them to around 70 AD. If he is right, the latest they are likely to date is within fifty years of Jesus' death, making them even older than the Rylands papyrus. As one Magdalen fellow has put it, this 'means that the people in the story must have been around when this [the Matthew gospel] was being written. It means they were there.'

Now it would be quite wrong to conclude that Dr Thiede has anything like proven the dating he claims. While some leading scholars have tentatively voiced their support, others, such as the formidable Graham Stanton, Professor of New Testament Studies at King's College, London, have been more than vociferous in their opposition. On the issue of whether Magdalen's Matthew papyrus genuinely dates from within a generation or so of Jesus' lifetime, the jury has to be considered still out.

But even without the Magdalen papyrus the discoveries of Jesus-related documents during the last hundred years have been impressive to say the least. As few realize, whereas we have just a single manuscript, copied around the twelfth century, for Tacitus' history of the early Roman emperors, of canonical material alone attesting to Jesus' existence there are some 274 vellum manuscripts, brothers and sisters of *Sinaiticus*, dating from between the fourth and the eleventh centuries, and 88 papyrus fragments datable to between the second and the fourth centuries (among these latter, of course, the Rylands and Magdalen examples). Additionally, as we have already seen, there is an intriguing variety of non-canonical material.

We can therefore be sure that the gospel texts were genuinely early. From the relatively minor text differences to be found even in the earliest versions, we can also be confident that those who copied them one from another did so mostly reasonably accurately. But what of the actual origination of the gospels? Who wrote them? And when? Even more crucially, how much can we trust them? For the answers to these questions we need to look to another specialist discipline, the work of New Testament theologians.

Papyrus fragments of the gospel of Matthew, preserved in the library at Magdalen College, Oxford. Like the Rylands papyrus, these were found in Egypt and derive from a codex once bound in the manner of a book. According to papyrologist Dr Carsten Thiede they date to around 70 AD.

2

HOW MUCH CAN THE GOSPELS BE TRUSTED?

Few, if any, pieces of writing can have received greater scrutiny than the traditional, canonical gospel stories of Jesus. Printed copies of them, translated into almost every language, are to be found in hundreds of millions of homes across the world. Thousands of professional theologians are paid salaries to study them, and to teach and write about them. Many thousands more are paid, as vicars, chaplains and priests, to read and review a passage from them each week for the purposes of conducting a Christian service and preaching a sermon.

It can therefore come as quite a shock to discover that no-one can even be sure who wrote the gospels. Despite the versions printed in our Bibles long having borne the names Matthew, Mark, Luke and John, these names are mere attributions, and even as such are rather less reliable than attributions given to unsigned works of art. Many of the earliest writers to refer to the gospels notably failed to mention the authors' names. Each gospel, whether among the canonical 'big four', or among those that failed to gain general acceptance, seems to have been designed as the teaching about Jesus for an early Christian community, with whoever wrote it seeming relatively unimportant. And only gradually did the canon of the 'big four' drift into general usage, each gospel at the

Opposite *Caves of the Scrolls. In 1947 a Bedouin goatherd's chance exploration of these caves overlooking the Dead Sea brought to light Jewish documents from close to the time of Jesus, the famous Dead Sea Scrolls. The caves are here viewed from the adjoining first-century AD Jewish settlement of Qumran, where the scrolls are thought to have been written.*

same time becoming linked with specific names from Christianity's earliest years.

It also needs bearing in mind that the earliest texts had none of the easy reading and reference features that they bear now. Without exception, everything was written in capital letters, the uncials referred to in the last chapter. There were neither headings, nor chapter divisions, nor verse divisions. Refinements such as these did not appear until the Middle Ages. Adding further to the difficulties both for people of the earliest years and for specialist scholars of today, there was practically no punctuation or space between words.

Given such a background, it may come as little surprise, particularly for sceptics, to discover that there can be inconsistencies between one gospel and another. While according to the Mark and Luke gospels Jesus stayed in Peter's house, and only afterwards healed the leper (Mark 1: 29-45; Luke 4: 38 ff.; Luke 5: 12 ff.), according to the Matthew gospel (8: 1-4 and 14ff.) Jesus healed the leper first. While according to Matthew the Capernaum centurion spoke man-to-man with Jesus (Matthew 8: 5 ff.), according to Luke (7: 1 ff.) he sent some Jewish elders and friends to speak on his behalf. Whereas according to Matthew (5: 1) Jesus delivered his Beatitudes on a hill (hence the Sermon on the Mount), according to Luke (6: 17) he gave what seems to have been the same discourse after he had come 'down with them and stopped at a level piece of ground'. Although according to Acts Judas Iscariot died from an accidental fall after betraying Jesus (Acts 1: 18), according to Matthew he went and hanged himself (Matthew 27: 5).

There are also differences in the reporting of Jesus' sayings, even in respect of some of the most central of these. Thus while Matthew's 'Our Father' prayer (6: 9-13) has seven petitions and begins 'Our Father in heaven' Luke's (11: 2-4) begins simply 'Father' and has only five. With regard to Jesus' institution of the Eucharist, Matthew has Jesus say 'Take it and eat, this is my body', while Mark has 'Take it, this is my body', and Luke 'This is my body'.

Of course the reasonable and fair-minded approach to such discrepancies is to regard them as no worse than the minor reporting errors which occur daily even in our more respected modern newspapers. But over the last couple of centuries New Testament criticism has gone much deeper, and in some quarters there is a fashion for each new critic to try to outdo his predecessors in casting doubt on the gospels' authenticity.

The first such forays into trying to get back to the true facts behind the gospels began harmlessly enough. Many incidents concerning Jesus are related in two or more of the gospels, and an early research method, still extremely valuable, was to study the corresponding passages side by side, the so-called 'parallel passage' technique. This is very useful for showing up which episodes are common to all gospels, which are peculiar to a single gospel, the variation of interest or emphasis between one writer and another and so on. And to anyone who tries it, immediately obvious is the fact that

THE PARALLEL PASSAGE TECHNIQUE

MARK 16: 2–5	LUKE 24: 1–4	MATTHEW 28: 1–4
... very early in the morning on the first day of the week they went to the tomb just as the sun was rising. They had been saying to one another 'Who will roll away the stone for us from the entrance to the tomb? But when they looked they could see that the stone - which was very big - had already been rolled back. On entering the tomb they saw a young man in a white robe seated at the right-hand side.	*On the first day of the week, at the first sign of dawn, they went to the tomb with the spices they had prepared. They found that the stone had been rolled away from the tomb, but on entering discovered that the body of the Lord Jesus was not there. As they stood there not knowing what to think, two men in brilliant clothes suddenly appeared at their side...*	*... towards dawn on the first day of the week Mary of Magdala and the other Mary went to visit the sepulchre. And all at once there was a violent earthquake, for the angel of the Lord, descending from heaven, came and rolled away the stone and sat on it. His face was like lightning, his robe white as snow...*

the Matthew, Mark and Luke gospels are the three that have most in common with each other. They report the same 'miracles'. They quote the same sayings. Essentially they share a common narrative framework, and in about 1774 the pioneering German scholar Johann Griesbach coined the word 'synoptic' for them, from the Greek for 'seen together'.

The John gospel, on the other hand, often referred to as the Fourth Gospel, seems to be some sort of maverick. With the exception of the events surrounding Jesus' death, it mostly describes quite different incidents of Jesus' life. Much of it is taken up with lengthy, apparently verbatim speeches that seem quite unlike Jesus' pithy utterances reported elsewhere. It is as if its author has chosen to present a side of Jesus that is different from that of the three synoptics, and the gospel has thereby mostly been regarded as having been written later than the other three.

The seeming flaws in the trustworthiness of the gospels began to emerge as critics, particularly in Germany, started to develop and apply more and more rigorous analysis techniques in order to get back to the original gospel writers and their closeness or otherwise to the events they reported. During the eighteenth century a faltering start on such techniques was made by Hamburg University oriental languages professor Hermann Samuel Reimarus. Working in secret, Reimarus wrote *On the Aims of Jesus and his Disciples*, arguing that Jesus was merely a failed Jewish revolutionary, and that after his death his disciples cunningly stole his body from the tomb in order to concoct the whole story of his resurrection. So concerned was Reimarus to avoid recriminations that he would only allow the book to be published after his death.

Following in this controversial tradition, in the years 1835-6 Tübingen University tutor David Friedrich Strauss launched his two-volume *Life of*

Careful comparison of the three gospel passages above reveals a fundamental common grond - the time of the morning, the day of the week, the rolling away of the stone, the visit to the tomb by women. But it also discloses some equally fundamental differences which serve to tell us something about the gospel writers. The Mark author, for instance, speaks merely of 'a young man in a white robe', with no suggestion that this individual was anything other than an ordinary human being. In the Luke version we find 'two men in brilliant clothes' who appear 'suddenly'. Although not absolutely explicit, there is already a strong hint of the supernatural. But for the Matthew writer all restraints are abandoned. A violent earthquake has been introduced into the story; Mark's mere 'young man' has become a dazzling 'angel of the Lord... from heaven'; and this explicitly extra-terrestrial visitor is accredited with the rolling away of the stone. Such comparisons provide important insights into the gospel writers' differing personalities and interests.

Jesus Critically Examined, making particularly penetrating use of the parallel passage technique. Because of the discrepancies he found, he cogently argued that none of the gospels could have been by eyewitnesses. Instead they must have been the work of writers of a much later generation who freely constructed their material from probably garbled traditions about Jesus in circulation in the early Church. Inspired by the materialistic rationalism of the philosophers Kant and Hegel – 'the real is the rational and the rational is the real' – Strauss uncompromisingly dismissed the gospel miracle stories as mere myths invented to give Jesus greater importance. For such findings Strauss was dismissed from his tutorship at Tübingen, and later failed, for the same reason, to gain an important professorship at Zurich.

But such sanctions merely served to intensify the efforts of those, particularly Protestants, who felt that they had some sort of mission to strip the gospel accounts of Jesus back to what they considered, in their theological judgment, to have been the original facts. Under the professorship of the redoubtable Ferdinand Christian Baur, a prodigiously productive theologian who was at his desk by 4 o'clock each morning, Tübingen University in particular acquired a reputation for a ruthlessly iconoclastic approach, one which spread not only throughout Germany, but also into the universities of other predominantly Protestant countries.

Some of this iconoclasm was undeniably useful and valid. The Matthew gospel, for instance, had long been considered as the earliest of the four New Testament gospels and to have been composed by none other than Matthew, the tax-collector disciple of Jesus. Then in 1835 Berlin philologist Karl Lachmann showed that the Matthew and Luke gospels, which each contained material (mostly sayings) that Mark's did not have, agreed in their order only when they followed Mark's. Only three years later the theologian Christian Wilke drew from this and similar deductions the firm conclusion that the Mark gospel had to have been written first among the three synoptics.

Now from both internal and external clues, the Mark gospel, simpler and more primitive than the other two, was almost certainly written in Rome. Among the three synoptics it ostensibly has the least claim to eyewitness reporting, for even according to tradition, the best said about its authorship is that Mark was some sort of secretary or interpreter for Peter. And even if this were so, at best Peter can hardly have carefully supervised the gospel's writing, for it shows some serious ignorance of the geography of Jesus' haunts. In the 7th chapter, for instance, Jesus is reported going through Sidon on his way to Tyre and to the Sea of Galilee. Not only is Sidon in the opposite direction, but there was no road from Sidon to the Sea of Galilee in the first century AD, only one from Tyre. Similarly the 5th chapter refers to the Sea of Galilee's eastern shore as the country of the Gerasenes. Yet Gerasa, today's Jerash in Jordan, is more than thirty miles to the south-east, too far away for a story which, in any case, requires the setting of a city not far from a steep slope down to the sea. Aside from geography, Mark represents Jesus as saying: 'If a woman divorces her husband and marries another she is guilty of adultery' (Mark 10: 12). Such a precept would have been meaningless for Jesus' Jewish world, where women had no rights of divorce, so whoever wrote the Mark gospel, addressing a Gentile readership, seemingly put into Jesus' mouth what he might have said on this issue.

The interesting question that now arises is where all this leaves the Matthew gospel. Since it can be seen that Matthew's author drew a substantial amount of his material from the Mark gospel, it is difficult to see how he can have been Jesus' original tax-collector disciple Matthew. For would this Matthew, a man represented as having known Jesus personally, and had travelled with him, have based his gospel on the work of someone who had no such firsthand knowledge and who made errors of basic fact? For such reasons theological opinion has largely, though not entirely, rejected the idea that the original disciple Matthew could have written the gospel that bears the same name. Whoever did so must have brought it out after the Mark gospel had already appeared, and this led the German theologians increasingly to date the composition of all three synoptic gospels to well into the second century AD.

Then the John gospel, in its turn, came under close scrutiny. The long speeches that its writer put into the mouth of Jesus, all quoted in fluent Greek, seemed Hellenistic in character, corresponding to the gospel's traditional place of authorship, the Hellenistic city of Ephesus in Asia Minor. Since even Church tradition acknowledged the John gospel to have been written later than the rest, the Germans concluded that it must date from close to the end of the second century.

Even one of the Mark gospel's more convincing features, its air of primitive 'matter-of-factness', became weakened with the publication, in 1901, of Breslau professor Wilhelm Wrede's *The Secret of the Messiahship*. In this Wrede argued powerfully that whoever wrote Mark tried to represent Jesus as making a secret that he was the Messiah while he was alive, so much so that even most of his disciples failed to recognize this until after his death. While not necessarily giving this idea their full endorsement, most modern scholars accept that Wrede may well have been right in regarding Mark's author as more concerned with putting over theology than with writing straight history. Five years after Wrede's publication, in a closely written treatise *From Reimarus to Wrede*, translated into English as *The Quest for the Historical Jesus*, Albert Schweitzer, later to become the world-famous Lambarene missionary, summarized the work of his fellow Germans in these terms:

There is nothing more negative than the result of the critical study of the life of Jesus. The Jesus of Nazareth who came forward publicly as the Messiah, who preached the ethic of the Kingdom of God, who founded the Kingdom of Heaven upon earth, and died to give his work its final consecration, never had any existence…This image has not been destroyed from without, it has fallen to pieces, cleft and disintegrated by the concrete historical problems which came to the surface one after another…

As if this were not damage enough, onto the scene stepped Rudolf Bultmann of Germany's Marburg University with a new and yet more devastating weapon, *Formgeschichte* or 'form criticism'. Before Bultmann, the German pastor Karl Ludwig Schmidt had noted that in all the gospels, but in Mark's gospel in particular, there were link passages that seemed to have been invented to give an impression of continuity between one episode or saying and the next. So Bultmann set his sights on determining what if anything might be authentic about the links, looking at each of the elements in each gospel – birth stories, miracle stories, ethical sayings, etc. – from the point of view of whether they might be original, or borrowed from the Old Testament, or from contemporary Jewish thought, or merely invented to suit some particular theological line which early Christian preachers wanted to promulgate.

Nothing if not Procrustean, Bultmann firmly discarded anything that savoured of the miraculous – the gospels' nativity stories, references to angels, accounts of wondrous cures of the sick, and the like – on the grounds that these were simply the gospel writers' attempts to make Jesus seem divine. Anything that appeared to him to fulfil an Old Testament prophecy – Jesus' birth in Bethlehem, his entry into Jerusalem on a donkey, his betrayal, and much else – he threw out as a mere attempt to represent Jesus' life as fulfilling such prophecies. Any of what Jesus reportedly said that could be traced to the general Jewish thinking of his time, Bultmann rejected likewise. For instance, Jesus' reported saying '…always treat others as you would like them to treat you; that is the meaning of the Law and the Prophets' (Matthew 7: 12) Bultmann ruled as inadmissible because it is mirrored almost exactly in a saying of the great first-century BC Jewish Rabbi Hillel: 'Whatever is hateful to you, do not do to your fellow-man. This is the whole Law [Torah] …'

Another example, from Mark's gospel, concerns the incident in which Jesus reportedly told a paralytic: 'Your sins are forgiven' (Mark 2: 5), causing the Jewish scribes to quibble that only God could forgive sins, and prompting Jesus to go ahead and cure the man anyway. In Bultmann's logic, early Christians probably invented this incident in order to bolster their own claim to be able to forgive sins. By a series of deductions of this kind he concluded that much of what appears in the gospels was not what Jesus had actually said and done, but what Christians at least two generations removed had invented about him, or had inferred from what early preachers had told them. Not surprisingly, the approach left intact all too little that might have derived from the original Jesus – not much more than the parables, Jesus' baptism, his Galilean and Judaean ministries and his crucifixion. Recognizing this himself, Bultmann condemned as useless further attempts to try to reconstruct the Jesus of history:

> I do indeed think that we can now know almost nothing concerning the life and personality of Jesus, since the early Christian sources show no interest in either, are moreover fragmentary and often legendary.

Somewhat ludicrously, all this damage was done by men who counted themselves good Protestant Christians, Bultmann, for instance, defending his destruction of so much that had been considered historical about Jesus on the grounds that still intact was his own Lutheran Christ of faith. As the leading Jewish scholar Dr Geza Vermes has most aptly remarked of the German theologians' position, it was like having 'their feet off the ground of history and their heads in the clouds of faith'.

Even so, when Bultmann died in 1976, at the age of ninety-two, he left behind a whole generation of mostly still active New Testament scholars – his Marburg successor Werner Kümmel, Bristol University's Dennis Nineham, Harvard University's Helmut Koester, and others – almost all of whom acknowledge him as the twentieth century's most influential theological thinker. But did he and his fellow-German predecessors go too far? Have their attitudes been too Teutonically rigid and unshakeable?

Throughout, there have been other scholars, often less fashionable, who have certainly felt this, acknowledging that while each gospel per se may have been written at second hand, they nonetheless contain substantial underlying elements of genuine first-hand reporting.

Thus not long after Bultmann had begun his professorship at Marburg, across the Channel at Queen's College, Oxford, a shy and retiring Englishman, Canon Burnett Streeter, quietly put the finishing touches to *The Four Gospels – A Study in Origins*. Thanks to both British and German theological research, it had already become recognized that the authors of Matthew and Luke, in addition to drawing on the gospel of Mark, must have used a second Greek source, long lost, but familiarly referred to by scholars as 'Q' (from the German *Quelle*, meaning source). Something of Q's original text was even reconstructible from some two hundred verses of the Matthew and Luke gospels, mostly relating to the teachings of Jesus, which bear a close resemblance to each other, but are absent from Mark, thereby suggesting a common written source. Supporting this thinking, Streeter went further to postulate at least two additional lost sources: 'M', which had provided material peculiar to the Matthew gospel, and 'L' which had furnished passages exclusive to that attributed to Luke. To clarify his arguments Streeter produced a chart showing the synoptic gospels' apparent relationship to these lost sources, and suggested that 'M' and 'L' may well have been written in Aramaic, the spoken language of Jesus and his disciples.

Streeter died in 1937, but his line of thought was continued by other

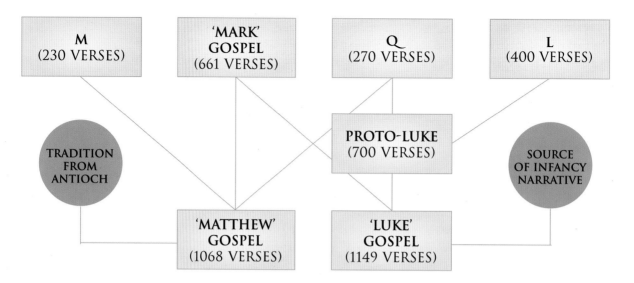

Sources of influence on the synoptic gospels as deduced by Canon Burnett Streeter. 'Proto Luke' is a theoretical early gospel, comprising Q plus the special Luke source L, which Streeter believed to have been a prototype for the so-called 'Luke' gospel.

major British theological scholars, among them Professor Charles Dodd, who went on to make his own special contribution to an understanding of the John gospel. To this day the broad outlines of Streeter's hypothesis remain the basis for much synoptic literary criticism, and the clues to underlying Aramaic sources are indeed there. In the Luke gospel, for instance, which includes 'exclusives' such as the parables of the Good Samaritan and the Prodigal Son, there occurs the following saying:

> Oh, you Pharisees! You clean the outside of cup and plate, while inside yourselves you are filled with extortion and wickedness... Instead *give alms* from what you have and then indeed everything will be clean for you. (Luke 11: 39-41)

Although 'give alms' appears to make no sense, it occurs in the very earliest available Greek texts, thereby showing that any error in transcription has to have occurred at a very early stage. All then becomes clear when we discover that the Aramaic *zakkau* (to give alms) looks very similar to *dakkau* (to cleanse). That the original saying genuinely did refer to 'cleansing' rather than 'giving alms' can be checked because Matthew includes a parallel passage in what we may now judge to have been the correct form: 'Blind Pharisee! Clean the inside of cup and dish first so that the outside may become clean as well...' (Matthew 23: 26). As has been remarked by Cambridge theologian Don Cupitt, this conveys more clearly than any amount of Bultmannesque theology that whoever wrote Luke in its 'original' Greek did not compose his material out of nothing, but had struggled with an earlier Aramaic *written* source that he was obviously determined to follow even if he did not fully understand it.

A similar misunderstanding is detectable in the Matthew gospel, notable for its remarkable 'Sermon on the Mount' passages. When translated from Greek into Aramaic, some of these passages take on such a distinctive verse form that Aramaic must have been the language in which they were first framed, rather as happens when the ostensibly dull-sounding words 'On the bridge at Avignon' are translated back into their original French. According to the Dutch Roman Catholic scholar Edward Schillebeeckx, the lost 'Q' also seems to have had an original Aramaic text, then, as in the case of the synoptic gospels, becoming translated into Greek and adapted for Gentile consumption.

Surprisingly, despite having been dismissed by the Germans as very late and very Greek, the gospel which would seem, in part at least, to have the most authentic underlying Aramaic flavour of all is that of John. The first shock to the Germans, with their so dismissive attitudes towards this gospel, came with the papyrologist Colin Roberts' publication of the Rylands fragment, and his closely argued insistence on its early date. For if a copy of the John gospel had reached as far as provincial Egypt by between 100 and 125 AD, then its original, if it were composed at Ephesus (and at least no-one has suggested it was written in Egypt), could only have been written significantly earlier, probably at least a decade before 100 AD, and thereby a century before the sort of late dating the Germans had been suggesting.

A second shock to the Germans came with the discovery of the much publicized Dead Sea Scrolls that had been stored in caves in the hillside surrounding Qumran on the Dead Sea. Despite many sensationalist claims, fuelled by several decades in which much of their content remained unpublished, the Scrolls can now be determined to contain absolutely no readily recognizable mention of Jesus (see fragment on p.35), even though there is general agreement that they date from very close to his time. But the intriguing feature of the Scrolls is that their authors, generally thought to have been the community which lived at Qumran in a settlement dating no later than 70 AD (often but by no means conclusively identified with a Jewish sect called the Essenes), were using already in Jesus' time precisely the same type of language and imagery that had previously been dismissed as late and 'Hellenistic' in John. As is well known, the John gospel prologue speaks of a conflict between light and darkness, and the whole gospel is replete with phrases such as 'the spirit of truth', 'the light of life', 'walking in the darkness', 'children of light', and 'eternal life'. A welter of such phrases and imagery occur in the Dead Sea Scrolls' Manual of Discipline. For instance the John gospel's prologue,

> He was with God in the beginning.
> Through him all things came to be,
> Not one thing had its being but through him.
>
> (John I: 2-3)

is strikingly close to the Manual of Discipline's

Steps to the Qumran community's cistern, showing fault from earthquake damage. Although the community who lived at Qumran, and were therefore most likely responsible for the Dead Sea Scrolls, are generally believed to have been monastic Essenes, in recent years there have been a variety of alternative theories for the settlement's main purpose, from luxury villa to guerrilla fortress. The cistern steps were repaired following a devastating earthquake of 31 BC which toppled the community's main building, and left the terrace's eastern half (seen at left), two feet lower than before. The community repaired their buildings after the damage, but were subsequently snuffed out by the Romans shortly before 70 AD.

All things come to pass by his knowledge,
He establishes all things by his design
And without him nothing is done.

(Manual 11: 11)

This is but one example of a striking similarity of cadence and choice of words obvious to anyone reading gospel and Manual side by side.

Even before such discoveries the Oxford scholar C.F. Burney and ancient historian A.T. Olmstead had begun arguing forcibly that the John gospel's narrative element at least must originally have been composed in Aramaic, probably not much later than 40 AD. One ingenious researcher, Dr Aileen Guilding, has shown in *The Fourth Gospel and Jewish Worship* that the gospel's whole construction is based on the Jewish cycle of feasts, and the practice of completing the reading of the Law, or Torah, in a three-year cycle. That the gospel's author incorporated accounts provided by close eyewitnesses to the events described is further indicated by detailed and accurate references to geographical features of Jerusalem and its environs before the city and its Temple were destroyed by the Romans in 70 AD, following their suppression of the Jewish Revolt which had broken out four years earlier. It is John who mentions a Pool of Siloam (John 9: 7), the remains of which are thought to have been discovered in Jerusalem, also a 'Gabbatha' or pavement, where Pilate is said to have sat in judgment over Jesus (John 19: 13), generally identified as a substantial area of Roman

Reference to Jesus in a Dead Sea Scroll fragment? According to Californian Robert Eisenman, this fragment refers to a Jesus-like 'pierced messiah', the 4th and 5th lines reading, in his translation: 'and they put to death [shall put to death?] the leader of the community, the Bran[ch of David] ... with wounds [stripes? piercings?], and the Priest [the High Priest] shall order...' But according to Oxford University's Dr Geza Vermes this particular messiah appears to do the piercing, Vermes' translation reading: 'and the Prince of the Congregation, the Bran[ch of David] will kill him by [stroke]s and by wounds. And a Priest [of renown?] will command...' Scholarly consensus seems to be on the side of Vermes, and the Scrolls therefore seem to contain no readily recognizable mention of Jesus.

paving now in the crypt of the Convent of the Sisters of Our Lady of Sion in Jerusalem.

From the historical point of view, therefore, while some elements in the gospels are undeniably clumsily handled and suggest that their authors were far removed in time and distance from the events they are describing, others have such a strikingly original and authentic ring that it is as if a second generation has come along and adulterated genuine first-hand material. In the case of the Matthew gospel at least this idea is certainly supported by a cryptic remark by the early Bishop Papias (c. 60-130 AD):

> Matthew compiled the Sayings in the Aramaic language, and everyone translated them as well as he could.

As some have interpreted this, the disciple Matthew himself may have genuinely set down in his native Aramaic those sayings of Jesus that he had heard at first hand (perhaps in a form very like the 'Thomas' sayings discovered at Nag Hammadi), then others translated them and adapted them for their own literary purposes. This would readily explain the Matthew gospel's traditional attribution to Matthew without its having been written by him, at least in the form it has come down to us. The crunch question, though, is why this situation should have come about. Why should original eyewitness material, emanating from genuine original Jewish followers of Jesus, have been editorially adulterated and

Carved for posterity on Titus' triumphal arch in Rome, the Roman army that crushed the Jews processes through Rome's streets carrying spoils from the Jerusalem Temple, among these the great menorah or seven-branched candelabrum, the gold table, and musical instruments. This representation of the menorah may not be exact, as it is thought to have been three-footed, rather than with the six-sided stand represented by the Roman artist.

swamped by interference from Gentile writers of a later time?

The answer almost certainly lies in one event, the Jewish Revolt of 66 AD, which had its culmination four years later in the sacking of Jerusalem, the burning and subsequent total razing to the ground of its Temple and the widespread extermination and humiliation of the Jewish people. As is historically well attested, in 70 AD the Roman general Titus returned in triumph to Rome, parading through the streets such Jewish treasures as the *menorah* (the huge seven-branched candelabrum of the Temple), and enacting tableaux demonstrating how he and his armies had overcome savage, ill-advised resistance from this renegade group of the Empire's subjects, many of whom they had had to crucify wholesale. At the height of the celebrations the captured Jewish leader, Simon bar Giora, was dragged to the Forum, abused and executed. In Titus' honour Rome's mints issued commemorative sestertii coins with the inscriptions 'JUDAEA DEVICTA' and 'JUDAEA CAPTA', and within a few years a magnificent commemorative arch was erected next to the Temple of Venus.

Intimately linked to this episode, according to at least one British authority, the late Professor S. G. F. Brandon, was the writing of the key canonical gospel of Mark. Generally recognized as having been written in Rome, according to most present-day thinking it was composed around the time of the Revolt and Titus' triumph, and it certainly displays one overwhelming characteristic, a denigration of Jews and whitewashing of Romans. Whoever wrote 'Mark' portrays Jesus' Jewish disciples as a dull, quarrelsome lot, always jockeying for position, failing to understand Jesus, denying him when they are in trouble (as in the case of Peter) and finally deserting him at the time of his arrest. The entire Jewish establishment, Pharisees, Sadducees, chief priests and scribes, is represented as being out to kill Jesus. Even his own family think him 'out of his mind' and want 'to take charge of him'. By contrast Pilate, the Roman, is portrayed as positively pleading for Jesus' life: 'What harm has he done?' (Mark 15: 14). At the very moment when Jesus, amid Jewish taunts, breathes his last it is a Roman centurion, standing at the foot of the cross, who is represented as the first man in history to recognize Jesus as divine: 'In truth this man was a Son of God' (Mark 15: 39).

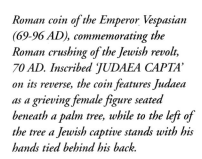

Roman coin of the Emperor Vespasian (69-96 AD), commemorating the Roman crushing of the Jewish revolt, 70 AD. Inscribed 'JUDAEA CAPTA' on its reverse, the coin features Judaea as a grieving female figure seated beneath a palm tree, while to the left of the tree a Jewish captive stands with his hands tied behind his back.

Given the background of the Jewish Revolt and the Roman triumph, it is not too difficult to understand why someone writing the Mark gospel in Rome might choose to bias his story in this way. For the Rome community of Gentile Christians, who would have been still reeling from the atrocities that the Emperor Nero reportedly inflicted upon them in 64 AD, it could only have been acutely embarrassing that the very founder of their religion had been a member of this accursed Jewish people, crucified at Roman hands like so many of the recent rebels. How could one hope to win more converts in such a situation? Arguably, for whoever wrote 'Mark', and for those who followed him, there could be only one answer: to de-Judaize Jesus by representing him as a reject of, and utterly divorced from, his own people. In like vein, the Luke gospel even avoids representing Roman soldiers as crucifying Jesus, while that of Matthew quotes what seems to be the Jewish people directly assuming responsibility for Jesus' death with the words: 'His blood be on us and on our children' (Matthew 27: 25). There is also a strikingly anti-Jewish character to the speeches attributed to Jesus in the John gospel, where Jesus is recorded as condemning 'the Jews' in the most vituperative way, using the words 'your Law', when referring to the Torah, as if this were no part of his own beliefs, and telling them that they are uncompromisingly evil, with the devil as their father (John 8: 43-7).

The Jewish Revolt therefore needs to be seen as a possibly important key to an understanding of how and when the canonical gospels came to be written. Trying to reconcile Bultmann's thinking with the papyrologists' early datings of some of the gospel scraps, the influential New Testament

DATINGS FOR THE WRITING OF THE CANONICAL GOSPELS

Earliest to latest dates for the writing of the canonical gospels, according to the late Dr John Robinson

Earliest to latest dates for the writing of the canonical gospels, according to Werner Kümmel

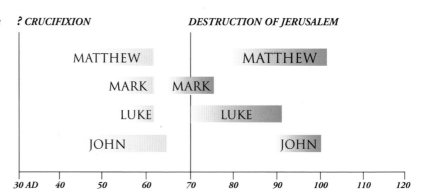

scholar Werner Kümmel has set widely accepted datings for each of the gospels (see above), based largely on the idea that Jesus' apparent prophecies of the fall of Jerusalem and destruction of the Temple (Matthew 24: 1-3; Mark 13: 1-4; Luke 21: 5-7) were 'written in' by the gospel writers after the event.

But such are the uncertainties that this dating peg cannot be regarded as assured. As came to be asked by the late Dr John Robinson of Trinity College, Cambridge, famed for his controversial *Honest to God*, what if Jesus' prophecies of Jerusalem's destruction were real prophecies – ones uttered a whole generation before the event actually happened? In his *Redating the New Testament*, published in 1976, Dr Robinson pointed out that if the gospels were not written until after Jerusalem's fall, it was surely surprising that the writers should not have capitalized on this amazing piece of fulfilment. Yet the Revolt and destruction as past events go entirely unmentioned. Among other indications of the gospels' origins before 70 AD, Robinson noted the Matthew gospel's reference to the Jews' obligation to pay the Temple tax (Matthew 17: 24-7), a burden which disappeared after the Temple's destruction. Similarly, if the gospels were written after 70 AD, why should their writers have represented Jesus as predicting his return 'before this generation has passed away' (Matthew 24: 34-6; Mark 13: 30-2; Luke 21: 32-3), surely already somewhat late for anyone living in the generation after the Jewish Revolt? Accordingly, and in the teeth of Kümmel's chronology, John Robinson drew up a radical 'new' scheme of dating showing the writing of all the gospels to have been completed by around 65 AD (see chart). Although there remain many of today's New Testament scholars who would reject this, and who continue to prefer Kümmel's scheme, even before John Robinson the distinguished biblical archaeologist William Albright had remarked on the basis of his quite independent archaeological insights:

> We can already say emphatically that there is no longer any solid basis for dating any book of the New Testament after about AD 80, two full generations before the date between 130 and 150 given by the more radical New Testament critics of today.

Accordingly, while the canonical gospels may not be quite the one hundred per cent contemporary eyewitness descriptions that sceptics demand, neither are they the tissue of late second-century fabrications that Strauss and other German theologians once tried hard to promulgate. Ironically, it has not been theologians but outsiders, such as scholars of ancient history, well used to imperfections in the works of the pagan writers of antiquity, who have been most prepared to recognize the gospels' strong underlying vein of genuine history. E.M. Blaiklock, Professor of Classics at Auckland University, has argued:

> I claim to be an historian. My approach to the Classics is historical. And I tell you that the evidence for the life, the death, and the resurrection of Christ is better authenticated than most of the facts of ancient history.

Likewise Nicholas Sherwin-White, writing in *Roman Society and Roman Law in the New Testament*:

> ... it can be maintained that those who had a passionate interest in the story of Christ, even if their interest in events was parabolical and didactic rather than historical, would not be led by that very fact to pervert and utterly destroy the historical kernel of their material.

Not least, the Oxford English don C.S. Lewis, speaking particularly of the John gospel, expressed it particularly beautifully:

> I have been reading poems, romances, vision literature, legends, myths all my life. I know what they are like. I know that none of them is like this. Of this text there are only two possible views. Either this is reportage – though it may no doubt contain errors – pretty close to the facts; nearly as close as Boswell. Or else, some unknown writer in the second century, without known predecessors or successors, suddenly anticipated the whole technique of modern, novelistic, realistic narrative. If it is untrue, it must be narrative of that kind. The reader who doesn't see this simply has not learned to read.

Overall, then, there is a good case for more than a little trust of the canonical gospels – particularly that, whoever were their actual authors in the form we now have them, they were written genuinely close to the time of the events they describe and were founded on the recollections of individuals who had directly known the living Jesus.

Even so, do they carry the authority of the sort of historical biography that we would expect of, say, a modern-day public figure? At the most basic level of information, do they tell us even when Jesus was born? And are they reliable about the circumstances surrounding this?

3

CAN WE BE SURE OF ANYTHING ABOUT JESUS' BIRTH?

We have seen that the surviving documentation for Jesus is surprisingly early and plentiful. We have also noted good grounds for believing that much of this is based on earlier, first-hand witnesses. Even so, some refuse to take for granted even that Jesus ever existed as a human being. In the former Soviet Union it used to be a basic part of Communist education that Jesus was invented in the second century AD as the hero of an early proletarian communist movement. In 1970 Manchester University oriental studies specialist John Allegro argued in all seriousness in his *The Sacred Mushroom and the Cross* that Christianity began as a secret cult of the sacred mushroom, and that the name 'Jesus' was a code word for this. During the late 1970s and early 1980s championship of the 'Jesus did not exist' school was taken over by G.A.Wells, professor of German at Birkbeck College, London, author of no less than three scholarly-looking books on the theme.

With regard to Wells's arguments, their linchpin is the writings of the apostle Paul, an individual whom Wells does admit to have existed, and to have authored at least some of the New Testament letters attributed to him.

Opposite *Adoration of the Magi: detail of fresco of the first half of the third century in the Capella Graeca, cemetery of Priscilla, Rome. The early date of this fresco is one attestation of how the Matthew gospel story of Jesus' birth had become well established within less than two hundred years of Jesus' death.*

But because Paul's letters are generally agreed to have been written before the canonical gospels (at least as based on Kümmel's chronology), for Wells their interest lies in their apparent ignorance of any detail of Jesus' earthly life. As he has pointed out, Paul does not name Jesus' parents, does not say where he was born, where he lived, even when he lived. Although his writings comprise a substantial proportion of the New Testament, they contain no mention of Jesus' parables or 'miracles'. They make no reference to his trial before Pilate, nor of Jerusalem as the place of his execution.

No-one can seriously deny any of this, for Paul freely admitted that he had never known Jesus in his lifetime, his conversion having come about sometime afterwards as a result of a claimed vision of Jesus in his resurrected form. It is therefore hardly to be expected that he would be full of chapter and verse on Jesus' biography. Nevertheless for Wells the inescapable deduction to be drawn was that Jesus was a mere figment of Paul's imagination who, when people began to believe in him, had to be made to seem a real-life historical individual. The writing of convincing-sounding pseudo-biographies thereupon became the task of the gospel writers, who drew upon all sorts of Old Testament material to give flesh to these, crowning them with the similarly invented story of the fictional hero being executed during the Roman governorship of Pontius Pilate.

Whatever view may be taken on Wells, few but the most die-hard of Christians can deny that some of the seemingly most essential facts concerning Jesus and his life are remarkably difficult to come by. At first sight this appears to be borne out by the lack of references to Jesus outside the gospels. For instance, although the great Roman historian Tacitus is often quoted as having mentioned Jesus, close scrutiny of the original reference reveals this to speak merely of certain Christians, barbarically put to death on Nero's orders, whose 'originator, Christ, had been executed in Tiberius' reign by the governor of Judaea, Pontius Pilate'.

For Professor Wells and like detractors Tacitus' vagueness and his undoubted distance from events in the Jewish world is sufficient to argue that a totally illusory belief in Jesus as a historical figure might have grown up by the second century in which he lived. For instance he referred to Jesus as 'Christ', as if this were his proper name, in apparent ignorance that it is a Greek form of the Hebrew *Māshīāh* (Messiah), or 'anointed one'. Nor does Tacitus' near contemporary Suetonius seem to have been better informed, referring merely to some Jews of Rome who, during the reign of Claudius (41-54 AD), rebelled at the instigation of one 'Chrestus'. The only other early classical reference is that of Pliny the Younger, who, as a rather fussy governor of Bithynia, wrote to Trajan in 112 AD reporting Christians to be an apparently harmless people who met at daybreak and sang hymns in which they appealed to their 'Christus' as God. Pliny commented of them, 'I found only a depraved superstition carried to extreme lengths'.

In all this, therefore, there might seem precious little to compel a belief that Jesus ever existed. But where we meet evidence of an altogether different order is in the writings of the Jewish historian Josephus. Born in 37 or 38 AD, the son of a Judaean priest, Josephus was educated as a Pharisee. In 66 AD he helped defend Galilee against the Romans during the Jewish Revolt, but when he was captured he took the realistic, though bitterly resented step of defecting to the Romans, subsequently pleading with his countrymen that further resistance was useless. In 70 AD, after acting as interpreter to Titus who besieged Jerusalem, he moved to Rome, and was there well looked after by successive Roman emperors, enjoying the leisure to write *The Jewish War*, which he completed around 77 or 78 AD, followed about fifteen years later by his monumental *The Antiquities of the Jews*. Both these works, packed with contemporary detail that is often confirmed by modern-day archaeological discoveries, have survived via later copies, and they represent our prime sources of information on the history of the Jewish people during the very period that Jesus, if indeed he existed, lived and breathed in what we now call the Holy Land.

If therefore we look at Josephus for some mention of a historical Jesus and his followers – which we might expect, since his interest in religious matters is evident from his having spent three of his early years living in the desert with a hermit called Bannos – we are certainly not disappointed. In the surviving text of the *Antiquities* there appears this passage:

> At about this time lived Jesus, a wise man, if indeed one might call him a man. For he was one who accomplished surprising feats and was a teacher of such people as are eager for novelties. He won over many of the Jews and many of the Greeks. He was the Messiah. When Pilate, upon an indictment brought by the principal men among us, condemned him to the cross, those who had loved him from the very first did not cease to be attached to him. On the third day he appeared to them restored to life, for the holy prophets had foretold this and myriads of other marvels concerning him. And the tribe of the Christians, so called after him, has to this day still not disappeared.

Now since the rest of Josephus' writings make it quite clear that he was not a Christian, there can be no doubt that some copyist of his manuscript must either have interpolated this passage or adulterated it, very clumsily, in a pro-Christian way. And this inevitably gives the likes of Professor Wells ready excuse to discount it altogether. But later in *Antiquities* Josephus includes a lengthy reference to the unjust execution in Jerusalem in 62 AD of James, whom he describes as 'the brother of Jesus called the Christ'. Of course this too might be dismissed as an interpolation, except that it does not sound like one, because it refers to Jesus merely as 'called the Christ', inconsistent with the earlier passage, and just the sort of remark that Josephus might well have made, given his non-Christian standpoint. Furthermore, we can be quite sure that this particular passage existed in a

Roman bust in the Ny Carlsberg Glypotek, Copenhagen, thought to represent Flavius Josephus (c.37-100 AD), whose prolific writings provide the main source of information on Jewish history of the first century AD. Josephus' reference to Jesus, although unmistakably adulterated by later Christian copyists, provides important attestation of Jesus' existence independent and supplementary to that of the Christian gospels.

very early version of his text, together with some separate passage casting doubt on Jesus' Messiahship, since in the third century the Christian writer Origen expressed his astonishment that Josephus, while disbelieving that Jesus was the Messiah, should have spoken so warmly about his brother. This information effectively therefore confirms that Josephus did make a reference to Jesus, albeit without regarding him as Messiah, before any Christian copyist had a chance to make alterations.

So with this established, is it still possible to reconstruct what Josephus may originally have said about Jesus in the first *Antiquities* passage, before it was tampered with? Encouragement for this is provided by the opening description of Jesus as 'a wise man', a comment that we would not expect from any Christian writer, but that was definitely characteristic of Josephus. This has encouraged completely uncommitted scholars such as the Jewish Dr Geza Vermes to try removing all pro-Christian elements from the passage, resulting in what has become accepted as a close approximation, though not necessarily complete, of what Josephus originally wrote:

> At about this time lived Jesus, a wise man ... He performed astonishing feats (and was a teacher of such people as are eager for novelties?). He attracted many Jews and many of the Greeks ... Upon an indictment brought by leading members of our society, Pilate sentenced him to the cross, but those who had loved him from the very first did not cease to be attached to him ... The brotherhood of the Christians, named after him, is still in existence ...

There is excellent justification for such a restoration, for the words 'astonishing feats', or more literally 'paradoxical deeds', are precisely the same as those used by Josephus to describe the healings of Elisha. The reconstructed text corresponds closely with a possibly unadulterated version preserved in the writings of the tenth-century Arabic Christian Agapius, which also includes the following:

> his disciples ... reported that he had appeared to them three days after his crucifixion and that he was alive; accordingly he was perhaps the Messiah, concerning whom the prophets have recounted wonders.

If Josephus originally wrote something approximating to these words – and as we have seen, Jewish as well as Christian scholars have been prepared to affirm that he did – then we have positive and authoritative corroboration of Jesus' existence from very nearly the best possible independent source, a man who actually lived in Galilee well within the lifetimes of individuals who would have known Jesus at first hand.

Other early Jewish sources too, while similarly saying nothing very favourable about Jesus, also at least tacitly acknowledge that he existed. Among both Christians and Jews these references are all too little known because, as a result of Christian persecution, Jewish religious books came under repeated attack during the Middle Ages, and references of all kinds were censored and not restored. But the last two generations of Jewish scholars, anxious to discover who Jesus was, have done much to retrieve them. As they have recognized, the name by which Jesus would have been known by his own Jewish contemporaries was not 'Jesus' – which is merely an adaptation for Graeco-Roman usage – but 'Yeshu'. Meaning 'God Saves', this was a common enough name in the first-century Jewish world, being found among several of the individuals referred to in Josephus' *Antiquities*, including no less than four of the Jerusalem Temple's line of twenty-eight high priests.

But specifically thought to refer to the Christians' 'Jesus' are at least five references to a 'Yeshu' in the *Baraitha* and *Tosefta*, supplements to the *Mishnah*, the great collection of Jewish religious literature compiled after what Christians know as the Old Testament, and mostly before 200 AD. The following are examples:

1. It has been taught: On the eve of Passover they hanged Yeshu…because he practised sorcery and enticed and led Israel astray.
2. Our rabbis taught: Yeshu had five disciples – Mattai, Nakkai, Netzer, Buni and Todah.
3. It happened with Rabbi Elazar ben Damah, whom a serpent bit, that Jacob, a man of Kefar Soma, came to heal him in the name of Yeshu[a] ben Pantera; but Rabbi Ishmael did not let him. He said 'You are not permitted, Ben Damah'. He answered, 'I will bring you proof that he may heal me.' But he had no opportunity to bring proof, for he died.
4. Once I was walking on the upper street of Sepphoris [capital of Galilee] and found one of the disciples of Yeshu the Nazarene, by the name of Jacob, a man of Kefar Sechanya. He said to me: 'It is written in your Torah: "Thou shalt not bring the hire of a harlot, etc." How about making with it a privy for the high priest?' But I did not answer him at all. He told me 'Thus did Yeshu the Nazarene teach me: "For the hire of a harlot hath she gathered them, And unto the hire of a harlot shall they return, from the place of filth they come, and unto the place of filth they shall go." And the utterance pleased me …'

Clearly the references do not sound particularly warm towards 'Yeshu', and the quoted number and names of his disciples are somewhat astray with what we learn from the gospels. But the other details, such as his 'hanging' on the eve of the Passover, the specific appellation 'Yeshu the Nazarene', his association with Galilee, and his accrediting with healings and 'sorcery' (another word for miracles), all indicate beyond reasonable doubt that the Yeshu of the *Mishnah* supplements was one and the same as the Jesus of the gospels. Arguably, therefore, there is sufficient acknowledgement of Jesus' existence from very early non-Christian sources for his one-time presence on earth to be beyond all reasonable doubt.

But what about our knowledge of how and when he was born? Because of the Western world's commercialization of Christmas, images of Jesus' birth in a stable, with visiting kings and shepherds, are among the most popularly known aspects of his life, readily familiar even to the many non-Christians who observe the festival, albeit in the old pagan way. Even many practising Christians, however, all too rarely appreciate that two of the gospels, those of Mark and John, carry absolutely no information about the human circumstances of Jesus' birth, while the other two, Matthew and Luke, contradict each other in several important particulars.

Historian and writer Marina Warner, in her highly acclaimed study *Alone of all her Sex – the Myth and Cult of the Virgin Mary*, has produced an excellent, yet inevitably disquieting summary of the main discrepancies. For instance, according to Matthew's gospel, the news of Jesus' impending birth is conveyed to Mary's husband, Joseph, in a dream, while according to Luke it is conveyed directly to Mary by the 'Angel Gabriel'. According to Luke, Jesus' parents had to travel from their home in Nazareth to Bethlehem for the Roman census, while according to Matthew they lived in Bethlehem already, and were only obliged to leave when King Herod began killing off the children. Although in Luke Jesus is represented as God's son by Mary, his ancestry is illogically traced back to King David via his human father Joseph. While Matthew's gospel similarly gives Jesus' genealogy via the male line, it provides a list of antecedents so different from those in Luke that even Joseph's father appears with a different name – Jacob instead of Heli.

Nor are these the greatest of the Matthew and Luke nativity stories' weaknesses. For instance, Matthew tries to justify Jesus' apparent divine parentage from Isaiah's famous prophecy: 'The virgin will conceive and give birth to a son' (Isaiah 7: 14).

Unfortunately this all too clearly reveals that whoever wrote at least this part of Matthew's gospel was no true Jew. In the original Hebrew text of Isaiah the crucial word *'almah* is used, which simply means 'young woman'. While it carries a general connotation of eligibility for marriage, this does not necessarily mean virginity. Only when, in the third century BC, the Hebrew scriptures were translated into Greek, to become the Septuagint – the bible of those Jews so absorbed into Greek-speaking communities that they had lost much of their Hebrew – was the Greek word *parthenos* inaccurately used as a translation of *'almah*, carrying with it a strong implication of untouched virginity absent from the original Hebrew. To this day, no true Jew expects the Messiah of Isaiah's prophecy, whoever he may be, and whenever he may appear, to be conceived by anything other than normal means, and it is to be noted that the writers of the Mark and John gospels show no awareness of anything unusual about Jesus' human parentage, and neither does Paul. Similarly, Mary's famous words of the *Magnificat* in the Luke gospel (Luke 1: 46-55) seem rather too close for comfort to the sentiments of the song of Hannah in I Samuel 2: 1-10.

What confidence can we have that we know the year when Jesus was born? Every day of their lives, everyone in the Western world organizes themselves according to a calendar that is ultimately based on the supposed year of Jesus' birth, and although it is often supposed that this must have been 0 AD, or 'the year dot', in fact our calendar system as devised by a sixth-century Byzantine monk, Dionysius Exiguus, has Jesus born in 1 AD, a year immediately succeeding 1 BC. But with regard to whether this was the true year of Jesus' birth, when we turn to the Matthew and Luke gospels, we find this is immediately contradicted, since Matthew, for one, very firmly sets Jesus' birth in the reign of Herod the Great, who died in 4 BC, while Luke likewise has the births of both Jesus and John the Baptist announced in Herod's reign (Luke 1: 5). Complicating Luke's information on the date, however, he then ruins any seeming point of agreement with Matthew by relating an apparent impressive historical detail:

> Now at this time Caesar Augustus issued a decree for a census of the whole world to be taken. This census – the first – took place while Quirinius was governor of Syria, and everyone went to his home town to be registered … (Luke 2: 1-3).

The problem here is that while the first-ever census among Jews did indeed take place during Quirinius' governorship, this did not happen until at least 6 AD, the first year that Judaea came under direct Roman rule. This was reliably reported by Josephus as an unprecedented event of that year. There is an unavoidable inference, therefore, that the Luke gospel's author may have been trying to make it appear that he knew more about Jesus' birth than he actually did.

Roman Census Order. According to the Luke gospel, Jesus was born at the time of a census (apographes) of the Roman world ordered by the Emperor Augustus (27 BC-14 AD). Such a census is known to have been called in 6 AD, but for an actual surviving census decree the example shown here dates from 104 AD, the time of Trajan. Found in Egypt, it is an order from the Prefect Gaius Vibius Maximus requiring all those in his terrritory to return to their homes to be counted, a situation clearly analogous to that described in the Luke gospel.

As for the actual day of Jesus' birth, both the Matthew and Luke gospels tell us absolutely nothing, but quite undeniably today's annual festivities focused on 25 December have their basis not in any early Christian tradition, but in the Roman festival of the Saturnalia, which celebrated the (re)birth of the sun. According to the Romans' Julian calendar the winter solstice, or shortest day of the year, was 25 December, after which days began to lengthen and become warmer, leading towards summer. December 25 was therefore regarded as the sun's birthday, a time for celebration, the exchange of gifts, and the decoration of temples with greenery, and because the festival was as popular in Roman times as 'Christmas' is today, when the Roman Empire went over to Christianity, it was shrewdly decided to assimilate it by celebrating Jesus' birth on the same day. This could of course have been justified then because of the concept of Jesus as the 'light of the world', though there are no known grounds for arguing that such justification actually took place.

The best we have then is that if there is any historical truth at all in the Matthew and Luke nativity stories, Jesus was born in the reign of Herod the Great, requiring us to look to a year sometime before 4 BC. With a view to pinpointing this, even possibly to the day, the Matthew gospel's references to the unusual star which hung over Bethlehem (Matthew 2: 2-11) have been a subject of intense interest on the part of the more astronomi-cally minded. As long ago as 1603 the astronomer John Kepler, observing a striking conjunction of the planets Saturn and Jupiter in the constellation Pisces on 17 December of that year, calculated that a very similar conjunc-tion must have occurred in 7 BC. Accordingly he speculated that this might have been the true year of Jesus' birth, even finding support in a Jewish rabbinical reference to the Messiah appearing when Saturn and Jupiter were in conjunction in the constellation of Pisces. When seventy-nine years later English astronomer Edmund Halley discovered the comet that now bears his name, it was calculated that one of its periodic fly-pasts must have occurred in 12 BC. It too was suggested as the star of Bethlehem, while much more recently three British astronomers, David Clark of the Royal Greenwich Observatory, John Parkinson of Dorking's Mullard Space Science Laboratory and Richard Stephenson of Newcastle University, have offered yet another theory – that the star of Bethlehem was a nova, or exploding star, which Chinese astronomers of the Han dynasty observed 'for more than seventy days' in 5 BC.

While any or all of such speculations are possible – and each of them of course has an important bearing on the age of Jesus at the time of his death – the hard reality is that neither the Matthew nor the Luke nativity stories offers sufficient historicity (and the story of the wise men and the star appears only in Matthew) for anyone to be confident that there was a star at all. And this lack of confidence extends to aspects such as Matthew's story that King Herod was so anxious to kill the infant Jesus that he ordered the slaughter of all recently born children in the hope of eliminating Jesus. Certainly the historical record as we have it from authorities such as Josephus makes clear that Herod the Great was no paragon of virtue. A wily Idumaean politician appointed by the Romans to rule the Jews on their behalf, Herod was loathed by his subjects from the first, and with good reason. While, as we shall see, he initiated some daringly ambitious and innovative building projects, not least the rebuilding of Jerusalem's Temple, he also surrounded himself with a shadowy network of informers and secret police with whose aid he systematically liquidated all whom he considered potentially dangerous to him, including his own wife and two of his sons. There is no difficulty, therefore, in thinking him capable of ordering the wholesale murder of infants, particularly if he felt the personal gain would outweigh the inevitable public antipathy. But whether he actually did so is very much more debatable. Josephus, who never shrank from cataloguing Herod's crimes, has no mention of such an atrocity, yet had anything like it actually occurred it would surely have rated among the best-remembered of Herod's misdeeds.

Adoration of the Magi, Capella Graeca, cemetery of Priscilla, Rome.

These by no means exhaust the uncertainties relating to the Matthew and Luke nativity stories. According to Luke, Jesus was circumcised in accordance with Jewish custom eight days after his birth (Luke 2: 21), after which he was presented in the Jerusalem temple on the fortieth. Only after these observances of the Jewish religion did Jesus' parents make a seemingly leisurely and peaceful return with him 'to their own town of Nazareth' (Luke 2: 39), in Galilee. Yet according to Matthew this was the very time that the trio fled to Egypt from what had been their home in Bethlehem to escape Herod's massacre of the new-born, remaining there for an unspecified period until the news reached them that Herod had died, whereupon they returned, settling not in Bethlehem as it was still too dangerous, but in Galilean Nazareth instead (Matthew 2: 22-3).

Of the circumstances surrounding Jesus' birth, therefore, the two gospel narratives that give us any information on this lack adequate assurance that they are based on reliable eyewitness reporting, even at second or third hand. The very fact that the two nativity stories sit somewhat uncomfortably in their gospels' opening chapters, and are never referred to again, adds to a genuine cause for disquiet. But it has to be remembered that if Jesus lived to, say, his mid-thirties (assuming he was born before 4 BC), then any memories from around the time of what may have seemed an unremarkable birth would have worn distinctly thin by the time of his death, and even thinner with every decade later than this that the gospels became committed to writing. Any inadequacies in the credibility of the Matthew and Luke nativity stories may therefore be accounted but a minor blip in relation to the content of the four gospels as a whole.

4

WHAT OF JESUS' UPBRINGING?

Even aside from our lack of reliable information on Jesus' birth, of the rest of his life Canon Streeter once calculated that aside from the forty days and nights in the wilderness (of which in any case we are told all too little), virtually everything described in the gospels could be compressed into a time scale of just three weeks, leaving by far the greater part of Jesus' life unrecorded.

That there is far too much we do not know is undeniable. For instance, not one of the four gospel writers seems to have given a thought to setting down even the tiniest morsel of information about what the adult Jesus looked like – whether he was tall or short, bearded or clean shaven, handsome or ugly. Because the Hebrew scriptures expressly forbade portraiture (Exodus 20: 4), the earliest surviving artistic depictions of him are Gentile works dating from the third century onwards, and such are the variations among these – in some of them vaguely he appears bearded (see p.172), but most depict him as beardless (whereas as a Jew, he would almost certainly have worn a beard) – that it is clear that even early on any reliable idea of what he looked like had already been lost.

Similarly, aside from readily predictable details, such as that as required by the Jewish Law he was circumcised on the eighth day after his birth

Opposite *Caesarea seen from the air, showing the sites of several of Herod the Great's ever-ambitious engineering projects. To the north is the harbour, one of the largest in the Mediterranean of Jesus' time, formed, according to Josephus, by a Herodian breakwater comprising huge blocks 50 feet long, 18 feet wide and 10 feet high, much of which later came to be destroyed in an earthquake. To the south an irregular landmass jutting into the sea marks the site of Herod's Promontory Palace, the dining room of which faced a large pool. The fine 4,000-seat theatre in the foreground is also of Herodian origin.*

(Luke 2: 21), the gospels tell us almost nothing about Jesus' upbringing, inevitably giving rise to some way-out theories. For instance, often put about is the idea that he spent his formative years in India, Tibet or China. According to one such argument, when he was two years old the 'three wise men' journeyed from India to identify him as a Dalai Lama-like high incarnation, whereupon, when he was thirteen years old, he followed the Silk Road to India, studied Buddhism, and thereby learnt his trade as a spiritual master. In reality such theories are extremely thin on substance, not least because Jesus is never recorded alluding to any life experience outside his own immediate Judaeo-Galilean environs, and nor do his highly individual teachings have their foundation in any religion other than that of his own characteristically Jewish roots.

With regard to even those roots, however, it is prudent not to take too literally the two gospel versions of Jesus' ancestry, the first as given in the Matthew nativity story (Matthew 1: 1-17) and the second as given in the Luke gospel associated with Jesus' baptism (Luke 3: 23-38). The Matthew gospel, for instance, makes some serious omissions from its Old Testament sources in order to have the magic number of exactly fourteen generations from Abraham to King David, from King David to the time of the Jewish exile and from the exile to Jesus. Furthermore, this descent from King David, so very important for Jesus' subsequent Messiahship claim, is somewhat incongruously given as via Joseph – whom the same gospel insists had not been responsible for Jesus' paternity.

On this issue of paternity it may be remembered from the documentary references in the Jewish *Mishnah* to the 'Yeshu' identified with Jesus, that he was given the patronymic 'ben Pantera' or 'son of Pantera' in one of the references (see p.45). Scurrilous Jewish stories about Jesus from the later Tannaitic period in fact claim that Jesus was the illegitimate son of a union between his mother Miriam or Mary and a Roman soldier variously called Pandera, Pantera or Panthera. That a rumour of this kind was early is confirmed by the Christian writer Origen who mentioned that he had heard it from the second-century philosopher Celsus, suggesting that it was already circulating before 150 AD. Equally undeniable is that at Bingerbrück in Germany there came to light the tombstone of one Tiberius Julius Abdes Pantera, the inscription on which shows that its owner was a Roman soldier from Sidon whose cohort of archers is historically known to have been posted to the Rhine in 9 AD. It is therefore just conceivable that this Pantera could have been Jesus' true father.

In fact, once this rumour and the gospel writers' somewhat flaky genealogies are set aside, there is much to suggest that Jesus was genuinely descended from King David, son of Jesse, as prophets such as Isaiah and Jeremiah had specifically predicted of the Messiah whose coming they promised (Isaiah 11: 1-10; Jeremiah 33: 15-22). Notably Jesus would later, on his entry to Jerusalem, be specifically hailed as 'Son of David' (e.g. Matthew 21: 9). St Paul, despite the little he seemed to know about the human Jesus, insisted that he was descended from David (Romans 1: 3). And perhaps most tellingly of all, the very scholarly and reputable church historian Eusebius, writing in the fourth century, quoted from the second-century church historian Hegesippus (whose works are now lost) how even in the reign of the Emperor Domitian (81-96 AD) close relations of Jesus were arrested specifically because they were known descendants of King David, then released because they seemed no more than harmless peasants.

If we rule out exotic Tibet or India, where was it that Jesus had his upbringing? Traditionally Jesus' family has long been associated with Nazareth (Luke 2: 4-5) , which is set on a hill overlooking what is today called the Bet Netofa Valley, though it is important to stress that this association is by no means as firm as the present-day town's tourist trade and modern New Testament translations' repeated reference to 'Jesus of Nazareth' might imply. This is partly because 'Jesus the Nazarene' is the more common form of the words in the original Greek, while in the Jewish record it is 'Hanotzri' – not particularly meaningful even for Jews. As Rabbi Morris Goldstein has commented:

> It might refer to *netzer*, as in Isaiah 11: 1, to mean 'a branch', used in Christian tradition with a messianic connotation. It might allude to Jesus as the source of the Nazarene sect. It might be a derivation from *noter*, which would describe those who keep the [new] Law of Jesus. It might mean, as is generally understood, 'of Nazareth'.

Another problem is that, as earlier noted, although the Luke gospel insists that Nazareth was Jesus' parents' home town, the second chapter of the Matthew gospel strongly suggests that Bethlehem was their original place of residence, and that they only settled in Nazareth following their return from Egypt. There has even been a suggestion that Nazareth may not even have existed in the first century; Josephus, in his listing of what appear to be all Galilee's main towns and villages (and he was the region's commander during the Jewish revolt), fails even to give it any mention throughout his writings, and the earliest Jewish literary reference (in a poem) does not occur until about the seventh century AD.

However, such negative thinking has been decisively changed by excavations carried out at Nazareth in the 1950s by the Franciscan Bellarmino

Was Jesus' father a Roman archer? According to one widespread early Jewish story, Jesus was the illegitimate son of a Roman soldier called Pantera or Panthera. The name is an unusal one, and was thought to be an invention until this first-century tombstone came to light at Bingerbrück, Germany. The inscription reads: 'Tiberius Julius Abdes Pantera of Sidon, aged 62, a soldier of 40 years' service, of the 1st cohort of archers, lies here.'

Bagatti. Digging both beneath and in the environs of the town's Church of the Annunciation – built above much older Crusader and Byzantine shrines reputedly marking where Jesus' mother Mary was told of the son she was to bear (Luke 1: 26-38) – Bagatti found wells, granaries and olive presses that seemed to date from around the first-century period. But these also clearly denoted that early Nazareth's economy was essentially rustic, and that at best it was a very small and insignificant place.

Readily corroborating Jesus' upbringing in precisely such environs is the easy familiarity with country life that he displays throughout the sayings that the gospels attribute to him. Within just a single chapter of the Luke gospel (Luke 13) he is depicted as knowing how to revive a barren fig tree (vv. 6-9), as being sensitive to farm animals' need for watering (v. 15), as being aware of the remarkable growth propensity of mustard seed (v. 19), being well informed on the amount of yeast needed to leaven dough (v. 21) and as keenly observant of the characteristic manner in which a hen gathers

The shores of the Sea of Galilee (also referred to in Luke 5: 1 as the 'Lake of Gennesaret'), the setting for most of what is known of Jesus' early life. The Sea of Galilee abounds in fish, and the historian Josephus, who lived just a generation after Jesus, described its environs as 'excellent for crops or cattle and rich in forests of every kind ... every inch has been cultivated by the inhabitants'.

her brood under her wings (v. 34). In the Matthew gospel he is the first man to go on record as interpreting a red sky at night as a portent for good weather the following day (Matthew 16: 1-3). Furthermore, we know from Josephus that almost the whole of Galilee, in which Nazareth was set, was a prolifically agricultural region – in Josephus' words:

> … excellent for crops or cattle and rich in forests of every kind, so that by its adaptability it invites even those least inclined to work on the land. Consequently every inch has been cultivated by the inhabitants and not a corner goes to waste.

If, therefore, as we have good reason to believe, Jesus grew up in such a rustic environment, then we can count it as also very likely that he spoke with the notorious Galilean accent. From sources quite independent of the New Testament it is known that certainly some of his fellow-Galileans greatly amused the snobbish southerners of Jerusalem by their characteristic sloppiness in pronouncing Aramaic, as, but one example, dropping their aitches, or more accurately, their alephs. As noted by the Jewish scholar Dr Geza Vermes, the Talmud features a typical Galilean being ridiculed in the Jerusalem market-place for trying to buy what he called *amar*. He was chided: 'You stupid Galilean, do you want something to ride on [*hamar*: a donkey]? Or something to drink [*hamár*: wine]? Or something for clothing [*'amar*: wool]? Or something for a sacrifice [*immar*: a lamb]?' The Matthew gospel mentions that Jesus' disciple Peter was specifically remarked upon in Jerusalem because of his accent: 'You are one of them for sure! Why your accent gives you away' (Matthew 26: 73).

This Galilean flavour is even conveyed by the gospels' references to two different individuals called Lazarus, one the poor man of Luke 16: 19-31, the other the man raised from the dead, John 11: 1-44. As various surviving funerary inscriptions make clear, in Jerusalem the name took the form 'Eleazar' or 'Elazar', with the initial aleph, but in Galilee this same name is found as 'Lazar' or 'Laze', just like the Lazarus of the gospels. Despite the gospels being written in Greek, therefore, they carry clear indications of Jesus' Galilean roots.

But to limit Jesus' background to that of just some Galilean rustic would be quite inadequate. Today, visible as little more than a pine-clad hillock four miles from Nazareth, is the site of ancient Sepphoris, which according to one Christian tradition was where Jesus' mother Mary was born. All too few Christians have even heard of Sepphoris, which is hardly surprising, since it goes entirely unmentioned in the gospels. But it was mentioned, it may be recalled, in one of the earlier quoted Mishnaic references to 'Yeshu'/Jesus, viz: 'I was walking on the upper street of Sepphoris and found one of the disciples of Yeshu the Nazarene, by the name of Jacob [i.e. James]' (see p.45). And while scholars have long known from Josephus and others that Sepphoris was the administrative capital of the Galilee

Nazareth as it looks today, a busy provincial town, with, visible in the background at three miles' distance, the green hillock with lone Crusader tower marking the site of Sepphoris. In Jesus' time the rôles were reversed, with Nazareth the rustic Galilean village and Sepphoris (traditionally the birthplace of Jesus' mother, Mary) the sophisticated Graeco-Roman administrative capital of the Galilee and Perea regions, complete with theatre and classically designed public buildings.

region, only very recently, and thanks to American-led archaeological excavations carried out since the early 1980s, have they appreciated the cultural timbre which went with that status.

For under the trowels of South Florida University's James Strange and Duke University's Eric and Carol Meyers have been steadily coming to light the remains of a one-time substantial Roman provincial capital of very considerable style and sophistication. Although the work is being painstak-

ingly conducted, and much remains to be uncovered, it is already evident that the Sepphoris of Jesus' time sported an acropolis; a colonnaded east-west main street, bordered by shops and public buildings, leading to a forum; pools; fountains; public baths; community ritual baths; a royal palace; and by no means least, a 4,000-seat theatre – a capacity vying with those among London or New York's largest.

All this just four miles from Jesus' Nazareth, yet without the slightest mention from a single gospel writer? As has been remarked by Dr Geza Vermes, the omission can hardly have been accidental. So who was responsible for initiating Sepphoris' hilltop magnificence and urban affluence? And how would this have been viewed by those, such as the young Jesus and his family, who lived less than an hour's walk away in rustic Nazareth?

For this we need to be aware of the Jewish people's long and often extremely painful struggle to preserve their religious and cultural identity in the face of what was, to them, the often offensive paganism of the surrounding peoples with whom they came into contact and too often conflict. Even when, as their tradition told, Moses had led them out of Egypt, some of their number had wanted to worship a golden calf in the manner of the Canaanites. Then, after the all too brief heyday of their independent kingdom under David and Solomon, the Babylonians had swept in, destroyed the beautiful Jerusalem Temple that Solomon had built, and deported all but the lowest-born to Babylonian exile. Not long after the Persians had released them, along came Alexander the Great, whose generals now brought in all the refinements of Hellenistic culture, such as bronze statues, public baths and gymnasia where athletes sported themselves stark

Offensive to Jews, Greek athletes exercising totally naked, from a Greek vase painting. Such nudity, the expected norm for the male athletics events and public bathing widely enjoyed in the Graeco-Roman world, embarrassed Jews observant of the Mosaic Law.

naked. Such a lifestyle was anathema to the Jews, whose Law forbade depictions of the human face and form, and whose practice of male circumcision could only make them conspicuous in any all-nude sporting event.

To make matters even worse, in 167 BC the Seleucid King Antiochus IV Epiphanes went to the lengths of specifically prohibiting circumcisions, abolishing the Sabbath as a day of rest, erecting Zeus' statue in the restored Jerusalem Temple, and sacrificing pigs on its altars – all more than enough to provoke the Jews to revolt. In the event they were successful in this, the Maccabee family who led it founding the Hasmonean dynasty which preserved a fragile independence for just over a century. But in 63 BC in burst the Romans – quite literally, with the inquisitive general Pompey, having captured Jerusalem, striding into the Temple's Holy of Holies.

Finding to his disappointment that this was no more than a small, empty room, without even a window, Pompey had the prudence to withdraw, and in conformity with Roman toleration, leave the Temple intact. But by 40 BC the Romans brought in Herod the Great, an Idumaean who had wormed his way into the Hasmonean dynasty, as their local client-king to rule the Jews. And although Herod provoked much hatred among those he ruled, he managed remarkably cleverly to preserve at least the appearance of traditional Jewish religion, while bringing in every refinement of the Rome-sponsored Graeco-Roman culture.

In the latter, there can be absolutely no doubt that Herod excelled to the point of genius. Besides his spectacular remodelling of the Jerusalem Temple, which we will look at in a later chapter, at Caesarea he built a complete port with accompanying Graeco-Roman installations (see p.50), including a theatre and a superbly appointed palace for himself, which incorporated a large fresh-water swimming pool almost completely surrounded by the sea (see overleaf). On Masada, high in the desert overlooking the Dead Sea, he taxed Roman engineering to its limits by again insisting on the installation of a 60-foot swimming pool. As for his Jerusalem palace, according to Josephus this was

> baffling all description: indeed in extravagance and equipment no building surpassed it. It was completely enclosed with a wall thirty cubits high, broken at equal distances by ornamental towers, and contained immense banqueting halls and bedchambers for a hundred guests. The interior fittings are indescribable – the variety of the stones (for species rare in every other country were here collected in abundance), ceilings wonderful both for the length of the beams and the splendour of their surface decoration, the host of apartments with their infinite varieties of design, all amply furnished, while most objects in each of them were of silver and gold … There were groves of various trees intersected by long walks, which were bordered by deep canals, and ponds everywhere studded with bronze figures, through which the water was discharged …

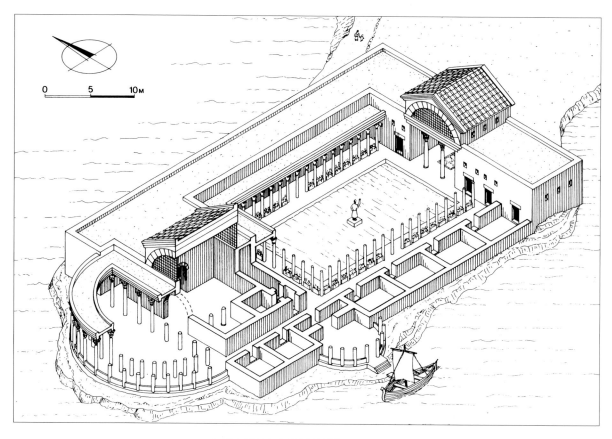

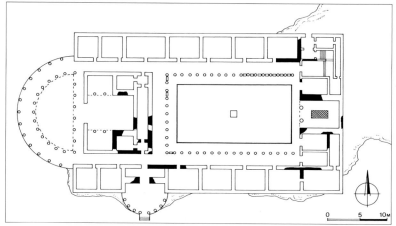

Reconstruction of Herod the Great's Promontory Palace at Caesarea, in an artist's rendition (above) and in plan form (right). With typical Herodian flamboyance, the palace was surrounded on three sides by the sea and had a special landing stage for visitors to arrive by water. Dominating the palace's interior was a near Olympic-sized swimming pool, 115 feet long, 59 feet wide and at least 8 feet deep, which some excavators think may have been filled with fresh water piped from the mainland.

Testimony to Herod's political grip while initiating such splendour (albeit aided by the power of Rome) is the fact that only when he died – after a 36-year-long reign – did pockets of rebellion break out, particularly strongly in Galilee where Sepphoris, which had an arsenal of weapons the rebels captured, became a major centre of resistance. With characteristic efficiency the Romans ruthlessly crushed this revolt, reducing Sepphoris to a smouldering ruin. And it was Herod's son, Antipas, whom they appointed to restore political order, and who decided to rebuild Sepphoris as his new capital with much the same enthusiasm for Graeco-Roman style and opulence as exhibited by his father. The magnificent city currently being revealed by the American archaeological excavations led by James Strange was therefore largely built at Herod Antipas' instigation. Like his father, he enjoyed a long life, his reign, and thereby his Sepphoris building projects, extending to 39 AD, and thereby throughout and beyond the entire known lifetime of Jesus.

So we now know that just four miles from Jesus' Nazareth there lived in considerable splendour a king over the Galileans whose thirst for stylish edifices in his new capital would have demanded the labour of many a skilled construction worker for miles around – including of course Nazareth, where there lived just such workers in the persons of Joseph and (probably) his son Jesus. Although the Matthew and Mark texts which refer to Jesus' family's mode of business leave it unclear whether Jesus was himself a carpenter (Mark 6: 3), or merely a carpenter's son (Matthew 13: 55; Mark 6: 3 variant texts), whichever was the case the word in the original Greek meant something closer to our 'builder' or 'construction worker' than the rather more limited word 'carpenter' by which it is now so often translated.

And in this regard, just as we noted how the imagery of a countryman is present in Jesus' sayings, so too is that of a carpenter, and/or construction worker. Hence in Luke's gospel alone there is reference to the planning needed by a man building a tower (14: 28-30); the parable of a house built on rock (6: 47-9); and allusion to Psalm 118, 'It was the stone rejected by the builders that became the keystone' (20: 17 and also in other gospels). Also, if we still prefer to see Jesus' father and/or Jesus as just carpenters in the more traditional sense, there is the saying: 'Why do you observe the splinter in your brother's eye and never notice the plank in your own' (6: 41, also Matthew 7: 3-5).

Accordingly, Shirley Jackson Case, Professor of New Testament studies at the University of Chicago, has noted that Sepphoris' proximity to Nazareth makes it 'no very daring flight of the imagination' that Jesus, and probably Joseph as well, may have played some part in Antipas' construction schemes there. For Jesus to have worked in a cosmopolitan city would also make sense, for instance, of the way, in the parables with which he later illustrated his teaching, he displayed easy familiarity with a keenly observed cast of characters far removed from any to be found in rustic Nazareth: kings, tax-collectors, unscrupulous judges, crafty stewards, virtuous Pharisees and many more. Likewise, in the Matthew gospel, when he is represented as addressing John the Baptist's disciples, he asks them what manner of man they had sought in the desert: 'A man wearing fine clothes? Oh no, those who wear fine clothes are to be found in palaces' (Matthew 11: 8). When Jesus spoke those words, it is not unreasonable to suppose that he had in mind the people in fine clothes that he had seen while working in Herod Antipas' palace at Sepphoris.

In this regard, a particular Sepphoris location where the archaeologist

James Strange has suggested Jesus and/or his father may have worked is the city's theatre. Although in their excavations of it Strange and his fellow archaeologists found the original stage's front and back walls, they did not find any part of its floor, suggesting that this had probably been of wood. So might Joseph and/or his son have crafted some of the planking? Speculative as this might seem, one fascinating indication of Jesus' apparent familiarity with Graeco-Roman theatre, and also of the possibility that he may well have been able to speak rather more than just the local Galilean version of Aramaic, derives from the notable frequency in the gospels in which he is represented as using the word 'hypocrite'. This occurs no less than seventeen times in sayings of his throughout the synoptic gospels, most frequently appearing as an expression of disapproval directed either towards the Pharisees (Matthew 6: 2, 5, 16; 7: 5; 15: 7; 22: 18; 23: 13, 14, 15; Mark 7: 6; Luke 6: 42; 13: 15), or, as in two instances in the Luke gospel, towards 'the crowds' (6: 17; 12: 56). Because the word derives from Greek, English New Testament translations almost invariably give it unchanged from this. But what this fails to convey is that in Jesus' time the image it carried was that of a play-actor, one who spoke behind a dramatic mask, and thereby a pretender. So Jesus seems to have been using specifically theatrical imagery – and pejoratively. Equally important, modern scholars have pointed out that 'hypocrite' has no equivalent in either Hebrew or Aramaic. So Jesus had either to be bringing in a specifically Greek word to make his point – or actually to have been fully speaking Greek at the time.

This raises the interesting point as to whether Jesus' upbringing included the learning of Greek. As has recently been argued by Joseph A. Fitzmyer, Jesuit Professor of Biblical Studies at the Catholic University of America, Washington DC, this is looking increasingly probable. Because of the powerful impact of Graeco-Roman culture, even many of Lower Galilee's funerary inscriptions of Jews of around Jesus' time were written in Greek, and when later in the gospels Jesus is represented as conversing, apparently easily, both with a Roman centurion and with Pontius Pilate, it seems very much more likely that these exchanges would have been in Greek rather than Aramaic. This does not mean to say that when Jesus used the term 'hypocrite' he did not simply introduce it among words spoken in Aramaic, just as Parisians blithely use English words such as 'football' and 'weekend' when speaking French. But there are certainly signs that Jesus had experienced the Graeco-Roman culture at close hand. There are also signs that he pointedly distanced himself from those Jews who embraced this rather too warmly at the expense of their own culturo-religious heritage.

Amidst the new importance that must now be attached to Sepphoris as a formative influence on Jesus's life, we might ask whatever happened to his father, Joseph? Once we set the nativity stories aside, Joseph effectively disappears from the gospels, suggesting that by the time that Jesus emerged to commence the rôle he felt he was destined for, Joseph was by then already dead. At this point it would seem to have been Jesus, as the eldest of four brothers and at least two sisters (Matthew 13: 55-6; Mark 6: 3–see family tree p.159), who became head of the family, for there are several instances in the gospels in which his family seem to look to him for leadership (e.g. Mark 3: 31-5), and these indications of an apparent family line of succession are important, because they effectively give the lie to the later Jewish stories of Jesus being the son of a Roman soldier. Had Jesus genuinely been known to have been born illegitimate, the eldest legitimate brother would have taken charge after Joseph's death, which certainly does not appear to have been the case.

None of this, however, answers one most fundamental question: just how did a construction worker's son from tiny Nazareth, even if he had the blood of King David running through his veins, acquire the sense of mission to give up the family trade and begin attracting ordinary men and women to follow him and his teaching?

5

HOW DID
HE ACQUIRE
HIS SENSE
OF MISSION?

As we have already seen, the authors of both the Mark and the John gospels chose not to commence their accounts of Jesus with the story of any seemingly miraculous nativity. Instead, aside from the John gospel's remarkable proiogue they begin with the wild man John the Baptist proclaiming the coming of 'someone more powerful than I am'. Immediately following this, both gospels tell of the apparently adult Jesus' arrival (from Nazareth, according to Mark), on the banks of the Jordan, a Jesus who to all appearances wants to be baptized by John, just as many others had been, for the forgiveness of sins.

Now there can be no doubt that John the Baptist's one-time existence is historically very well attested. Throughout early Christian literature he was referred to as a man of whom everyone had heard, and according to the New Testament book of Acts his disciples carried his teachings as far afield as Alexandria and Ephesus (Acts 18: 25; 19: 2). All four gospel authors referred to him at some length, and although naturally their prime focus was on Jesus (and there are hints of even a little rivalry between John's disciples and those of Jesus), they freely acknowledged that great crowds had flocked to John from 'Jerusalem and all Judaea and the whole Jordan

Opposite *Jesus' baptism by John the Baptist, from a fifth-century mosaic in Santa Maria in Cosmedin, Ravenna. John the Baptist's existence is independently attested by Josephus and others. Note Jesus' nudity and the 'spirit of God' descending in the form of a bird.*

district' (Matthew 3: 5). Furthermore, from quite outside the Christian milieu, the first-century historian Josephus mentioned John the Baptist in a passage that scholars generally agree is not a copyist's interpolation:

> He [John] was a good man, and exhorted the Jews to lead righteous lives, practise justice towards one another and piety towards God, and so to join in baptism. In his view this was a necessary preliminary if baptism was to be acceptable to God. They must not use it to gain pardon for whatever sins they committed, but as a consecration of the body, implying that the soul was thoroughly purified beforehand by right behaviour.

As has been argued by Dr Martin Purbrook of Maynooth, Ireland, and others, the full extent of John the Baptist's influence on Jesus has probably been played down in the gospels, particularly by the synoptic authors. But besides John's baptism of Jesus being the first event on which all four gospels are in agreement, one reason for confidence that this baptism actually happened lies in the fact that there was no advantage to be gained by the gospel writers from inventing it. Rather the reverse, as it implied that Jesus had past sins that needed washing away. A hint even of early Christian sensitivity on this matter is to be found in the Matthew gospel, which represents John the Baptist as saying to Jesus: 'It is I who need baptism from you', and Jesus replying, 'Leave it like this for the time being...' (Matthew 3: 15).

So if John's baptism of Jesus actually occurred, what sort of event was it? The John gospel remarks that one of the settings in which John the Baptist conducted his work was 'Aenon, near Salim, where there was plenty of water' (John 3: 23), and as was pointed out half a century ago by the noted American archaeologist Professor W. F. Albright, this particular spot can almost certainly still be identified:

> ... Salim cannot be separated from the well-known ancient town of that name, south-east of Nablus, nor can it be quite accidental that there is an 'Ainun in the immediate vicinity. The nearby sources of the Wadi Far'ah are extremely well provided with water.

In fact, the gospels are fairly explicit that the specific baptism of Jesus was somewhere else along the Jordan, rather than at 'Ainun, but an obvious deduction to be drawn is that an open-air location and a plentiful supply of fresh water were required, the intention, clearly, being total immersion. John or one of his disciples appears to have needed to officiate, and for each recipient the event appears to have been a unique, once in a lifetime ritual, there being no accounts of anyone returning for a second baptism.

It is important to notice that in each of these respects the John baptism seems to have distinctively differed from the routine, self-administered ritual ablutions long commonplace for religious purification among Jews of all denominations. Directly challenging the Jerusalem Temple's claimed monopoly on the cleansing of sins, it seems to have been a form of consecration or initiation by which, after repentance, an individual could feel purified from his past sins in preparation for a better life thereafter.

Of John's baptism of Jesus, the gospels tell us enough to be able to envisage something of the scene, the hairy John in his camel-skins and Jesus himself most likely naked, for according to early churchman Hippolytus, and references to 'complete stripping' by Paul (I Colossians 2: 11), that is how the earliest Christian baptisms seem to have been conducted. Since no source specifically describes witnesses at John's baptisms, some degree of privacy may have been managed, thereby adding to the ceremony's element of mystery.

The very popularity of John's baptisms suggests that they had a powerful impact on those who received them and, we may assume, on no-one more so than on Jesus, for we are told that as he surfaced after immersion he seemed to receive a vision in the form of a dove, accompanied by a heavenly voice announcing: 'You are my son...' (Mark 1: 11). While sceptics might dismiss this as an obvious piece of Christian deification of Jesus, it cannot be tossed aside altogether lightly, for in the traditional Jewish royal ritual a perfectly human King of the Jews became 'Son of God' at the time of his anointing as Messiah. And an especially intriguing feature of Jesus' baptism, to be found in all four canonical gospels (also in non-canonical ones such as the Gospel of the Ebionites), is the association of a bird with his reported vision. As pointed out by an American scholar, the late Dr Morton Smith, the vision of a bird also occurs in early mystery religion initiations, as in one Greek magical papyrus description in which an initiate, after lying naked in a sheet and repeating a prescribed chant, is told to expect to see 'a sea-hawk flying down' as a sign that union with the deity had been achieved.

Accordingly, it would not be at all unreasonable to interpret Jesus' baptism, his first real appearance on the stage of history, as hugely life-changing. According to the Mark gospel, it was immediately after this that he spent his forty days in the wilderness. The John gospel even seems to suggest that initially he became one of the Baptist's disciples, spreading his work into other areas (John 3: 22-4), and becoming even more successful at it (John 4 : 1), although we are somewhat contradictorily told 'in fact it was his [Jesus'] disciples who baptised, not Jesus himself' (John 4: 2).

Whatever may have been the exact relationship between John the Baptist and Jesus, circumstances were to be dramatically changed by John's arrest and subsequent execution. It is the Mark gospel that very matter-of-factly gives us the fullest account, in which, in very unsavoury and tragic circumstances, we renew our acquaintance with the now familiar Herod Antipas:

Now... Herod [Antipas]... had sent to have John arrested, and had him chained up in prison because of Herodias, his brother Philip's wife whom he had married. For John had told Herod, 'It is against the Law for you to have your brother's wife'. As for Herodias, she was furious with him and wanted to kill him, but she was not able to, because Herod was afraid of John, knowing him to be a good and holy man, and gave him his protection. When he had heard him speak, he was greatly perplexed, and yet he liked to listen to him.

An opportunity came on Herod's birthday when he gave a banquet for the nobles of his court, for his army officers and for the leading figures in Galilee. When the daughter of this same Herodias came in and danced, she delighted Herod and his guests, so the king said to the girl, 'Ask me anything you like and I will give it to you'. And he swore her an oath, 'I will give you anything you ask, even half my kingdom'. She went out and said to her mother, 'What shall I ask for?' She replied, 'The head of John the Baptist'. The girl hurried straight back to the king and made her request, 'I want you to give me John the Baptist's head, here and now, on a dish.' The king was deeply distressed but, thinking of the oaths he had sworn, and of his guests, he was reluctant to break his word to her. So the king at once sent one of his bodyguard with orders to bring John's head. The man went off and beheaded him in prison; then he brought the head on a dish and gave it to the girl, and the girl gave it to her mother. When John's disciples heard about this, they came and took his body, and laid it in a tomb. (Mark 6: 17-29)

Now the basic facts are firmly historical. Josephus, for instance, supplemented the gospels by even providing the name of Herodias' daughter, Salome, also the information that the location was Machaerus, Herod Antipas' palace-fortress near the Dead Sea. Overall also quite clear is that John the Baptist had taken upon himself the rôle of one of the Jewish people's 'prophets' – men and women referred to rather more accurately in Hebrew as *nabi'im*, literally 'mouthpieces of God', to interpret the Law of Moses as it applied to everyday life problems. Unlike the Temple's priests, who were mere functionaries, essentially supervisors of animal sacrifices, *nabi'im* were individuals who could step from any background and fearlessly speak as if for God before the highest and mightiest in the land. One such had been Nathan, who openly denounced King David's duplicity over his adultery with an officer's wife; another the goatskin-clad Elijah the Tishbite, who similarly condemned Israel's ninth-century King Ahab and his flagrantly pagan Queen Jezebel. Such encounters always ran high risks of blood being spilt, and for John the Baptist this particular confrontation with Herod Antipas and his Herodias ended with the ultimate penalty, death. Not without good reason was it widely put about after John's death that he had been Elijah born again (Matthew 17: 12), for if he had been Elijah, then according to some schools of thought, this meant that the whole purpose of his return would have been to recognize and anoint the promised new Messiah – an individual who may not even have known his identity himself.

At the very least, therefore, Jesus would have been deeply moved and affected by the news of John's so unjust execution. Despite the Mark gospel's detailed account of how John died, its seemingly Rome-based author characteristically avoided stating anything too overtly political. Only in the Luke gospel are we told of Jesus' attitude to Antipas as expressed in just two words: 'that fox…' (Luke 13: 32). However what Mark's author did describe, in very next breath, was a large crowd 'like sheep without a shepherd' who, with scant thought for provisions, immediately journeyed to a 'lonely place' to seek out Jesus. There were five thousand of them, and Dr John Robinson pointed out that the original Greek makes clear that they were all men (Mark 6: 44). Although exactly what happened on this occasion has been somewhat obscured in the gospels by the accompanying 'miracle' – the feeding of the five thousand – the story's origins are undoubtedly early, for it can be seen that Mark drew on no less than two previous accounts of the happening, one referring to five thousand people, the other to four thousand. And the strong inference is that the popular following which John the Baptist had stirred up had turned to Jesus, both as John's natural successor, and as the potential Messiah so badly needed to free the Jewish people from the yoke of Rome and from self-seeking Roman-collaborator lackeys like Herod Antipas.

But what would Jesus do with this following? We are told that in common with John the Baptist before him he called upon them to repent, and proclaimed the closeness of what he called the Kingdom of God (Mark 1: 15). He also quite evidently impressed them, hence the story of the feeding miracle, whatever kind of explanation may be attributed to this (see chapter 7). But if those who had sought Jesus out expected him, as they surely did, to lead them in some sort of armed insurrection, then they were in for dis-

'They collected twelve basketfuls of scraps of bread and pieces of fish' (Mark 6: 43). Remarkably modern in appearance, this Jewish basket, dating from within a century of Jesus' lifetime, was found in caves in which rebels hid from the Romans during the Second Jewish Revolt. It vividly evokes the baskets described as being used during Jesus' feeding 'miracle'.

appointment. According to the John gospel, immediately after the food left over from the feeding miracle had been gathered up in baskets, 'Jesus could see they were about to come and take him by force and make him king' (John 6: 15) – whereupon his response was to make a swift diplomatic exit to the hills.

And in this lies one of the most explicit indications of Jesus' purpose. Had he been a mere guerrilla leader, undoubtedly he would have seized upon the wave of popular support, and there and then drawn up plans for a blood-letting rebellion. But whatever the effect of John's baptism upon him, what he was about was not of this order. A succession of post-war writers, among them Manchester University's Professor S.G.F. Brandon and Jewish scholars Hyam Maccoby and Joel Carmichael, have all tried to represent Jesus as an ardent Jewish nationalist whom the gospel writers deliberately misrepresented as a pacifist in order to make him more acceptable to Gentiles. If this were so, Jesus' pacifism would stand out as a glaring inconsistency with the rest of his message. Instead it seems all of a piece with everything else that he was about.

For if we try to define the essence of Jesus as at his succession to the mantle left by John the Baptist, it was his claim of the nearness of what he called the 'Kingdom of God'. And very clear in his mind was that this 'Kingdom' was not anything pertaining to the world of fancy palaces and fine clothes that (as we have suggested) he had seen displayed in Herod Antipas' Sepphoris. As related in the Mark gospel when the five thousand sought Jesus out in the 'lonely place', he 'set himself to teach them at some length' (Mark 6: 34), and although there is no record of his exact message on that occasion, it may readily be deduced from such texts as the Matthew 'Sermon on the Mount':

> Do not store up treasures for yourself on earth, where moths and wood-worm destroy them and thieves can break in and steal … You cannot be the slave both of God and money. That is why I am telling you not to worry about your life and what you are to eat, nor about your body and how you are to clothe it. Surely life means more than food and the body more than clothing? Look at the birds in the sky. They do not sow or reap or gather into barns; yet your heavenly Father feeds them. Are you not worth much more than they are? Can any of you, for all his worrying, add one single cubit to his span of life? And why worry about clothing? Think of the flowers in the fields, they never have to work or spin; yet I assure you that not even Solomon in all his regalia was robed like one of these. (Matthew 6: 19-29)

Aerial view of the Judaean wilderness. Despite its apparent remoteness, this 'wilderness' is located only a few miles south of Jerusalem, and is in similar close proximity to the Dead Sea Scrolls community at Qumran. After John the Baptist's death, Jesus was sought out by a reputed five thousand male Jews at a place such as this.

This so striking and compelling message, at once both so simple to preach and so extraordinarily difficult to put into practice, has never appealed to any vainglorious power-seeker, whether a Louis XIV or a Herod Antipas. Even in conventional Christianity it has too often been neglected, not least by Renaissance popes. But from time to time it has been taken to heart by men and women from as variegated backgrounds as St Francis of Assisi, William Blake, Tolstoy, Mother Teresa of Calcutta and Mahatma Gandhi. And ultimately it may be distilled into a simple attitude of mind: self-abnegation, shedding the earthly bonds of property, clothes, family ties and the like, and dwelling in a heaven of the mind. Almost everything that Jesus would say and do can be related to this utterly simple and consistent way of thought, including the counselling of extreme pacifism by which he spurned the sentiments of those who wanted him to overthrow the Romans by force: 'offer the wicked man no resistance. On the contrary, if anyone hits you on the right cheek, offer him the other also' (Matthew 5: 39).

Fired by their evangelical fervour, Christian writers have sometimes tried to claim that Jesus introduced such doctrines as total novelties into a world that had heard nothing like them before. But this needs some rather careful qualification. For instance, the New Testament book of Acts has a description of how Jesus' followers lived in Jerusalem after his death: '… all lived together and owned everything in common; they sold their goods and possessions and shared out the proceeds among themselves according to what each one needed' (Acts 2 : 45). This is effectively little different from what we are told of the Essenes by Josephus: 'each man's possessions go into the pool', and as with brothers their entire property belongs to them all. Similarly, just as Jesus sent his disciples on their missions 'with no haversack for the journey or spare tunic or footwear' (Matthew 10: 10), so we are told of the Essenes, '…when they travel they carry no baggage at all, but only weapons to keep off bandits… Neither garments nor shoes are changed till they are dropping to pieces or worn out with age'.

But although such parallels might seem to detract from Jesus' originality, reducing his ideas to ones simply typical of the Jewish spiritual thought of his time, also clear is that time and again Jesus did give such existing ideas a new twist, and not always in the same direction. While John the Baptist asked for the man with two tunics to give away the one he did not need – 'If anyone has two tunics he must share with the man who has none', Jesus asked him, if called upon, to give away both: 'If a man … would have your tunic, let him have your cloak as well' (Matthew 5: 41). Likewise, whereas the book of Leviticus ruled: 'You must love your neighbour as yourself' (Leviticus 19: 18), Jesus urged, 'Love your enemies, and pray for those who persecute you' (Matthew 5: 44). Precepts such as these, so far as can be ascertained, were utterly new, and exclusive to the gospel Jesus. They have no obvious counterparts in the teachings of either the Pharisees or the Essenes. Humane and inspired as the old Mosaic code was, Jesus' code went far beyond it.

But there was a further element. As we have already noted, John the Baptist had seen himself as being in the tradition of the Old Testament *nabi'im*, men and women who felt that God spoke through them on fundamental issues. Quite clearly Jesus too felt he could and did speak for God, but even more intensely. The gospels notably include a scattering of his utterances left in their original Aramaic, ones that because of this, even the Bultmann school of thought has recognized as having the greatest claim to authenticity. Among these undoubtedly one of the most striking is his apparent addressing God as *'Abba'*, 'Father'. This has caused more than a little controversy because, while some commentators have claimed that as a mode of address to God this carried a sense of familiarity virtually equivalent to 'Daddy', others have seen this as somewhat exaggerated, *'Abba'* as a way of addressing God, for instance, certainly being used a century before by the grandson of a Jewish holy man, Honi the Circle Drawer.

This qualification aside, however, there can be little doubt about the contrast between this apparent intimacy and the normal Jewish tradition. Traditionally for Jews the name of God carried such awe and mystique that no ordinary man could either utter it, or set it in writing. Thus the earliest manuscript copies of the books of the Old Testament feature God's name in the form of the 'Tetragrammaton', four Hebrew letters, the equivalents of YHWH , or Yahweh with the vowels omitted, and usually written in a more archaic form than the rest of the text, the custom being that when readers in the synagogue came to these letters they would automatically substitute *Adonai*, Hebrew for Lord.

And that Jesus did see himself as very special, sufficient to cause deep offence even to those with whom he had grown up in Nazareth, is quite evident from the Luke gospel's account of him reading in his local Nazareth synagogue a passage from Jewish scripture as if it pertained to himself. Whatever may survive of Nazareth's synagogue as it existed in Jesus' time has not yet been located, and indeed in all Galilee the only first-century synagogue remains for the tourist to see are at Gamla, on the slopes of the Golan with distant views of the Sea of Galilee. However, the Gamla remains show that early synagogue designs differed comparatively little from those known from later centuries, and by way of further background Professor Alan Millard of Liverpool University has painted the following vivid picture of the typical Sabbath day scene as Jesus would have known it at Nazareth:

> Entering, they [the congregation] climbed the steps and walked along to find a place to sit. Men and women may have had separate sections; that is not clear. They sat in rows along the steps, leaving the central area empty. The floor there was probably covered with rugs, giving a splash of colour. Men wore shawls, white, some with long fringes (Matthew 23: 5). When everyone was seated, the leader could begin the service. An important moment was the reading of the Bible lessons. The Scrolls of the Law and the Prophets would be brought respectfully from their ark or cupboard, carried through the congregation and laid on the reading desk in the centre.

Thanks to the discovery of the Dead Sea Scrolls, the visitor to Jerusalem

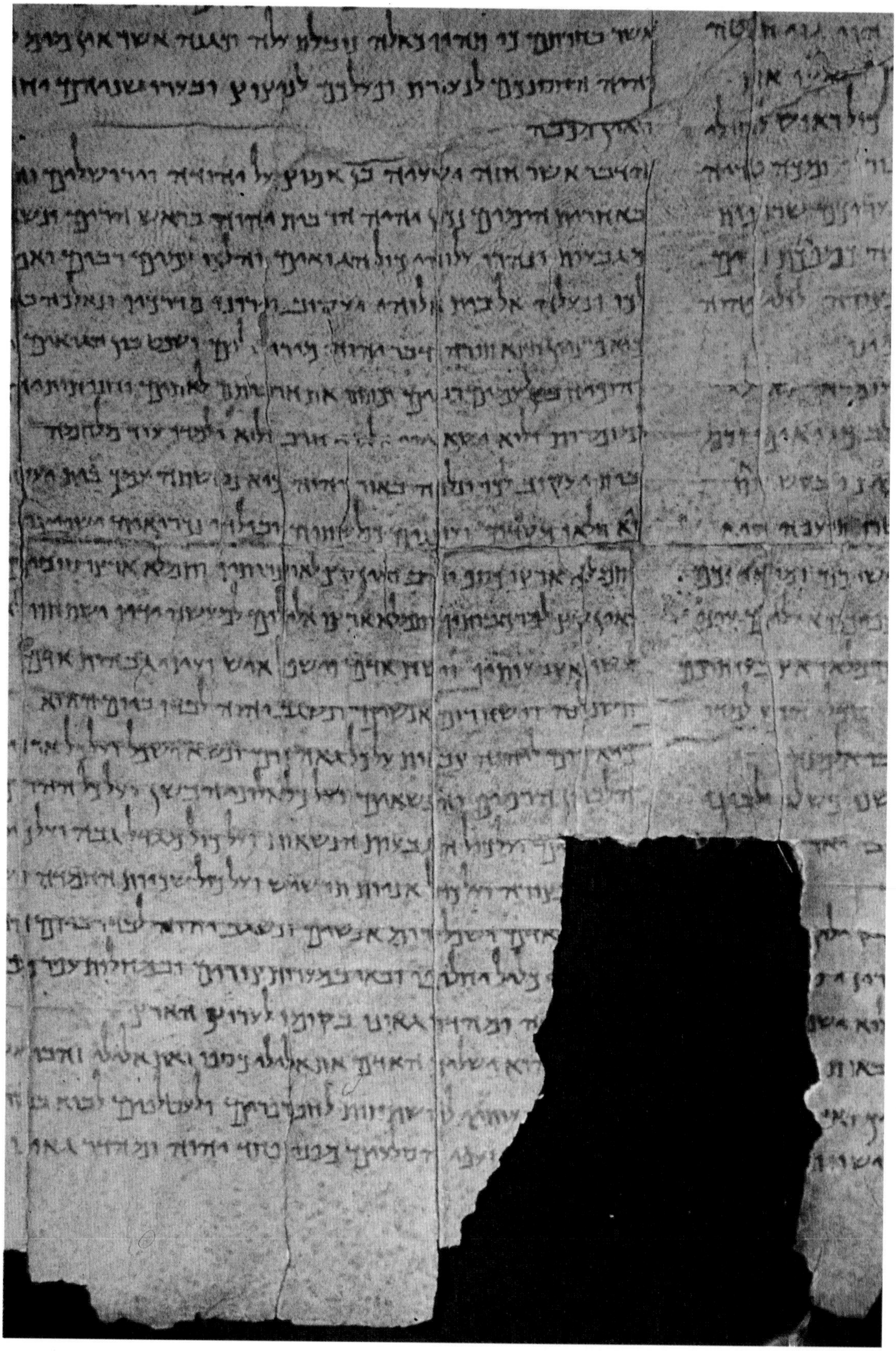

can today examine, rolled around a great drum in the centre of the city's Shrine of the Book, at least a facsimile of a scroll of the prophet Isaiah of the kind that would have been read in synagogues around Jesus' time. Sadly, the original developed cracks from having been forced into the very reverse of the way that it had been rolled up for nearly two thousand years, but it would have been from just such a scroll that, as described by the Luke author, Jesus read to fellow-Nazarenes Isaiah's long familiar passage relating to the promised Messiah:

The Isaiah Scroll, from the Dead Sea Scrolls. From such a scroll Jesus read out the text that (because he identified it with himself) led to his forcible expulsion from the Nazareth synagogue. A thousand years older than any previously known biblical text in Hebrew, this and the other biblical scrolls found at Qumran show that the Old Testament 'Bible' was faithfully transmitted from Jesus' time to our own.

> The spirit of the Lord has been given to me,
> for he has anointed me.
> He has sent me to bring the good news to the poor,
> to proclaim liberty to captives
> and to the blind new sight,
> to set the downtrodden free,
> to proclaim the Lord's year of favour.
>
> (Isaiah 61: 1-2)

According to the Luke author Jesus then rolled up the scroll, gave it back to the assistant, sat down and told his audience: 'This text is being fulfilled today even as you listen'. Although whatever happened next has almost certainly been somewhat fudged by the gospel writers, it can hardly have been anything less than ugly, for after first learning that Jesus 'won the approval of all', we are next told of the Nazarenes muttering 'This is Joseph's son, surely?' None too diplomatically, Jesus reportedly pointed out to them the persistence with which the Jews rejected their *nabi'im*, whereupon in the Luke author's words:

> Everyone in the synagogue was enraged. They sprang to their feet and hustled him out of the town; and they took him up to the brow of the hill their town was built on, intending to throw him down the cliff, but he slipped through the crowd and walked away. (Luke 4: 28-30)

Readily apparent from this, even though it derives from one of the two gospels that have a nativity story, is the conviction that in his home-town of Nazareth Jesus enjoyed nothing of any protective cocoon of stories of his miraculous birth accompanied by visitations of angels. In rude country fashion Jesus' fellow-Nazarenes saw one of their own number, 'Joseph's son', affecting to be a far more important and indeed sacred person than they knew him to be, and their reaction was the thoroughly understandable one of disbelief. Yet as we are about to see, others, from outside Nazareth, would react to him altogether differently.

6

FISHER OF MEN–AND WOMEN

Howerver negative may have been the impact that Jesus made upon those with whom he grew up in Nazareth, the gospels convey that he had no difficulty drawing followers from elsewhere. In the Mark author's very first chapter he is described seemingly casually strolling 'along by the sea of Galilee' and coming across two different pairs of fishermen brothers, Simon (Peter) and Andrew, and James and John, apparently easily persuading them to join him.

We are given no clear explanation for how Jesus exerted so instant an attraction upon these fishermen, nor upon the other eight male disciples whom he similarly gathered. Nor it is at all obvious even how and where Jesus was living at this point. According to the John gospel the two pairs of fishermen brothers came from Bethsaida (John 1: 44), which may or may not be the Bethsaida on the east bank of the River Jordan, where it enters the Sea of Galilee. But, when in the synoptic gospels Jesus is described as beginning his active ministry, both he and these same disciples seem to be living in Capernaum. The Matthew and Mark gospels both indicate that it was at Capernaum, and specifically Simon Peter and Andrew's house there, that Jesus healed Simon Peter's mother-in-law of a fever (Matthew 8: 14-

Opposite *Remains of New Testament-period Capernaum seen from the air, looking towards the Sea of Galilee. The octagonal-shaped foundations closest to the tree-lined lakeside are those of the Byzantine church marking what has come to be called 'St Peter's house'. The large edifice on the lighter-coloured ground is the fourth-century synagogue, thought to be the successor to the one in which Jesus taught (Mark 1: 21). Other remains found at Capernaum indicate that the town was the base for a Roman garrison, arguably that commanded by the very centurion whose servant was reportedly cured by Jesus (Matthew 8: 5-13 et al.).*

15; Mark 1: 29-31). Earlier the Matthew version relates that Jesus had gone to live in Capernaum after leaving Nazareth (Matthew 4: 13). The John gospel describes Jesus and his disciples, after the feeding of the five thousand, rowing across the Sea of Galilee to Capernaum as if they were returning home (John 6: 15). The Mark gospel suggests that Jesus somehow owned a Capernaum house sufficiently large to accommodate quite a gathering of disciples, tax-collectors and sinners (Mark 2: 15). Again according to Mark, Jesus taught in the Capernaum synagogue, reportedly sustaining a rather more favourable impression than he had in Nazareth (Mark 1: 21). Furthermore, this Capernaum synagogue appears to have been built by a locally based Roman centurion or royal official whose servant Jesus reportedly cured of his sickness in an intriguing incident that is described in no less than three of the gospels (Matthew 8: 5-13; Luke 7: 2-29; John 4: 46-53).

So where in present-day Israel was this Capernaum with so many close associations with Jesus? After many centuries in which its whereabouts remained unknown, in 1866 the British engineer and biblical enthusiast Captain Charles Wilson identified it with a site the local Arabs called Tel-Hum on the shores of the Sea of Galilee. An important clue lay in the Arab name, preserving the original Hebrew *Kfar Nahum* or 'village of Nahum' (in Greek, Capernaum), and the accuracy of Wilson's identification has been readily demonstrated by more recent archaeological excavations.

For instance, although the well-preserved Capernaum synagogue that today's tourists flock to see dates only to the fourth century, beneath this archaeologists have found the traces of an earlier, circa first-century version that is arguably the very one built by the Roman centurion whose servant Jesus healed. The presence of Roman occupants of Capernaum is further indicated by the remains of a 64-foot long bath-house of unmistakably Roman, rather than Jewish design. Although this dated from the second or third centuries, beneath it were again found indications of a similar building from the first century. The inference is that there was a substantial Roman presence – and thereby very likely a garrison commanded by a centurion – stationed at the Capernaum of Jesus' time, almost certainly as support troops to the Herod Antipas regime.

Yet more pertinently, within the last two decades archaeologists digging below the foundations of Capernaum's long-gone fifth-century Byzantine octagonal church came across the remains of a large and yet more ancient private house that the church had clearly been intended to honour. This was found to date to the first century, thereby to around the time of Jesus, and to have been specially rebuilt, even at that early date, to transform it into a large meeting place whose early Christian function was clearly indicated by unmistakably Christian inscriptions (such as 'Lord Jesus Christ help your servant ...' and 'Christ have mercy'), some in Aramaic, Syriac and Hebrew, scratched into what remained of its walls. A key question therefore arises as to what made this dwelling so special for it to have been transformed into such a 'house-church' at so early a period? One possibility is that it belonged to Jesus' disciple, Simon Peter, who as we have already noted, seems to have had a house in Capernaum, and for tourism purposes the house is indeed popularly dubbed 'St Peter's house'. Another possibility – and no less credible – is that it was the very house in which Jesus himself lived while in Capernaum, and in which he held the gatherings of the tax-collectors and sinners already noted from the Mark gospel.

But these possibilities aside, why among his fellow-Jews did Jesus choose Galilean fishermen to be the most prominent occupational group among his disciples? A leading classical historian has recently pointed out that in antiquity fishermen were regarded as socially very much the bottom of the scale, and Jesus' selection of them may have been part of his policy of seeking out such social outcasts. But the particular fishermen with whom Jesus associated may not necessarily have been quite as humble as they have sometimes been painted. In January 1986 an unusually severe drought lowered the level of the Sea of Galilee, whereupon the outlines of a clearly long-buried boat became revealed in the mud just five miles east of Capernaum. A quick expert appraisal revealed that it had been made in the ancient manner, the planks of the hull being edge-joined with 'mortise-and-tenon' joints held in place by wooden pegs. Not least because it was the first ancient boat ever known to have been found in the Sea of Galilee, immediate steps were taken to get it to shore for proper conservation and study before rains could restore the Sea's usual level.

This proved no small problem for the appointed Israeli government archaeologist, Shelley Wachsmann, and his hastily assembled team of

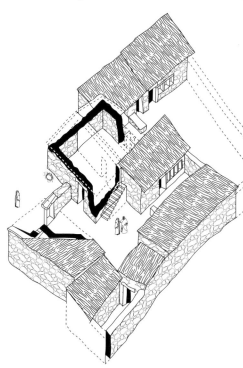

Artist's reconstruction of the original appearance of a first-century house as found beneath the foundations of Capernaum's octagonal Byzantine church (as seen below left). According to the archaeological findings, Judaeo-Christians remodelled this house sometime in the first century, removing some walls (shown by dotted lines) to convert it into a **domus ecclesia,** *or very early house-church. Indicative of this early Judaeo-Christian usage were symbols and inscriptions found on the walls. In the fourth century, the time of the first Christian Emperor Constantine the Great, the building was substantially altered. Then in the first half of the fifth century almost all the previous structure was demolished in favour of the octagonal-shaped church.*

Left: *Close-up of the excavated foundations of the fifth-century octagonal Byzantine church found at Capernaum. At that time the octagonal shape denoted a particularly holy site.*

volunteers. They found that although the boat's timber was reassuringly in good overall shape, its long immersion had saturated it to the consistency of wet cardboard, meaning that it was too soft to move by normal means. Yet, as they were all too well aware, if it were allowed to dry out its entire cellular structure would collapse. They had but days to come up with a solution, but ingeniously conservator Orna Cohen devised a method of spraying liquid polyurethane over the already exposed inner portions of the vessel, and letting this harden to the boat's exact shape. Protected by an impromptu 'dry dock' of sandbags the volunteers then dug tunnels below the outer part of the boat still embedded in the mud, and threaded fibreglass through these which, with the addition of more polyurethane, provided supportive trusses. After clearing the rest of the mud and spraying on yet more polyurethane, creating a complete protective cocoon, they then removed the sandbags and gently floated the whole ensemble to the nearby Kibbutz Ginnosar, where Yigal Allon Museum staff were waiting to receive it.

Although at the time of writing, the Galilee boat is still at the Yigal

The Galilee boat, the outlines of which became exposed early in 1986 when the Sea of Galilee's water-level was at a record low due to drought. From its mortise-and-tenon joint construction, this boat was quickly identified as being of a very early date, and here on only its second day of excavation its 26-foot length is already revealed. Each bucket of mud removed was carefully numbered so that its contents could be later sifted and the location of any small artefacts identified with precision.

Allon Museum undergoing conservation treatment of a kind similar to that used for England's sixteenth-century *Mary Rose*, it is already clear from the radiocarbon dating of its wood, mostly cedar planking with oak frames, that this dates from between 40 BC and 40 AD, its working life hence having been very close to, if not actually contemporary with, the lifetime of Jesus. Furthermore it has already been sufficiently well studied for an assessment to be made that it is similar, if not identical to the type of vessel repeatedly described in the gospels as used by Jesus and his disciples (Matthew 8: 18, 23-7; 9: 1; 14: 13-14, 22-32; 15: 39; 16: 5; Mark 4: 35-41; 5: 18, 21; 6: 32-4, 45-51; 8: 9-10, 13-14; Luke 6: 1; 8: 22-5, 37, 40; John 6: 16-21). It is twenty-six and a half feet long, seven and a half feet wide and four and a half feet high, with a rounded stern and well-crafted bow, and nautical experts have determined that it could be both sailed and rowed, and would have needed a crew of five, four rowers and a helmsman who steered with a specially shaped steering oar. Additionally it could have carried either a substantial cargo or some ten passengers. The crew complement readily corresponds to the Mark gospel's account of Zebedee's sons James and John leaving their father 'in the boat with the men he employed' when Jesus recruited them (Mark 1: 20), and indicates that those who operated such vessels were by no means at the lowest level of subsistence, but must have needed to be at least moderately well-placed in order to be able to invest in such transport.

Nine days after the commencement of the excavation, and protected by a polyurethane cocoon, the Galilee boat is gently floated to shore before being lifted onto dry land for conservation. From pottery and coins in the mud surrounding the boat, it was tentatively dated to the first century AD, and radiocarbon dating has supported this.

Mosaic of a small boat, as found in a first-century AD house at Migdal, the ancient Magdala, home of Jesus' woman follower Mary Magdalen. Migdal is only a mile from where the Galilee boat was found. The mosaic shows that the boat was powered by four rowers, two on each side, with a fifth man controlling the steering oar, or rudder. This corresponds well with the fishing boat crew indicated in Mark 1: 20.

The gospels also convey vivid images of people for whom fish were a central part of their diet and economy, as in the Luke gospel's description of Jesus somehow arranging a record catch of fish after Peter and the others had been out all night in two boats and caught nothing (Luke 5: 1-7). Important for buttressing the gospels' credibility, these elements are not regarded as fanciful even by non-Christians. As has been pointed out by Mendel Nun, a modern-day authority on the Galilee fishing industry, for two boats to have been out overnight, seemingly working in partnership, is totally accurate for the traditional Galilean way of fishing for a large, wily and very edible fish known as musht. Musht (see p.84) are shoal-loving plankton-eaters who will shy from any net deployed during the day, as a result of which the long-established way

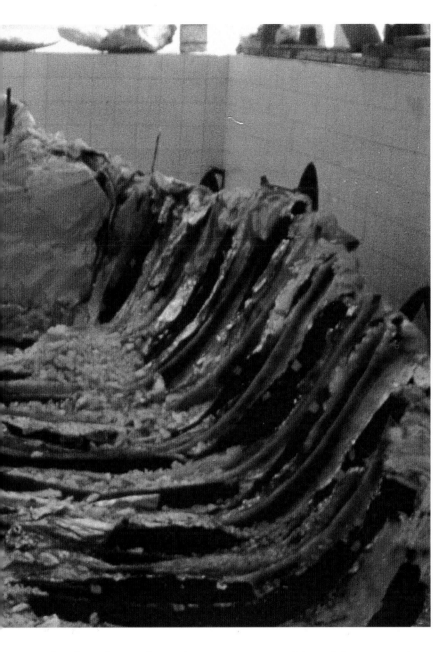

Its protective cocoon removed, the Galilee boat undergoing conservation at the Yigal Allon Museum, where its timbers are being carefully re-consolidated with the aid of the synthetic wax polyethylene glycol. This will eventually enable the boat to be displayed in a dry atmosphere, providing the closest glimpse of the sort of boat in which Jesus travelled with his disciples on the Sea of Galilee.

of catching them is for two boats to go out overnight and fan a trammel net around any shoal they find, trapping the fish in an underwater 'barrel' stretching from the lake bottom to the surface (see p.85). It is an all-or-nothing operation, and as Mendel Nun insists, this is almost certainly what Peter and his companions had been trying unsuccessfully to do until Jesus' apparently miraculous intervention. Elsewhere in the gospels we are told of Jesus eating barbecued fish with his disciples (e.g. John 21: 9). And Migdal, on the Sea of Galilee's eastern shore, where the gospels' Mary Magdalen almost certainly had her origin, has long been where the very plentiful Galilee sardines have been brought for pickling, this variety of fish still representing some half the annual total of those commercially caught in the Sea of Galilee.

Musht, large, edible and shoal-loving fish that have remained very plentiful in the Sea of Galilee from Jesus' time to our own. Often called 'St Peter's fish', this is definitely a misnomer, since musht are not caught singly with hook and line as in the incident with Simon Peter described in Matthew 17: 24-7. However, because of their shoal-loving characteristics, they were almost certainly the particular fish netted in the 'miraculous' catch described in Luke 5: 1-7.

But whatever may have been the status (or lack of it) of Galilean fishermen in Jesus' time, also clear is that these were by no means the only individuals of low esteem whom Jesus gathered to him. According to the Matthew gospel, John the Baptist had attracted 'tax-collectors and prostitutes' (21: 32), and it is very evident that Jesus pointedly drew to him disciples and hangers-on of similar ilk, in line with his openly declared policy that these people were most in need of what he had to offer. Thus it was again from what seems to have been Capernaum, and specifically from the town's customs house, that Jesus reportedly recruited the tax-collector Matthew (Matthew 9: 9), a man who would have been widely disliked because of his necessary collaboration with the forces of occupation. Likewise, immediately after the story of this Matthew's recruitment, we are told of Jesus' entertaining to dinner 'a number of tax-collectors and sinners' at what seems to have been his Capernaum house.

In fact, so frequently do the gospels report Jesus' socializing with obvious undesirables, enjoying meals with them, speaking of himself as 'a glutton and a drunkard' (Luke 7: 34), even declining to join in fasts observed by John the Baptist's disciples, that there can be little doubt that he did behave in precisely this way, the most extreme example of this being his reported acceptance of particularly intimate favours from 'a woman … who had a bad name in the town' (Luke 7: 37-8). The woman is described as wiping Jesus' feet with her hair, massaging his feet and/or his head with an expensive lotion, and lavishing kisses upon him, all so repugnant for the gospel writers and for the disciples alike that no two accounts are the same. While the Luke author noted the horror felt by Jesus' host at the fact that Jesus had allowed himself to be made impure, or ritually unclean, by such a woman, the Matthew, Mark and John writers all remarked on the disciples' indignation at the waste of money: 'Why this waste of ointment? Ointment like this could have been sold for over three hundred denarii and the money given to the poor' (Mark 14: 4-5). Only Jesus, amidst all the embarrassment and anger, seems to have accepted the woman's clearly sensual favours with a quite shameless equanimity.

For although association with a prostitute was clearly extreme behaviour, feelings would already have been heightened by the fact that in Jesus' day almost any association with a woman outside one's immediate family was frowned upon. For example, the Babylonian Talmud tells of the Galilean Rabbi Yose being scolded for merely asking a woman the way to Lydda: 'You stupid Galilean, have the Sages not commanded "Do not engage in a lengthy conversation with a woman?"' In first-century Jewish society women were second-class citizens, banned from the Inner Courts of the Temple, banned from any part of the Temple during their monthly periods, and, at any time, instantly divorceable by their husbands without any right of redress, merely by the writing of a notice to this effect. This has even given rise to inconsistencies within the New Testament, for because the apostle Paul had never known the human Jesus, and according to some arguments at least wrote before the gospels themselves had been written, he reflected the attitudes of contemporary society towards women rather than what we may now believe to have been Jesus' own ideas. Thus he wrote:

How two Galilean fishing boats would traditionally fish in partnership to catch musht. They would use one net to encircle a shoal in a barrel of mesh, then a second net would be spread on the water's surface and kept afloat with reeds, to trap any fish trying to escape by leaping out of the barrel.
The fish inside the barrel would then be caught with cast nets.

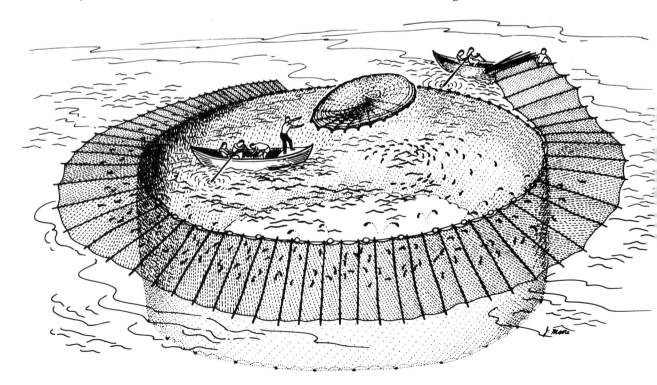

... women are to remain quiet at meetings since they have no permis-sion to speak; they must keep in the background as the Law itself lays it down. If they have any questions to ask, they should ask their husbands at home: it does not seem right for a woman to raise her voice at meetings. (1 Corinthians 14: 35)

By way of contrast, the gospel writers convey Jesus entering into deep conversations with women, as in John 4: 27, 'The disciples returned and were surprised to find him speaking to a woman' and in Luke 10: 38-42, in which he became involved in such a lengthy discourse with Mary, sister of Martha of Bethany, that even the practical Martha thought he had gone too far. And although in general the gospels gloss over the fact, the Luke author, who seems to have had a more liberated outlook than his fellow-evangelists, makes clear that Jesus attracted nearly as many women followers as he did men:

> With him went the twelve, as well as certain women who had been cured of evil spirits and ailments: Mary surnamed the Magdalen, from whom seven demons had gone out, Joanna the wife of Herod's steward Chuza, Susanna and several others who provided for them out of their own resources. (Luke 8: 1-3)

It is frustrating that we are told by no means nearly enough concerning these women, how they accompanied this large entourage day and night, and the strength of feelings they must have aroused in those whom they had left behind back home. Particularly interesting is the inclusion in the list of Joanna, the wife of Herod Antipas' steward, Chuza. From Luke's mention of her among 'certain women ... cured of evil spirits and ailments' it would seem that Jesus had relieved her of some mental or physical illness. But why are we not told more of Jesus' healing of such a well-to-do woman? It can hardly be doubted that some sort of fluttering in the Herod Antipas camp must have been caused by such a woman leaving her highly placed husband and going off to tramp Galilee's dusty by-ways with her healer.

The inclusion in the list of Mary Magdalen is another case in point. Of Jesus' precise relationship with her we are likewise told very little, but this has not stopped sensationalist writers – from Baigent, Leigh and Lincoln in their best-selling *The Holy Blood and the Holy Grail* to Australian Barbara Thiering in *Jesus The Man* making a whole industry out of speculations on this theme, particularly centring on the idea that Mary Magdalen and Jesus secretly married. A certain fuel to this was provided by the discovery, among the Nag Hammadi hoard, of a 'Gospel of Philip' in which occurs the passage:

> ... the companion of the [Saviour is] Mary Magdalen. [But Christ loved] her more than [all] the disciples, and asked to kiss her [often] on her [mouth]. The rest of [the disciples were offended] ... They said to

Jewish woman's hair, first century AD, from the excavations at Masada. Jesus was noted in the gospels for entering into deep conversations with women, and for treating them with far greater respect and consideration than was normal in his day. He allowed a woman to dry him with her hair (Luke 7: 38).

him, 'Why do you love her more than all of us?' The Saviour answered and said to them, 'Why do I not love you as [I love] her?'

In fact the 'Gospel of Philip', unlike its companion 'Gospel of Thomas', has no special claim to an early date, and seems to be merely a Mills & Boon-style fantasy of a type not at all uncommon among Christian apocryphal literature of the third and fourth centuries. Inevitably the very fact that Jesus was canonically described as being so intimate with women gives rise to the entirely legitimate question: if he did not marry – and there is absolutely no serious evidence that he did – why did he choose not to, particularly since Jewish priests and rabbis of his time were very much expected to do so, and also Peter at least among the disciples certainly had a wife, as revealed by Jesus' cure of his mother-in-law?

What may well be clues to Jesus' reasons lie in a cryptic remark in the Matthew gospel: '… there are eunuchs who make themselves that way for the sake of the kingdom of heaven' (Matthew 19: 12), together with an equally significant passage in the Luke gospel:

> The children of this world take wives and husbands, but those who are judged worthy of a place in the other world and in the resurrection from the dead do not marry because they can no longer die, for they are the same as angels, and being children of the resurrection they are sons of God. (Luke 20: 34-7)

Arguably, Jesus may here have been defining a blueprint for the purest and most immediate way of reaching the kingdom of God. For although for most Jews the kingdom of God, long spoken of by the *nabi'im*, was conceived as something between a politically independent state of Israel and a heavenly dream home for the righteous, for Jesus it seems to have been both of these – hence his talk of the 'coming' of the kingdom – but also something much more immediate and positive, a releasing of the self from all earthly ties, the prime among those being property, employment and wife, not necessarily in that order. As Dr John Robinson beautifully expressed it in his controversial *Honest to God*, Jesus 'emptied himself utterly of himself thus abandoning all self-consciousness, all shame, all self-seeking, in order that God and only God could shine through'. This same ideal, as translated into the rôle of a Catholic priest, was also superbly expressed in Morris West's *The Shoes of the Fisherman* in the response of a priest to a friend who felt that he, the priest, had thrown away his life the day he was ordained:

> It costs so much to be a full human being that there are very few who will have the courage to pay the price. One has to abandon altogether the search for security and embrace the world like a lover, and yet demand no easy return for love. One has to accept pain as a condition of existence. One has to court doubt and darkness as the cost of

knowing. One needs a will stubborn in conflict, but open always to every consequence of living and dying. If a man is centred on himself, the smallest risk is too great for him because both success and failure can destroy. But if he is completely centred on God ... then no risk is too great because success is already guaranteed.

It is important to emphasize, however, that this was an ideal for those who were free so to abandon themselves, as Catholic priests do to this day, rather than any recipe for universal communism and anarchy. For however offbeat and unconventional his behaviour may sometimes have been, Jesus nevertheless firmly upheld the Jewish Law (Matthew 5: 17, 18). Likewise while he may have told the adulterous woman that her sins were forgiven, he also asked her not to repeat them (John 18: 1, 2). Contrary to those who today try to push for more liberal divorce laws, Jesus insisted on stricter ones than those pertaining in his time (Mark 10: 10), pointedly removing the husband's then prerogative of being able to dismiss his wife without an equivalent right on her part. It would seem always to have been the underlying spirit of the Law that he wished to enforce rather than its letter.

Likewise, while Jesus openly and unashamedly consorted with prostitutes and tax-collectors, it was not only such people whom he won over. Those who went on, after his death, to carry out his message, often at great danger to themselves, were people leading ordinary lives who, though they may sometimes have been shocked to observe him saying and doing things not expected of a holy man, followed him nonetheless. And to these he likewise insisted on the nearness of the kingdom of God. The strength of this following by people of all kinds is in fact one of the most striking features of Jesus' recorded life. Repeatedly the gospels refer to the crowds which surrounded him wherever he went, crowds from whom, equally repeatedly, he felt obliged to slip away when the pressure became too great. As the Mark gospel specifically commented on the predicament this presented for him: 'Jesus could no longer go openly into any town, but had to stay outside in places where nobody lived. Even so, people from all around would come to him.' (Mark 1: 45)

So how was it that when Jesus wanted helpers he had merely to say: 'Follow me', and, as the gospels insist, hard-headed fishermen like Andrew and Simon Peter, James and John, mercenary tax-collectors like Matthew, and even suspected near-terrorists like Simon the Zealot (Zealots were a Jewish near-equivalent of the IRA) abandoned all else to do just that? Nor was Jesus' appeal only to Jews. As even Josephus, although a non-Christian, acknowledged in the brief reference to Jesus that we discussed in chapter 3: 'He [Jesus] won over many of the Jews and many of the Greeks'.

Now no teaching alone, however unconventional or innovative, could have made such an impact, particularly upon people who were not of the same nationality. So just what was it about Jesus that could have exerted such a magnetic appeal?

7
MAN OF
MAGIC

If there is one feature of Jesus' activities that repeatedly shines out from the gospels, it is his capacity to work acts of healing and other feats that men have called 'miracles'. The Mark gospel makes quite clear that it was his reputation for these which caused him to be the centre of so much popular attention: '… after sunset they brought to him all who were sick and those who were possessed by devils. The whole town came crowding round the door' (Mark 1: 32).

There was nothing completely new in this, for acts of healing were a common attribute of Jewish holy men both before and after Jesus. Moses and Elisha were accredited with curing a leper or two (Numbers 12: 13; 2 Kings 5: 1-4), and a generation after Jesus a *hasid* or holy man called Hanina ben Dosa, from Araba, ten miles to Nazareth's north, was also accredited with healings.

But the works reported of these were as nothing compared to the cures of paralysis, lameness, fever, catalepsy, haemorrhage, skin disease and mental disorder attributed to Jesus. Miracles were the first aspect of Jesus' ministry that the disciple Simon Peter reportedly recalled after Jesus' death:

Jesus the Nazarene was a man commended to you by God by the miracles and portents and signs that God worked through him when he was among you as you all know. (Acts 2: 22)

Opposite *Jesus depicted healing a woman with a chronic haemorrhaging disorder. From a fresco of the late third century, the cemetery of SS Peter and Marcellinus, Rome.*

This same reputation was clearly what Josephus had in mind when, as we noted earlier, he spoke of Jesus as 'a wise man' who performed 'astonishing feats', or 'paradoxical deeds', the word *paradoxon* that he used commonly denoting 'miracle' in Hellenistic Judaism. In the earliest Christian art, among the most frequent representations of Jesus are ones showing him with a magician's wand, usually being used for raising Lazarus. As reported in Luke's gospel, when asked by the imprisoned John the Baptist whether he was 'the one who is to come (i.e. the super-*nabi* prophesied by Moses, Deuteronomy 18: 15-18), Jesus' reply to John's messengers was, 'Go back and tell John what you have seen and heard: the blind see again, the lame walk, lepers are cleansed, and the deaf hear, the dead are raised to life ...' (Luke 7: 22)

That Jesus performed such deeds is therefore one of the best-attested items of information about him, yet paradoxically, it has been one of the least explored because, as Matthew Arnold succinctly expressed it, 'miracles do not happen'. Under the influence of Kant and Hegel, the German rationalist theologians steadfastly resisted treating the gospel miracle stories with any seriousness, and among many of today's theologians, quite aside from the ordinary general public, this resistance has continued. Nonetheless, some scholars are now favouring the idea that one of the very earliest lost gospels may have been one specifically devoted to accounts of Jesus' miracles. And the leading Anglican scholar Canon Anthony Harvey of Westminster Abbey has laid stress on the convincingness of the very matter-of-fact way in which the canonical gospels' miracle stories are described:

> In general one can say that the miracle stories in the gospels are unlike anything else in ancient literature ... They do not exaggerate the miracle or add sensational details, like the authors of early Christian hagiography [lives of the saints]; but nor do they show the kind of detachment, amounting at times to scepticism, which is found in Herodotus or Lucian ... To a degree that is rare in the writings of antiquity, we can say, to use a modern phrase, that they tell the story straight ...

And indeed if we allow ourselves at least temporarily to suspend incredulity towards miracles per se, we find that some of the gospel stories of this ilk have within them material which we simply cannot dismiss out of hand. For instance, in a manner rare among gospel stories, the writer of the John gospel, in one of his important narrative sections, sets the healing of the so-called paralytic in a historically identifiable building:

> Now at the Sheep Pool in Jerusalem there is a building, called Bethzatha in Hebrew, consisting of five porticoes; and under these were crowds of sick people – blind, lame, paralysed – waiting for the water to move; for at intervals ... the water was disturbed, and the first person to enter the water after this disturbance was cured of any ailment he suffered from ... (John 5: 1-4)

Remains of Herodian building (at the lowest level) thought to have been the five-porticoed edifice called Bethesda (or Beth-zatha) housing the so-called Sheep Pool at which Jesus reportedly healed the paralytic man (John 5: 1-9). Although only part of the original pool has been exposed beneath layers of Christian churches dating back to the fifth century AD, tunnels and soundings show that there were originally two very large pools cut deep into the bedrock, surrounded by porticoes with columns 25 feet high. Probably this same edifice is mentioned in the Dead Sea Scrolls' Copper Scroll as Beth Eshdathayin, or the 'House of the Twin Pools'.

As a result of exhaustive research by Professor Joachim Jeremias, there can be absolutely no doubt that there was a building of this kind in the Jerusalem of Jesus' time, the original natural pool having been used probably as early as the eighth century BC, and developed as two 'Great Pools' around 200 BC. Despite the depredations the city suffered as a result of the Romans' suppression of the Jewish Revolts, the Sheep Pool building of John's gospel seems still to have existed in the fourth century AD, for as reported at that time by Western Europe's earliest-known Christian pilgrim to the Holy Land, the so-called Bordeaux pilgrim:

> Further in the city are twin pools having five porticoes, which are called Bethsaida [from New Testament manuscripts, this seems to have been a corruption of Bethzatha]. There those who have been sick for many years are cured. The pools contain water which is red when it is disturbed.

Sadly, the five porticoes effectively disappeared during subsequent centuries upon the building's conversion into a church, this church in its turn suffering all sorts of vicissitudes as Jerusalem painfully and successively changed hands between Christians and Moslems. But the site has continued to be marked by a church, and just north of what is now the Crusader church of St Anne in Old City Jerusalem's Muslim Quarter, excavations earlier this century revealed two huge, deep rock-cut cisterns, with stairs that originally led to their bottoms, which undoubtedly once comprised the original Sheep Pool described by John, some of the surviving masonry being of the time of Herod the Great, who is known to have embellished the building.

But even if we can actually identify a building where Jesus once reputedly worked a miracle, why should we trust the story of the miracle itself? According to the author of John the paralysed man whom Jesus encountered at the Sheep Pool had had his condition for thirty-eight years, and Jesus cured him with the simple command: 'Get up, pick up your sleeping-mat and walk' (John 5: 8). Although this is obviously scant information on which to base any belief in the story, it is well-known medically that some paralyses are 'hysterical' in origin, that is they have a mental rather than physical cause, usually as a result of some severe emotional stress. Disfiguring skin conditions, blindness, apparent inability to hear or speak, and all manner of seeming mental disorders, can also be induced by hysteria, and while to the patient such ailments seem all too real, and may last for many years, they can sometimes be cured by a reversing or neutralizing of the original, debilitating emotional problem. Although treatment with drugs is of course the most usual way of doing this today, other nonetheless well-recognized approaches are via psychotherapy or hypnosis, the 'cure' as effected by the latter often being dramatically sudden.

It has to be acknowledged that even to this day no-one really knows what hypnosis is, whatever individual hypnotists themselves may claim they know. In essence hypnosis appears to be a belief system shared between two individuals, one, the subject, who abandons himself, in terms of his waking consciousness, to the other, the hypnotist, who by taking charge of the patient's unconscious mind may be able to free elements that the patient's consciousness has previously repressed or held back. So-called 'hysterical' individuals often seem to make particularly good hypnotic subjects and consistently the effects of hypnosis upon these can be in direct proportion to the degree of awe in which they hold the hypnotist. While scientists mostly remain reticent about stating anything too positive about hypnosis because of its continuing mysteries and uncertainties, few would deny that it can and does produce some remarkable phenomena, including spectacular 'cures'.

For instance, the now veteran British hypnotist Peter Casson has on his files the case of a woman who, for fifteen years after a major car accident, had been quite unable to close her hand or to grip with it. Several operations had failed to improve her condition, but on the strength of just one hypnosis session with Peter Casson she found that she could once again close her hand and use it normally. Effectively, Casson achieved her 'cure' by commands little different from those which Jesus is said to have used in curing the paralytic by Jerusalem's Sheep Pool.

An even better attestation of hypnosis's medical potential is a British doctor's highly dramatic use of it as a last resort for a particularly disfiguring skin condition that was well documented, with accompanying photographs, in the *British Medical Journal* of 23 August 1952. The patient was a sixteen-year-old boy who two years earlier had been admitted to East Grinstead's Royal Victoria Hospital suffering from ichthyosis, a most unsightly condition that from ever since he had been born had covered his body with a black, horny, reptilian layer that was as uncomfortable and evil-smelling as it was disfiguring. Although two attempts at plastic surgery had been made, in both the reptilian layer had quickly replaced the skin that had been freshly grafted, so that even Sir Archibald McIndoe, the most eminent plastic surgeon of the day, pronounced further conventional treatment useless.

By chance, however, the boy's plight came to the notice of a young physician with an interest in hypnosis, Dr A.A.Mason, today a psychoanalyst in Beverley Hills, California. Mason asked if he might at least try hypnosis, and on 10 February 1951, having induced a hypnotic state, he suggested to the youth that his left arm's reptilian layer would disappear. There ensued an extraordinary transformation. Within five days the horny covering on this arm simply fell away, and within a further few days the skin was soft, pink and normal for the first time in the boy's life. During the next few weeks hypnotic suggestion was given for the clearance of the reptilian layer on the right arm and then for specific remaining areas of his body, each time with between 50 per cent and 95 per cent success. Although the cure was slower than it might have been in the case of, say, a

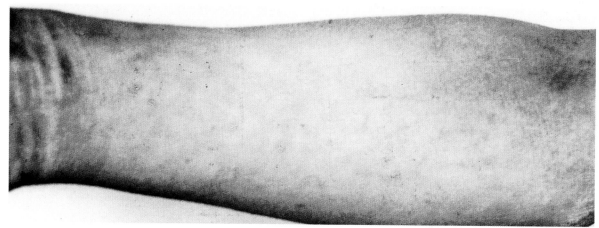

A modern-day 'miracle'? The legs and arms of a sixteen-year-old sufferer from the disfiguring and repulsive skin condition ichthyosis, as seen before and after his hypnotic treatment by the then British physician Dr A.A.Mason. Following Dr Mason's purely verbal suggestions, it took only a few weeks for the horny, reptilian layer to fall away and be replaced by clear, normal skin.

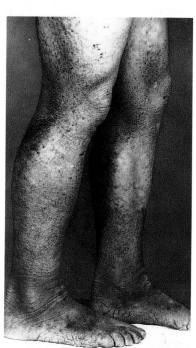

hysterical blindness or paralysis (almost certainly because of the very nature of the disease), it is little short of incredible that it should have happened at all. And a fascinating feature is the fact that, because of ichthyosis's rarity, Dr Mason did not even realize at the time that he was dealing with such a congenital, structural illness. As he has frankly admitted, had he realized he would most likely not have tried hypnosis, because he would have thought it unsuitable for anything so deep-seated. But because he believed he could do it, he succeeded. Accordingly, it is the most striking possible attestation of what mere words, given the hypnotic state, can do.

So could there have been a knowledge of hypnosis in ancient times upon which Jesus drew? Professor Lionel Haward of the University of Surrey psychology department has pointed out that there are Egyptian papyri, such as the Demotic Magical Papyrus preserved in the British Museum, which appear to describe hypnotic inductions and trance states and also classical frescoes that depict individuals in what looks like hypnotic trance. Furthermore, that whatever Jesus was using for his miracles derived not from any quasi-divine power, but could be well within the powers of ordinary men, is quite evident from the gospels themselves, which describe him sending out his disciples to do the same healing work that he undertook himself:

He summoned his twelve disciples, and gave them authority over unclean spirits with power to cast them out, and to cure all kinds of diseases and sickness. (Matthew 10: 1)

Likewise the book of Acts relates that the disciples were able to carry on his work after his death:

There were ... unclean spirits that came shrieking out of many who were possessed, and several paralytics and cripples were cured. (Acts 8: 7)

Arguably then, hypnosis may help us go at least some way towards recognizing, and believing, in a perfectly rational way, that at least some of Jesus' reputed healing miracles could and did happen along the lines the gospels describe. Furthermore, if we look more closely at one group of these, his exorcisms or cures from 'possession', we find that modern medical and psychological insights can again give us good reason for trusting the gospels' accounts of the disorders that Jesus tackled.

Thus back in the early 1920s, and ironically at the very University of Tübingen which was the setting for so many attacks on the gospels' credibility, psychology professor T.K. Oesterreich made an intensive study of the cases of possession encountered by Jesus. First published in the journal *Deutsche Psychologie*, then developed into a definitive 400-page book, *Possession, Demoniacal and Other*, Professor Oesterreich's findings were that the Mark gospel in particular is very impressive for its concise and

Jesus healing a so-called 'leper' (Mark 1: 40-2). In the ancient world the term 'leprosy' could denote a variety of serious skin disorders. From a fifth-century ivory from Palermo, Sicily, now in the Victoria and Albert Museum, London.

clinical reporting of the cases Jesus tackled. There was the so-called Gerasene demoniac:

> … no sooner had he [Jesus] left the boat than a man with an unclean spirit came out of the tombs towards him. The man lived in the tombs, and no-one could secure him any more, even with a chain; because he had often been secured with fetters and chains but had snapped the chains and broken the fetters and no-one had the strength to control him. All night and all day, among the tombs and in the mountains he would howl and gash himself with stones … (Mark 5: 1-10)

There was the man suffering from convulsions:

> In their synagogue … there was a man possessed by an unclean spirit and it shouted 'What do you want with us, Jesus of Nazareth? Have you come to destroy us?' … But Jesus said sharply 'Be quiet! Come out of him!' And the unclean spirit threw the man into convulsions and with a loud cry went out of him. (Mark 1: 23-7)

There was the youth who foamed at the mouth:

> A man answered him from the crowd, 'Master, I have brought my son to you; there is a spirit of dumbness in him, and when it takes hold of him it throws him to the ground, and he foams at the mouth and grinds his teeth and goes rigid. And I asked your disciples to cast it out and they were unable to' … They brought the boy to him and as soon as the spirit saw Jesus it threw the boy into convulsions, and he fell to the ground and lay writhing there, foaming at the mouth. Jesus asked the father: 'How long has this been happening to him?' 'From childhood', he replied, 'and it has often thrown him into the fire and into the water, in order to destroy him …' (Mark 9: 17-27)

As commented by Professor Oesterreich:

> … the succinct accounts of Jesus' relation to these events, his success and failure together with that of his disciples, as well as the particulars

of his cures, coincide so exactly with what we know of these states from the point of view of present-day psychology that it is impossible to avoid the impression that we are dealing with a tradition which is veracious.

Of course, neither Professor Oesterreich nor any other realistic individual would argue that real demons or unclean spirits were responsible for the disorders being dealt with, as the gospel writers and Jesus seem to suppose. But the point at issue is the power of the belief held by the sufferer, who had come to believe himself so much afflicted, usually as a result of some emotional stress. However extreme and fictional the book and film of William Blatty's *The Exorcist* might seem, it represents a very real phenomenon that has been reported century after century, throughout all sorts of cultures, both before and after the time of Jesus. Church of England vicar the Reverend Christopher Neil-Smith, now living in retirement in Ealing, claims to have been called upon to deal with up to five hundred 'possession' cases a year in just the area in and around London, and although it is a little-known part of its organization, since the 1970s the Church of England has appointed a consultant exorcist for every diocese. For if people try to solve such problems without professional help, sometimes things can go badly wrong, as in 1973, in West Yorkshire, when a 'possessed' young father murdered his wife and the family dog after a failed exorcism by local amateurs.

One form of 'possession' psychiatrically well-recognized is the condition known today as 'multiple personality', of which recent famous cases have been those of Virginia housewife Chris Sizemore (the original 'Eve' of *The Three Faces of Eve*) and Ohio rapist Billy Milligan, who in 1979 committed a series of robberies and rapes while apparently possessed by some nine alternating personalities, ranging from 'Ragan', an aggressive hit-man, to

Site of one of Jesus' healings? The remains of the Roman forum and a colonnaded street at Jerash, Jordan, the very hellenized 'Gerasa' of Jesus' time where, according to Mark 5: 1-10, he healed the deranged 'demoniac' who wandered among the tombs.

Jesus depicted healing a woman with a chronic haemorrhaging disorder. Her cure is described in all three synoptic gospels (Mathew 9: 20-22; Mark 5: 25-34; Luke 8: 43-8). According to later tradition, she came from Caesarea Philippi, and in gratitude erected a statue to Jesus there. From a fresco of the late third century, the cemetery of SS Peter and Marcellinus, Rome.

'Christine', a three-year-old obsessed with painting butterflies. Among many parallels between these cases and those reputedly cured by Jesus is a tendency for one of the personalities to speak for the rest by using the term 'us'. In the very first chapter of the Mark gospel, a possessed man in the Capernaum synagogue reportedly railed at Jesus: 'What do you want with us, Jesus of Nazareth? Have you come to destroy us?' (Mark 1: 24), and the Gerasene demoniac, asked his name by Jesus, responded: 'My name is legion … for there are many of us' (Mark 5: 10), and in the American multiple-personality case 'Sybil', Sybil's 'us' personality told her psychiatrist/ hypnotist '… the rest of us know about Sybil, she knows nothing about any of us …'.

In connection with Jesus' dealings with such phenomena we have no need to believe that he had any formal knowledge of what we now label hypnosis. But that his approach to the physically and mentally sick was powerfully and spontaneously hypnotic is absolutely self-evident from the gospel descriptions of the sharp, authoritative verbal manner in which he conducted his healings: 'Be quiet! Come out of him!' he reportedly told the possessed man in the Capernaum synagogue (Mark 1: 26), *'Ephphatha!'* ('Be opened!') he commanded of the eardrums of the deaf man brought to him in the Decapolis (Mark 7: 34), *'Talitha kum!'* ('Little girl, I tell you to get up!') he ordered the seemingly dead daughter of synagogue official Jairus (Mark 5: 41). The very fact that we have been given, in these last two examples, Jesus' apparent exact original words, untranslated from the Aramaic, is a powerful sign of just how awed had been those present at the time, seemingly prompting them to try to record these 'magical'-seeming formulas for posterity.

But what would it have been that gave Jesus the authority and confidence to be so naturally hypnotic? Two special attributes arguably at least helped. One was his personal conviction that God was speaking and working through him in a manner unparalleled since the days of Moses (the Luke author notably represents him as speaking of 'the finger of God' as being responsible for the success of his exorcisms, Luke 11 : 20). The other was an equally strong belief that at some unpredictable moment the dread 'Last Times' (already spoken of by earlier prophets) would begin, bringing eternal life for those who followed his words, and eternal damnation for those who did not. Fired by such convictions, Jesus would have been a difficult man to ignore, though as we saw earlier some were able to do so, most notably in his own home village of Nazareth.

Yet this very admission that there were circumstances in which he could and did fail is itself interesting for two reasons. First, it is an important indication of the basic honesty of the gospel writers' reporting that they could admit that Jesus had his limitations. And second, he failed precisely where *as a hypnotist* (albeit an unconscious one) we might most expect him to fail, among those who knew him best, those who had seen him grow up as an ordinary child, and knew all his human weaknesses. For largely responsible for any hypnotist's success are the awe and mystery with which he surrounds himself, and these essential factors would have been lacking in Jesus' home town.

Now this idea of Jesus' natural hypnotic talents can be carried further. For instance, his alleged first miracle, the changing of water into wine at Cana of Galilee, exclusively described in the narrative portion of the John gospel (John 2: 1-11), can easily lend itself to an explanation involving hypnosis. As every stage hypnotist knows, one of the most entertaining of demonstrations is to suggest to a group of hypnotized volunteers that they are drinking some highly alcoholic (but in reality totally harmless) liquid, and then watch them roll around the stage in comic states of 'inebriation'. With a set of already inebriated guests at a wedding feast Jesus would have had a very easy group of subjects to persuade that the water they were being given was the finest wine. Likewise, because so many illusions and fantasies are possible via hypnosis, it would be possible to argue that his so-called 'transfiguration' – the incident in which, on a high mountain, he reportedly turned into dazzling light before three disciples (Matthew 17: 1-8; Mark 9: 2-8; Luke 9: 28-36) - was engineered by some clever piece of hypnotic suggestion. Likewise, his apparent feeding of the five thousand, his walking on water, and much more.

Very important, however, is not to stray too far down this road. For, as is human nature, hypnotists, magicians and David Copperfield-type illusionists all perform their tricks and wonders for the normal human motives of commercial gain, entertainment, power, etc. But in Jesus' case, what did he have to gain? When instructing his disciples in healing, he told them, 'You received without charge, give without charge' (Matthew 10: 8). The gospels emphasize his total disinclination to make any personal capital from his miracles. We are told by the writer of John that the paralytic whom Jesus cured at the Sheep Pool did not even know who it was that had cured him: 'The man had no idea who it was, since Jesus had disappeared into the crowd that filled the place' (John 5: 14). Jesus mostly shunned publicity, as in the case of his cure of the deaf man: 'Jesus ordered them to tell no-one about it, but the more he insisted, the more widely they published it' (Mark 7: 36).

Equally importantly, even if all those diverse individuals to whom Jesus brought release from suffering were, in psychological terms, mere hysterics, the sheer scale of what Jesus managed to effect, and the spontaneity with which he is said to have achieved it, go far beyond what even the greatest braggadocio among hypnotists would profess to be able to achieve today.

There is a yet further, sombre, aspect of this issue. For had Jesus been just a clever hypnotist/exorcist he could no doubt have continued happily into old age making a comfortable living from his craft. But whatever Jesus' purpose was it was altogether more serious than this, as is apparent from the most well-attested feature of his life, the way of death that he now began to bring upon himself.

8

THE ROAD TO
JERUSALEM

As theologians have repeatedly emphasized, the gospels are not, and were never intended to be, biographies of Jesus, and it is therefore quite impossible to reconstruct from them any realistic timetable for the events between Jesus' baptism and his last, so fateful days in Jerusalem. Particularly highlighting our inadequate knowledge of such matters is an incident in the Luke gospel in which Jesus told an un-named but 'very rich' aristocrat that if he wanted to inherit eternal life he had to sell everything he owned and give the money to the poor. During the subsequent lively discussion Simon Peter reportedly remarked, on behalf of both himself and the rest of the disciples: 'What about us? We left all we had to follow you', prompting Jesus to respond 'I tell you solemnly, there is no-one who has left house, wife, brothers, parents or children for the sake of the kingdom of God who will not be given repayment many times over in this present time, and in the world to come ...' (Luke 18: 28-30).

Suddenly we are very forcefully reminded that the gospel episodes of Jesus seemingly so casually calling his disciples away from whatever they had previously been doing must in actuality have involved some very strong feelings between them and their families as they left their homes to

Opposite Aerial view of the Temple Mount as it looks today. In place of the former Jewish Temples built by King Solomon and King Herod, the platform is now dominated by the gold-domed Dome of the Rock, built in the seventh century by the Umayyad Caliph 'Abd-al-Malik, and by the more southerly el Aqsa mosque that occupies part of the site of Herod's Royal Stoa. In 70 AD the Romans flattened all the Herodian buildings throughout the entire 1,300,000-square-foot platform as a reprisal for the Jewish Revolt. On the Mount's western side is the part of the Temple platform, formerly known as the Wailing Wall, where devout Jews perform special devotions as a ritual reminder of the loss of their Temple. The southern part of the Temple platform was revealed by excavations directed by the Israeli archaeologist Benjamin Mazar after the Israelis' successful capture of this area in 1967.

go with him 'on the road', with 'no purse, no haversack, no sandals' as he would later insist (Luke 10: 4). As the Luke gospel conveys, Jesus even expected them to make their departures without a moment's hesitation or looking back to pay any last-minute respects (Luke 9: 61-2), and on the principle that he must surely have practised what he preached we can only presume that he too must have left his own family much in the same way. This makes it small wonder, as the Mark gospel imparts, that his family initially 'set out to take charge of him, convinced he was out of his mind' (Mark 3: 21).

However, although we are never until the very last hours of his life provided with any remotely sure timetable of what Jesus did when, the gospel writers do at least provide the glimmerings of an itinerary for his earlier travels, albeit subject to some of the geographical gaffes mentioned in an earlier chapter (see p.28). Thus within Galilee's immediate environs he reportedly turned the water into wine at Cana, some ten miles to the north of Nazareth (John 2: 1-12), and on a separate occasion cured a nobleman's son in the same town (John 4: 46-54). At Nain, about six miles to Nazareth's south-east, he brought a widow's son back to life (Luke 7: 11-16). At Bethsaida on the Sea of Galilee's northern shore he 'walked on the water'. And after a boat journey from Bethsaida, he apparently healed many sick at Gennesaret on the north-western shore.

Further afield, he reportedly ventured at least as far north-west as Tyre and Sidon, on the Phoenician coast (Mark 7: 24-30), where he healed the daughter of a Syro-Phoenician woman. To the north-east, the Mark gospel describes him as at least en route to Caesarea Philippi (Mark 8: 27), in which vicinity snow-capped Mount Hermon is favoured by several scholars for the location of his 'transfiguration' on an otherwise un-named 'high mountain' (Matthew 17: 1-13; Mark 9: 2-13; Luke 9: 28-36). The Matthew and Mark gospels also describe him visiting the Decapolis, a confederation of ten mainly Greek-speaking cities east of the Jordan, two of these being Gadara and Gerasa (today Jerash in Jordan), where he reportedly healed the possessed man who lived among the tombs.

Throughout all Jesus' journeys he not only healed, he taught, and one of his most distinctive modes of teaching was by the parable. He did not invent this art form, for earlier Jewish prophets such as Nathan in King David's time had used it, as had Gautama the Buddha back in the fifth century BC. Yet by the keenly observed characters with whom he peopled his parables, and the clever twist he gave to each plot, he exhibited an exceptionally wry and lively mind, and took the teaching aid to new heights.

But as Jesus seems to have been well aware, ultimately the journey that he had to make to fulfil his destiny was southwards, to the Jewish people's holy city of Jerusalem. More than a thousand years before, his reputed ancestor King David had captured Jerusalem from the Jebusites and had made it his capital, David's son, Solomon, thereupon building the first Temple there. The city had undergone a number of vicissitudes, both constructive and destructive, in the subsequent centuries, including savage sack by the Babylonians in 586 BC. But every bit as dramatic was the transformation that had happened to the city shortly before and during Jesus' own lifetime. Ironically it is mostly thanks to the present-day generation of Israelis, from a tradition perennially so disinclined to accept Jesus and his teachings, that our archaeological knowledge of the Jerusalem of Jesus' time has dramatically increased in recent years, particularly regarding places associated with the leading Jewish religious groups with whom Jesus found himself in opposition in the lead-up to his crucifixion.

For most Christians, the Pharisees are the Jewish religious faction most likely to spring to mind as opposing Jesus, not least because in the English language at least, their very name has become a pejorative term, largely owing to what Jesus had to say about them. As represented in the gospels, he lost no opportunity to fulminate against the Pharisees' love of external show (e.g. Matthew 23: 1-7); against their preoccupation for observing the letter rather than the spirit of the Jewish Law (Matthew 23: 13-32); and against their attitudes of self-righteousness towards others, as epitomized by Jesus' parable of the Pharisee and the tax-collector (Luke 18: 9-14). Yet for reasons that are by no means clear, this appears to have been more than a little unfair. Other sources, most notably Josephus and the Talmud, portray the Pharisees altogether more favourably, as experts in scriptural interpretation who remained in close touch with the ordinary people, working alongside them as humble tailors, shoemakers and the like, and engendering much affection for their education of children, for their founding of regional synagogues and for their development of an oral tradition of religious wisdom that despite every attempt (including Christian) to suppress it, flourished into mainstream present-day Judaism.

For in reality the Pharisees seem to have been vigorous and down-to-earth, 'with the multitude on their side', as Josephus expressed it. Although they made no greatly overt opposition to the Roman regime, they did not disguise their lack of love of it, and they even had a paramilitary wing, the Zealots, from whose ranks Jesus appears to have drawn at least one disciple, 'Simon called the Zealot' (Luke 6: 15), also possibly Judas Iscariot, whose surname is thought to mean 'daggerman'. It is a notable aside on the author of the Mark gospel that, ever sensitive to anything too political, he notably side-stepped translating the word for 'Zealot' from its original Aramaic. Particularly in the Luke gospel there are several reported instances in which Pharisees entertained Jesus socially and exhibited genuine concern for his safety (e.g. Luke 7: 36; 13: 31; 14: 1 and elsewhere), and according to Acts (thought also to have been written by the Luke author), it was a Pharisee called Gamaliel who shortly after Jesus' death stepped forward to defend Jerusalem's earliest Christian community before the Jewish Sanhedrin (Acts 5: 34-40). The Pharisees also seem to have shared with the first Christians a belief in both angels and spirits (Acts 23: 8) and a conviction that the body would physically rise from the grave at the end of time, for this reason

Carpet-style mosaic decorating the floor of one of the opulent and tastefully furnished houses in the priestly area of first-century Jerusalem excavated by Nahman Avigad. In keeping with the Second Commandment, the mosaics and frescoes adorning the houses in this area included no human or animal representations, only floral and geometric designs.

insisting that the dead should be buried, not cremated, and that all their bones should be left intact.

Instead, the Jewish religious faction who would seem to have been Jesus' real opponents were the Sadducees, the priestly aristocrats who controlled the Jerusalem Temple. Highly materialistic in their attitudes, they rejected angels and spirits (Acts 23: 8), and the idea of any physical resurrection (Matthew 22: 23), and their love of outward show was sufficient for this to have been written large even in the archaeological record. When in 1967 the Israelis captured Old City Jerusalem's Jewish Quarter, which had lain razed and neglected under Jordanian rule, the then already veteran archaeologist Nahman Avigad seized what seemed an ideal opportunity to excavate this historic area. Trying always to keep one step ahead of planned urban redevelopment, he and his team spent some fourteen years uncovering what can now be determined to be several of the houses owned by the Sadducean priestly aristocracy that lay just to the south-east of the Temple Mount. As today's visitors to Jerusalem can see for themselves from a permanent exhibition of the finds, and from the remains of the houses themselves, cleverly preserved in specially designed basements to modern-day buildings, these chief priests lived in princely style.

By far the most impressive of their houses, though today some twenty feet below the twentieth-century floor level, is the so-called Palatial Mansion, on the eastern edge of the Western Hill overlooking the Temple and the Lower City. With two thousand square feet of floor area, and built on two (possibly even three) storeys around a spacious paved courtyard, the fact that this was fitted out with several *mikveh*, or ritual baths, suggests that it may well have belonged to the Jerusalem Temple's highest functionary, the high priest, perhaps as his official residence, in the manner of the grace-and-favour homes provided for England's Lord Mayors. In every room used for living and for guest accommodation the archaeologists found plastering and traces of fine fresco decoration, which along with a superb glass pitcher and other clues make it quite evident that this house's one-time occupants enjoyed many of Graeco-Roman life's luxuries.

A little to the north-west of this mansion Avigad and his team uncovered another impressive villa, known as the Burnt House, because it had clearly been set ablaze and destroyed during the Roman sack of Jerusalem in 70 AD (see p.165). From the debris again ritual baths emerged, accompanied by the remains of fine furniture and everyday objects. Particularly enabling attribution to a priestly family, and one to which a name could be put, was the finding of a weight inscribed as belonging to the Kathros family. Known to have been one of the 'big four' among Jerusalem's Sadducean mafia of priestly families, the Kathroses feature unfavourably in a satiric folk-song preserved in the Talmud because they used their position for their own gain.

Indicating the rich but undeniably tasteful lifestyle enjoyed by the Palatial Mansion's priestly owners, a reconstruction of what was once a superb glass pitcher.

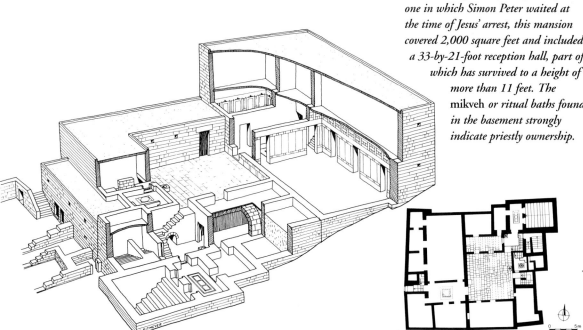

Plan/reconstruction of the so-called Palatial Mansion in Old City Jerusalem's priestly area. Centred around a large courtyard, possibly the one in which Simon Peter waited at the time of Jesus' arrest, this mansion covered 2,000 square feet and included a 33-by-21-foot reception hall, part of which has survived to a height of more than 11 feet. The mikveh or ritual baths found in the basement strongly indicate priestly ownership.

Last resting place of the Temple high priest of Jesus' time? Ornate limestone ossuary of the first century AD accidentally discovered in 1990 during the construction of a water park in the Peace Forest on the hill of Abu Tor immediately south of Jerusalem. The most elaborately carved of the dozen ossuaries found within the tomb, this particular example is inscribed 'Joseph bar Caiaphas' [Joseph, son of Caiaphas] and is thought to have belonged to the Caiaphas who controlled the Jerusalem Temple in Jesus' time.

This runs:

> Woe unto me because of the House of Kathros, woe unto me because of their reed pens … for they are high priests and their sons are treasurers and their sons-in-law are temple overseers, and their servants smite the people with sticks.

Reinforcing the folk-song's sentiments, the scholar Martin Goodman in his recent book *The Ruling Class of Judaea* has shown that these Temple priests operated a lucrative sideline using the taxes and tithes that they imposed upon the religious faithful in order to buy up small family holdings, resulting – as has happened so often in other countries throughout history – in themselves becoming richer and the poor poorer, with ordinary people who had once owned their own modest patches of land being reduced to tenant farmers or hired labourers.

In fact the gospels make clear that the Sadducean high priest when Jesus came into conflict with this breed was not Kathros but Caiaphas (Matthew 26: 3; also John 11: 49), who held the office c.18-37 AD. And although we cannot be totally sure that this Caiaphas was the occupant of the Palatial Mansion excavated by Avigad, there is now the strongest likelihood that archaeologists have found his bones. When in November 1990 Israeli workmen were building a water park as part of Jerusalem's Peace Forest, just to the south of the Old City, they came across an old cave with several limestone ossuaries or bone boxes in its central chamber. (In Jesus' time it was a common practice for the bones of the dead to be gathered in these often beautifully crafted containers after all the flesh had decomposed.)

As the archaeologists called to the scene quickly deduced, it was likely that these ossuaries dated from around the time of Jesus, since as funerary equipment they ceased in Jerusalem after 70 AD. But the find became really interesting when their study of the inscriptions revealed two to bear the name Qafa, or Caiaphas. The first box, simply inscribed 'Qafa' (ka-FA), contained just the skeletons of four children and an adult woman. But the second, with significantly superior decoration, and twice inscribed 'Yehosef bar Qayafa' (yeh-hoh-SEF bar ka-ya-FA), Joseph, son of Caiaphas, contained the bones of four children, an adult woman, and – most importantly – a man aged about 60. Although the New Testament simply gives the name Caiaphas (Matthew 26: 3, 57; Luke 3: 2; John 11: 49; 18: 13, 14, 24, 28; Acts 4: 6) to the high priest of Jesus' time, Josephus specifically refers to him as 'Joseph who was called Caiaphas of the high priesthood', 'Caiaphas' thereby seeming to have been either a family name or a nick-name. It is therefore a tantalizing possibility that the skeleton of the elderly man in the second ossuary was that of the very high priest of the time of Jesus. Sadly, however, the bones were very quickly re-interred at the behest of ultra-orthodox Jewish extremists, thus depriving both Christians and Jews of any chance of reconstructing Caiaphas' facial features using the methods that have recently been so successful with King Midas, King Philip of Macedon and others.

The control of the Jerusalem Temple's revenues, revenues directly deriving from that institution's monopoly as the only place where sacrifices could be made in atonement for sins, was therefore directly in the hands of men such as Kathros and Caiaphas. And what an emporium their allies, the Herod family, had made of the Temple in order to further this sort of trade! In keeping with his passion for ambitious building projects, back around 20-19 BC Herod the Great had set in motion plans for transforming Jerusalem's Second Temple from its somewhat modest rebuilding of King Solomon's version after the Jews' return from their Babylonian captivity, into the largest and most magnificent religious building in the world. Not satisfied with King Solomon's original foundations, which had partly utilized Jerusalem's highest hill, Herod decided to double this hill in extent, filling in natural valleys to the north and west, extending the original eastern wall and building new western, southern and northern foundation walls to create a vast man-made platform a quarter of a mile long by a fifth of a mile wide. Onto this platform Herod set his engineers to implement his grandest design, an enormous structure that he knew would not be completed in his lifetime, and indeed was continued throughout the time of Herod Antipas, and thereby throughout the lifetime of Jesus. What neither Herod could have believed was that in keeping with Jesus' apparent prophecy (see p.38), this man-made wonder would be all but completely destroyed by the Romans following the Jewish Revolt of 70 AD, so that trying to reconstruct the original by combining archaeological findings with descriptions by contemporary eyewitnesses such as Josephus demands a great deal of detective work.

However, thanks to exhaustive efforts by American archaeological architect Leen Ritmeyer and his Irish-born archaeologist wife Kathleen, and also by English model-maker Alec Garrard, enormous advances in recapturing the Herod Temple's magnificence have been made in recent years. As noted by the Ritmeyers, Josephus wrote of the Temple: 'To approaching strangers it appeared from a distance like a snow-clad mountain, for all that was not overlaid with gold was of purest white'. Making up much of the structure of this man-made mountain were precision-cut blocks of limestone, some up to thirty-five feet long and weighing up to eighty tons which had to be hauled by oxen from the nearest quarries over a mile distant. Even in the Temple's present near totally razed state some of these blocks remain over a hundred feet

Side-view of the same ossuary, showing the 'Joseph bar Caiaphas' inscription. The Matthew, Luke and John gospels all identify the high priest who presided over Jesus' interrogation simply as 'Caiaphas' (Matthew 26: 57; Luke 3: 2; John 18: 13-14). But according to Josephus' Antiquities *'Joseph Caiaphas' was the high priest from 18 to 36 AD, i.e. the period within which Jesus was crucified. And elsewhere in his* Antiquities *Josephus refers to this same individual as 'Joseph who was called Caiaphas of the high priesthood'. There is therefore a strong likelihood that the man of about sixty years old whose skeleton was among the six interred in this ossuary was indeed the Caiaphas who encountered Jesus.*

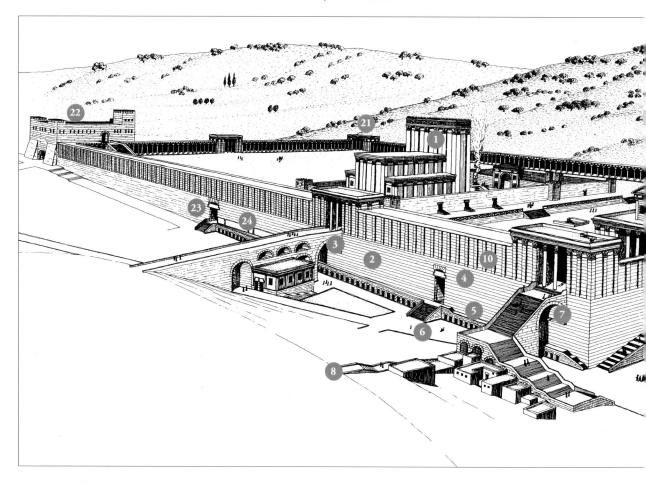

KEY TO THE TEMPLE MOUNT

1. THE SECOND TEMPLE
2. WESTERN WALL
3. WILSON'S ARCH
4. BARCLAY'S GATE
5. SMALL SHOPS
6. MAIN N-S STREET
7. ROBINSON'S ARCH
8. UPPER CITY
9. ROYAL STOA
10. PILASTERS
11. DOUBLE GATE
12. TRIPLE GATE
13. STAIRWAY
14. PLAZA
15. RITUAL BATHOUSE
16. COUNCIL HOUSE
17. ROW OF WINDOWS
18. BURNT ARCHES
19. BURNT ARCHES
20. STAIRWAY
21. HERODIAN TOWER
22. ANTONIA FORTRESS
23. WARREN'S GATE
24. LARGEST ASHLARS

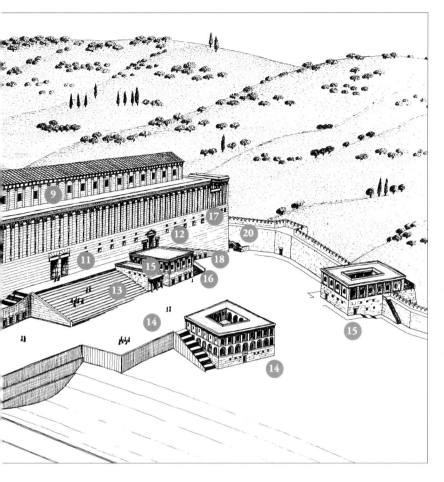

above the foundations, and the awe they created among Jesus' disciples is a matter of gospel record (e.g. Matthew 24: 1).

Also clear is that on the Temple Mount's western side Herod provided the chief priests and aristocracy with their own special bridge from the Upper City across the Tyropoeon valley and onto the Mount, while for those coming from the Lower City to the south, wide steps led up to a Double Gate and Triple Gate opening into what is called the Royal Stoa. This, a basilica-like structure, was lined with Corinthian columns which according to Josephus were so wide that it took three men with out-stretched arms to encircle them. Money-changers for changing image-bearing Roman coins for image-less ones approved by the Jewish Law, together with hawkers of animals and birds to be used for sacrifices, are thought to have plied their business in the aisles provided by these columns, one of several places around the Temple where they did so, while at the Stoa's eastern end was an assembly room for the Sanhedrin, the Jewish central religious and legislative council.

North of the Stoa lay a series of increasingly exclusive courts, the pro-hibition of Gentiles on pain of death being marked by special stone notices, two of which survive, one near complete in the Archaeological Museum,

Jesus almost certainly walked up and down these steps. These led to and from the southern entrance-way to the Temple, commanded by the Royal Stoa (see 13 on previous reconstruction), and are one of the very few usable areas to have survived. Although they are not high, Herod the Great's engineers carefully made them of alternating depths, one 12 inches deep, the next 35 inches deep, then back to 12 inches, preventing those ascending and descending from doing so in anything but a slow, methodical manner.

How Herod's stonemasons achieved very accurate rectangular shapes for the huge limestone blocks used in the Temple's construction. First a channel would be cut into the natural 'grain' line of a limestone block, then water poured over logs inserted the length of this channel. Swelling of the wood would cause the limestone to split along the relatively straight natural fault line, creating neat, rectangular blocks with relative ease. The quarries were only a mile from the Temple, and once stonecutters had properly dressed the blocks teams of oxen would then haul them to the site with the aid of wooden rollers.

Huge Herodian blocks still in situ as part of the platform of the Temple Mount. Some of these measure 39 feet in length, and weigh over 100 tons.

Istanbul, the other, more fragmentary, in the Rockefeller Museum, Jerusalem. At the approach to the Temple itself a so-called Court of the Women marked the point beyond which all women were excluded. From this court a portico led into the Court of the Priests (see reconstruction, p.122) where animals, from pigeons to heifers, many purchased from the traders in the preceding areas, were brought to be sacrificed on an altar on which two fires were kept constantly alight, and a third acted as an auxiliary. Reputedly the very spot where Abraham had once stayed his hand in sacrificing his son Isaac, this was the one place where every good Jew of Jesus' time was expected at least once a year to bring an animal sacrifice accompanied by suitable money offerings. Beyond this lay the Temple itself, with its mysterious Holy of Holies reserved only for the high priest. Some twenty thousand functionaries were said to be employed in the day-to-day running of this vast enterprise, and another sixteen thousand craftsmen and labourers kept busy on the construction work.

It is against this overall setting that we must now try to see Jesus and his disciples as they completed their fateful journey to Jerusalem, and to the Temple, that would culminate in Jesus' death. As with so many circumstances of Jesus' life, such as his enjoyment of food, and his acceptance of the endearments of prostitutes, we find him acting in a particularly offbeat

way on his arrival. Normally expected of any pilgrim on visiting the holy city of Jerusalem was that he or she would make the final stages of the journey on foot as a sign of respect and devotion. Thus even as recently as 1917 Britain's General Allenby,

ΜΗΘΕΝΑΑΛΛΟΓΕΝΗΕΙΣΠΟΡΕΥΕΣΘΑΙ
ΕΝΤΟΣΤΟΥΠΕΡΙΤΟΙΕΡΟΝΤΡΥ
ΦΑΚΤΟΥΚΑΙΠΕΡΙΒΟΛΟΥΟΣΔΑΝ
ΛΗΦΘΗΑΥΤΩΙΑΙΤΙΟΣΕΣΤΑΙ
ΔΙΑΤΟΕΞΑΚΟΛΟΥΘΕΙΝ
ΘΑΝΑΤΟΝ

Notice warning Gentiles on pain of death to keep out of the Temple's inner precincts. According to Josephus, several such notices were displayed on a screen surrounding the Temple courts, 'some in Greek and some in Roman characters', warning that 'no foreigner was to enter the holy area'. This example was found in 1935, near Jerusalem's St Stephen's Gate (the Lion's Gate) and is today in Jerusalem's Rockefeller Museum. Its reconstruction (below) is possible from a near-complete version found in the late nineteenth century and now in the Archaeological Museum, Istanbul.

Jesus rides into Jerusalem on a donkey (Matthew 21: 1-10). His riding into the Holy City in this way can only be interpreted as intentionally provocative, particularly towards the priestly aristocracy who controlled the Temple. From the sarcophagus of Junius Bassus, city prefect of Rome 359 AD, now preserved in the Vatican Grottoes, Rome.

upon capturing Jerusalem from the Turks, pointedly dismounted from his horse at the Jaffa Gate before making his entry.

Fascinatingly however, the gospels portray Jesus doing the very reverse. While throughout the rest of the gospels there is not the slightest reference to him ever using animal transport, for his entry into Jerusalem he is specifically described as going to elaborate lengths to procure a donkey to ride on (e.g. Luke 19: 28 ff.). And his choice of animal is particularly interesting. A horse would have seemed ostentatious, grandiose and militaristic. Indeed had Jesus chosen this we might have been obliged to treat more seriously the claims of Professor S.G.F. Brandon, Hyam Maccoby and others that Jesus was a guerrilla leader whose actual use of violence was written out by the gospel writers in order to make his message more acceptable to Gentiles.

But a donkey, as much in Jesus' time as now, could only be viewed as a humble beast. Furthermore, as Jesus would have been well aware, more than five hundred years earlier the *nabi* Zechariah had 'prophesied' that the promised Messiah's coming would be in precisely this manner:

> Shout with gladness, daughter of Jerusalem!
> See now, your king comes to you.
> He is victorious, he is triumphant,
> humble and riding on a donkey…
> He will proclaim peace for the nations.
> His empire will stretch from sea to sea…
>
> (Zechariah 9: 9-10)

Acclaiming Jesus on his entry, the gospels tell us, was a crowd waving palm branches and singing, 'Hosannah, blessed is he who comes in the name of the Lord', words from Psalm 118. As has been pointed out by Westminster Abbey's Canon Anthony Harvey, this scene strongly recalls the triumphant purification and rededication of the Jerusalem Temple by the Hasmonean Simon Maccabeus after it had been defiled by Antiochus Epiphanes in the second century BC, readily confirmed from even the most casual glance at the relevant passage in the first book of Maccabees: 'The Jews made their entry … with acclamations and carrying palms … chanting hymns and canticles.' (1 Maccabees 13: 51)

So if this was how Jesus entered Jerusalem, who was this gesture aimed at? Was it the occupying Romans, as might be expected if Jesus had genuinely been a guerrilla leader? Or was it the Sadducean aristocracy, with all their materialism, their lucrative concessions to money-changers and animal traders, and their concern only with the outward forms of religion? There can be no greater confirmation that it was the latter than the account (in all four gospels, though the John writer puts it almost at the very beginning of his) of Jesus' famous 'cleansing' of the Temple, the most violent physical act recorded of him throughout all four gospels. Reportedly he knocked over the money-changers' tables, laid about the traders themselves with whips, and released the animals and pigeons intended for sacrifice, loudly declaiming 'Take all this out of here and stop turning my Father's house into a market' (John 2: 16).

Now this was the man who, with John the Baptist, had already told the populace (following the theme, 'What I want is mercy not sacrifice', Matthew 9: 13 and elsewhere, after Hosea 6: 6) that repentance was what was truly necessary for the forgiveness of sins, not the paying of a Sadducean priest to sacrifice some innocent animal. So if this had not been challenge enough to the Sadducees' monopoly, now, by turning out the traders and money-changers, he had made his feelings crystal clear: to him the Sadducees' money-dominated running of the Temple was every bit as much a defilement and abomination of God's Holy Place as the pagan Antiochus Epiphanes' erection of a statue of Zeus had been two centuries before.

We have every reason to believe that the news of his high-handedness was quickly relayed to the chief priests and other members of the Sadducean aristocracy, for sure enough they were seemingly instantly upon the scene the very next time that Jesus showed his face in the Temple. According to the Mark gospel, 'the chief priests, and the scribes and the elders came to him' demanding 'What authority have you for acting like this?', prompting Jesus' characteristically cryptic response: 'John's baptism, did it come from heaven, or from man?' (Mark 11: 30). Modern-day psychologists are notoriously fond of answering a question with a question, and the gospels convey Jesus' mastery of this device long before them, making particularly adroit use of it when someone tried to trap him.

But of course the real import of Jesus' response was its challenge to his questioners' authority. If they had been prepared to acknowledge that John had been a mouthpiece of God, then Jesus, as John's successor, could have claimed the same, and thereby authority over matters concerning the Temple. We are told that those who had put their question to Jesus extricated themselves as best they could by mumbling that they did not know, but with little doubt they had sensed the trap and astutely recognized that they were dealing with a man who threatened their whole grip on the affairs of the Temple, and the comfortable living that went with this.

Accordingly, there can be absolutely no doubt that from this point on Jesus was a marked man. Because of the popular support he had attracted he represented such a serious danger to the ruling Sadducean and Herodian aristocracy that, as the John gospel chillingly conveys, they 'determined to kill him' (John 11: 52). So, this decision taken, their course now was to find the best means to effect this with the least opposition (Luke 19: 47, 48) and with the least blame falling upon themselves.

'Take all this out of here and stop turning my Father's house into a market!'
Jesus expelling the traders from the Temple, from the famous painting by El Greco in the National Gallery, London. The most violent act recorded of Jesus, it seems to have been this which prompted the Temple's controlling Sadducean priesthood to decide that he could no longer be allowed to live.

9

THE ROAD TO
THE CROSS

J ust as earlier in this book we found it impossible to determine the year in which Jesus was born, so similar uncertainty shrouds the exact year of his death, chiefly because of gospel contradictions. According to the authors of the four canonical gospels, also the Roman historian Tacitus and also the de-Christianized version of Josephus' text, Jesus was executed sometime during Pontius Pilate's governorship of Judaea. This Pontius Pilate's existence is readily confirmed by extensive mention of him in other contexts in the writings of Josephus. Also, in 1961, excavation of the ruins of a Roman temple at Caesarea revealed a Roman dedicatory inscription bearing Pilate's name as *praefectus* or governor of Judaea, the first known reference to him in a non-literary context. And his term as *praefectus* has been reliably determined as between 27 and 36 AD.

This term of office therefore usefully provides us with a narrower set of years for Jesus' death than the equivalent for Caiaphas as high priest, which was between c.18 and 37 AD. But it is still not narrow enough, for the gospels badly let us down on what might otherwise be a useful chrono-logical pointer provided by the Last Supper. According to all three synoptic gospels this Supper was very definitely the Passover Meal of Jesus and his disciples (Matthew 26: 17-20; Mark 14: 12-17; Luke 22: 7-14), a meal all

Above *Attestation of Pilate's governorship of Judaea, independent of the gospels, is provided by this fragmentary inscription discovered in 1961 in the first-century theatre at Caesarea Maritima during excavations by Italian archaeologists. The text appears to read '[CAESARIEN]S [IBUS] ... TIBERIEVM ... [PON]TIVS PILATVS [PRAEF]ECTVS IVDA[EA]E' ('To the people of Caesarea ...Tiberieum ... Pontius Pilate, Prefect of Judaea').*

Opposite *Among the very few contemporary visual representations of crucifixion, a crude graffito showing the victim with knees apart, and appearing to have been hung facing the cross. From Pozzuoli, near Naples.*

Jesus' Last Supper, in which he asked his followers to share bread and wine together, in memory of the sacrifice he was about to make of his body and blood. He closely modelled the rite on the Jewish Kiddush. From a fresco of the first half of the third century in the Capella Graeca, cemetery of Priscilla.

practising Jews know as the Seder and which they celebrate on a very specific night of the year to give thanks for their apparently divine deliverance from bondage in ancient Egypt. Since the Passover always falls on the Jewish 15 Nisan (Nisan roughly corresponds to our April), and all gospels are agreed that the day after Jesus' crucifixion was a Sabbath (making the crucifixion day a Friday and the day of the Last Supper a Thursday), it ought to be possible to fix the date of Jesus' death by finding on which year or years between 27 and 36 AD the 15 Nisan fell on a Thursday. However the author of the John gospel ruins any such calculations by stating that the day of the crucifixion, which he agrees to have been a Friday, was 'Passover Preparation Day' (John 19: 14), meaning, if he was right, that the Last Supper could not have been a Passover meal, and that we should be looking for a year in which 15 Nisan fell on a Friday.

Ingenious attempts have been made to reconcile the differences by suggesting that Jesus and his disciples, along with the Essenes of the Dead Sea Scrolls, may have celebrated the Passover according to an ancient solar calendar different from that observed by the Jews of Jerusalem. Another possibility is that Mark, as the first of the synoptics, simply got his facts wrong, and that the authors of Matthew and Luke, because they copied from Mark, made the same error, John thereby providing the only true date. Yet another possibility is that it was the author of John, in his desire to represent Jesus as the new 'paschal lamb', who distorted historical truth by altering the true moment of crucifixion to coincide with the time when lambs would have been slaughtered in the Jerusalem Temple in preparation for the Passover.

Equally fraught is any attempt to fix the year of Jesus' death from the Luke gospel's dating of Jesus' baptism to the fifteenth year of the reign of the Emperor Tiberius (Luke 3: 1). Since this is readily calculable as 29 AD, and the synoptic gospels suggest Jesus' public ministry lasted no longer than a year, this would mean that Jesus died in 30 AD. But again the John gospel complicates matters by suggesting that Jesus' ministry spanned some three years after his baptism. This has led to a widespread, but still thinly founded idea that the true year was 33 AD, hence the holding of a Holy Year in 1933. Among theologians the likeliest dates have been calculated to be 30, 33 and 27 AD, in that order of probability, though the late Hugh Schonfield, author of the famous *Passover Plot*, preferred 36 AD. But the only honest verdict can be that we simply do not know the exact year when Jesus died.

Whatever the exact year we are dealing with, however, it would seem to have been on a Thursday very close to Passover time that Jesus shared with his disciples the meal now known as the Last Supper. Supporting the synoptic view that this was the Passover meal we are told that there was wine on the table, indicating a celebration, and also that, by way of introducing the meal, Jesus reportedly used words very close to those of the Jewish Kiddush or Blessing, traditionally said by the head of a Jewish family before a Sabbath or on the eve of a major festival. This rooting of what we now know as the Christian Eucharist in the Jewish Kiddush is very obvious:

Jewish wooden eating bowls of the early second century AD, found among objects left in caves near the Dead Sea by Jewish guerrillas holding out against the Romans during the Second Jewish Revolt. Bowls such as these would very likely have been used at the Last Supper.

JEWISH KIDDUSH

Blessed are you, O Lord our God, King of the universe, who creates the fruit of the vine ...

Blessed are you, O Lord our God, King of the Universe, who brings forth bread from the earth.

CHRISTIAN EUCHARIST

Blessed are you, Lord, God of all creation, through your goodness we have this wine to offer, fruit of the vine and work of human hands ...

Blessed are you, Lord, God of all creation, through your goodness we have this bread to offer, which earth has given and human hands have made.

However, as in so much else that he said and did, Jesus introduced a quite new element into this rite, and an extremely chilling one, which was to liken the bread and wine that all were sharing with his own flesh and blood that was about to be sacrificed: 'This is my body which will be given for you' (Luke 22: 21); 'this is my blood, the blood of the covenant, which is to be poured out for many for the forgiveness of sins' (Matthew 26: 28).

There can be no mistaking the novelty of this way of thinking. While the Jewish Kiddush simply acknowledged God as Creator of bread and wine, ignoring the additional 'human hands' factor that contributed to both these products, Jesus pointedly recognized the additional human contribution, emphasizing that the same also applied to his own body and blood which was now, like the bread and wine, about to be sacrificed. Whereas perhaps two thousand years before – purportedly on the very spot occupied by the Jerusalem Temple – God had chosen to stay the Jews' ancestor Abraham from killing his son in sacrifice, now, with a little help from Joseph and Mary, God was providing the victim, for man to make his choice whether to stay his hand, or otherwise. So would Abraham's

The Jerusalem Temple's place of sacrifice, the inner court, or Court of the Priests, where animals brought in offering for the forgiveness of sins were slaughtered by the Temple priests. Detail from a meticulously researched reconstruction of the Temple made by East Anglian model-builder Alec Garrard.

descendants, in the form of the Jewish priesthood, continue with their declared aim to shed Jesus' blood – slaughtering him just as they daily slaughtered the animals and birds brought to them? Or would they stay their hand, just as God had done with Abraham's son, Isaac?

The Jewish priests, of course, had no conception that their killing of Jesus might have any role cleansing people's sins, in the manner of their more normal sacrificing of animals. But Jesus' insistence that his new version of the Kiddush and its accompanying celebratory meal was specifically for the forgiveness of sins, and that it should be repeated in perpetuity in his memory, underlines the importance that he attached to his words. His seriousness of purpose is also all too evident from the bloodiness of the events that so swiftly followed. According to the gospels it was one of his own disciples, Judas Iscariot, who turned traitor and sold the vital information that would enable the Temple priesthood to make their seizure when the ordinary people had the least opportunity to come to Jesus' aid. Although it is impossible to be sure exactly what went on in Judas' mind, the author of the John gospel, without stating as much, gave him a real motive apart from the famous 'thirty pieces of silver'. According to John, Judas' responsibility was looking after 'the common fund' (that is, the money that Jesus and all his followers shared between them for their needs), and a few days before the Passover he had been deeply angered by the wastefulness with which Jesus had allowed Mary of Bethany to lavish on him some highly expensive perfume, feeling that this went against all Jesus' avowed principles of giving all to the poor.

Whatever Judas' thinking, however, the gospels agree that Jesus and his disciples did not stay that night in the house where they had shared his Last Supper. Instead they went on to the Mount of Olives, to what the Matthew and Mark authors both describe as 'a small estate called Gethsemane' (Matthew 26: 36; Mark 14: 32). In the original Greek Gethsemane is described as a *chorion*, a very general term that simply denotes an estate or property. But because the John gospel (John 18: 1) mentions Jesus and his disciples going (in what seems to be the same context) 'into' a 'garden' (Greek *kepos*), it has long been assumed that Gethsemane was a garden, the oddity being that Jesus and his disciples should apparently quite regularly (John 18: 2) sleep rough in such a place at a time of year when Jerusalem could be very chilly, which we know from Peter being described as warming himself by a fire later that same night (Luke 22: 55-6).

As recently pointed out by New Zealand lecturer Joan Taylor, the explanation may be that Gethsemane, which (as *gat-shemanim* in Aramaic and Hebrew) means 'olive oil press', may not have been a garden at all but instead a large cave used for the pressing of olives into oil. Precisely such a cave, undoubtedly used in early centuries for pressing olives and equipped with a cistern for catching winter rainwater, is located just seventy yards north of the present-day 'garden'. Although in the autumn this would have been filled with olives awaiting processing, in Passover's springtime it would have been empty and ideal for overnight shelter, and historical sources strongly suggest that it was this, rather than the 'garden', that the earliest Christian pilgrims venerated as the true 'Gethsemane'. Certainly it is the sort of shelter that Jesus and his disciples might well have used overnight at a time when accommodation in Jerusalem would have been very scarce because of the crush of Passover pilgrims.

The Luke author informs us that on this occasion Jesus' group had two swords with them (Luke 22: 38), information that it is important to interpret carefully since some have used it to fuel arguments that Jesus was a guerrilla leader. In fact, Josephus says that even the monastic Essenes were allowed 'weapons to keep off bandits', as a result of which it seems perfectly reasonable to regard the swords as a sensible, minimal deterrence to protect the 'common fund' from being seized by undeserving hands. Even the philosophy of going the second mile and giving away cloak as well as tunic needed to be treated sensibly, rather than to the absolute letter.

Whatever number of swords Jesus' group had with them, there is no suggestion that Gethsemane, whether it was a cave or a garden, had any

The true location of Jesus' arrest? Gethsemane, where Jesus spent his last night with his disciples before his arrest, has long been supposed to have been a garden. But nowhere in the gospels is it directly described as a garden. Instead, the name actually means 'olive oil press', and new researches by Joan Taylor, of the University of Waikato, New Zealand, suggest that the true 'Gethsemane' of the gospels was this still extant natural cave 70 yards north of the present-day tourists' 'Garden of Gethsemane'. It was undoubtedly used in ancient times for pressing olives to produce oil, and in the spring months, as at Passover time, it would have lain idle and would have been ideal for overnight shelter for Jesus and his disciples. Today the cave is used as a chapel.

defence capabilities, seemingly prompting Judas, who we are told knew it well (John 18:2), to choose it as the best location for Jesus to be seized with the least amount of fuss. Ironically, there virtually had to be a Judas for Jesus to suffer the fate he clearly believed the Messiah had to suffer, and thirty years ago in his best-selling *The Passover Plot* Jewish writer the late Hugh J. Schonfield made a very plausible case for Jesus having almost psychologically pressured Judas into carrying out his unsavoury role. Certainly this remains rather more convincing than the argument by Schonfield's fellow-Jew Hyam Maccoby that Judas never did betray Jesus, as advanced in his recent *Judas Iscariot and the Myth of Jewish Evil.*

For certainly the Luke gospel in particular conveys Jesus as going through some very convincing human emotions during that last night of his life, as he waited for the results of that betrayal and the consequent harrowing fate which he had effectively brought upon himself. It is exclusively reported by the Luke writer, who in this instance certainly seems to have had access to someone who directly witnessed Jesus' plight, that: 'in his [Jesus'] anguish ... his sweat fell to the ground like great drops of blood' (Luke 22: 44). Considerable interest in this information has been expressed by forensic pathologist Dr Frederick Zugibe, Chief Medical Examiner of Rockland County, New York, who has pointed out that the 'bloody sweat' strongly suggests a rare medical condition called haematidrosis, in which anything from one to thousands of subcutaneous blood vessels rupture into the exocrine sweat glands, causing the sufferer literally to 'sweat blood'. Since the condition is comparatively little known, and is invariably triggered by extreme emotional stress, for someone to have observed Jesus suffering this at the crisis time at Gethsemane (and when he was supposed to be alone) gives us another of those tantalizing glimpses of him as a flesh-and-blood human being.

However inadequately, we are able to feel something of what a terrible moment of aloneness it must have been for Jesus. Knowing the physical torment that he had committed himself to, and knowing the disbelief and ignorance among his companions regarding what he had told them of his fate, he might easily at this moment have run away from it all, while there was still time. Yet he seems quite deliberately to have chosen this particular time and place for his ultimate act of self-sacrifice. As represented in the gospels, while many of his followers, even though they had been sleeping, took the opportunity to slip away as they heard the approach of the arrest squad, Jesus, who had reportedly so often made himself scarce on previous occasions with surprising ease (e.g. Luke 4: 30; John 10: 39), this time resolutely stood his ground, even forbidding any resistance on the part of those companions who temporarily stayed.

As the gospels also make clear, the arrest squad was composed of 'a number of men armed with swords and clubs, sent by the chief priests and the scribes and the elders' (Mark 14: 43; also with slight variants Matthew 26: 47 and Luke 22: 52). These therefore seem to have been the chief priests' servants behaving 'with sticks' in much the same manner portrayed in the Talmud's poem about the Kathros family (see p.108). And while we may question the John writer's isolated mention (John 18: 3) of the part that the Pharisees played in the arrest, also his equally isolated mention of the seemingly Roman 'cohort', the hand of the 'chief priests' in the operation is agreed by all.

Thus it was, therefore, that on that very same night Jesus found himself on trial for his life before the very men whose conduct of religious affairs he had so outspokenly questioned. Although according to Mark and the other synoptic writers, the trial was conducted by 'the chief priests and the elders and the scribes … the whole Sanhedrin' (Mark 14: 53-5), several Jewish scholars have convincingly argued that for the full Sanhedrin, the supreme Jewish council, to have held an overnight or even dawn meeting is historically extremely doubtful, since no normal Sanhedrin meeting ever took place at night, and the difficulties of summoning appropriate representatives from their beds at festival time would have been far greater than simply holding Jesus overnight, or indeed over several nights had there been any legitimate trial.

We may therefore find the John gospel's account rather more convincing, suggesting that there was no formal trial, but that Jesus was simply shuttled between two high priestly houses, that of Caiaphas and that of Caiaphas' father-in-law, Annas, both these individuals having much to lose if Jesus' popularity went unchecked. If this were the case then we may perhaps picture Jesus' 'trial' as little more than a hasty overnight interrogation by two Sadducees whose motives were rather more those of self-interest than a desire for justice. We may even quite reasonably conjecture

Jesus being brought before his accusers in one of the Palatial Mansion's upper rooms as revealed by Israeli archaeologist Nahman Avigad's excavations, while the chief disciple Peter waited 'below in the courtyard', just as described in Mark 14: 46.

But what of the charges on which Jesus is said to have been condemned? The Mark gospel represents the high priest as asking him: 'Are you the Messiah, the Son of the Blessed One?' (Mark 14: 61), thereupon tearing his robes at the apparent blasphemy when Jesus answers in the affirmative. As modern Jewish scholars have pointed out, it was surely not the Messiah claim as such that could have caused Caiaphas such offence, for someone, sometime, had to be he. For instance, according to the Jewish Midrash, at the time of the Second Jewish Revolt of 132 AD the great Rabbi Akiba specifically acclaimed rebel leader Simon Bar-Kokhba with the words: 'This is the king Messiah!', and although Akiba's companion reportedly scoffed: 'Akiba, grass will grow in your jawbones and he will still not have come!', Akiba's claim as such was no offence.

The John gospel, for its part, says the charge on which the priests brought Jesus before Pilate for execution was 'because he has claimed to be the Son of God' (John 19: 7), and here it seems to be the use of the definite article, i.e. the Son of God, as also in the Mark version, that brings us nearer to the issue on which Jesus' life hung. Any Messiah's claim to being a son of God was already recognized, the link being made in Psalm 2, for instance, and in some Dead Sea Scroll references. But as the high priest seems to have been already aware, perhaps via Judas, Jesus' claim for himself, overt or otherwise, went far deeper - to the extent, if accepted as such, of carrying authority in God's name over the whole enterprise that he, Caiaphas, currently controlled to such advantage.

Clearly this upstart Galilean could not be allowed to live, and with this decided Jesus' inquisitors are described as handing him over to Pilate because: 'We are not allowed to put a man to death' (John 18: 31). No doubt there was something to this effect in the small print of the alliance between the Temple authorities and the Romans, but that in practice the Temple authorities could put a man to death if they so chose is evident from the fact that the book of Acts describes the martyr Stephen being stoned by the Jerusalem Sanhedrin (Acts: 7: 59-60) for an apparently similar blasphemy shortly after Jesus' death. Although some have argued that this was a mere mob lynching, the likelihood that the Sadducean chief priests possessed at least some power of execution, albeit most likely reserved for special offences against the Temple, is further indicated by the Temple's still extant stone notices threatening death to any Gentile trespasser, as featured in the previous chapter (see p.113).

So whilst there is little doubt the 'chief priests' could have publicly killed Jesus there and then had they felt they were acting with the full approval of the Jewish people, there is every reason to suppose that they would have been extremely unpopular had they openly done so, and it must have seemed much more expedient for them to have Pontius Pilate take care of their dirty work. From the gospels' mention of the governor's custom of releasing a prisoner, Pilate seems to have made a regular practice to come to Jerusalem to keep an eye on events during Passover (he was normally based at Caesarea). And despite the chief priests' own Temple security force, it would have been Pilate who had the far superior military capability to deal with any disturbance.

But what of the gospels' portrayal of Pilate as finding no fault with Jesus, and pointedly washing his hands of any responsibility for Jesus' death? Fortunately the Jewish historian Josephus includes in his writings mention of two attempts by Pilate to put down demonstrations of Jewish passive resistance which provide important clues to the Roman's mentality. The first of these demonstrations had arisen because Pilate had provocatively ordered the display of his legion's image-bearing standards in Jerusalem. This had prompted an 'angry city mob ... joined by a huge influx of people from the country' to surround Pilate's residence in Caesarea, calling for him to remove the offending objects, whereupon on his refusal they all 'fell prone all round his house and remained motionless for five days and nights'. Concerned to rid himself of this nuisance, Pilate ordered the gathering to be surrounded by a ring of soldiers three deep, who advanced with drawn swords. But at this, according to Josephus,

> ... the Jews as though by agreement fell to the ground in a body and bent their necks, shouting that they were ready to be killed rather than transgress the Law. Amazed at the intensity of their fervour Pilate ordered the standards to be removed from Jerusalem forthwith.

The second demonstration described by Josephus was provoked by Pilate's use of some of the Temple tax for the building of an aqueduct. In his response to this Pilate seems to have tried hard to be more cunning, for he had his soldiers '... mix with the mob, wearing civilian clothing over their armour. Furthermore they were ordered not to draw their swords but to use clubs on the obstreperous'. Even so the result was hardly a triumph for public order. According to Josephus, '... many died from the blows, and many were trampled on by their friends as they fled.'

The interest value of these episodes is that first, and quite independently of anything in the gospels, the incident of the standards in particular shows Jews of Jesus' time using passive resistance methods of which even Mahatma Gandhi could scarce not have been proud. Although we are told nothing about who led those who bared their necks to Pilate's soldiers, their actions accord unerringly with the message of the man who taught: 'offer the wicked man no resistance ... if anyone hits you on the right cheek, offer him the other as well' (Matthew 5: 38).

Secondly, the incidents are mentioned by Josephus in his book *Antiquities* specifically just before his controversial reference to Jesus that was discussed

Roman dice found at Sepphoris, of a kind typical of the first century AD. Made of bone, such dice are often found at sites associated with Roman troops, and are arranged almost identically to modern dice (i.e. opposite faces always add up to seven). According to the John gospel the Roman soldiers responsible for Jesus' crucifixion used dice at the foot of his cross to decide who should have his 'seamless undergarment' (John 19: 24).

in chapter 3. As was noted there, this reference was tampered with, and most commentators, such as Paul Winter and others, recognize that part of the text is now missing. So in his original did Josephus directly link Jesus with some third popular demonstration that mediaeval Christian copyists felt obliged to suppress? Could this have been the incident Luke's gospel hints at: 'It was just about this time that some people arrived and told him [Jesus] about the Galileans whose blood Pilate had mingled with that of their sacrifices' (Luke 13: 1).

Likewise, is there some significance in Mark's cryptic reference to Barabbas as one who had been thrown into prison 'with the rioters who had committed murder during the uprising' (Mark 15: 7)? We may take comfort from the probability that whatever was suppressed is unlikely to have been earth-shattering, for we would otherwise have heard about it from those commentators on Josephus, such as Origen, who were writing before the text was mutilated. But even so there are grounds for suspicion that Jesus, albeit passively, had stirred up greater popular Jewish fervour than the Gentile gospels convey.

A third point of interest is Pilate's reaction to the passive resistance methods. He acts neither as the insensitive butcher that some modern authors have tried to label him, nor as the pusillanimous capitulator to mob demands portrayed by the gospel writers. A man clearly used to the ways of violence – he was, after all, regionally responsible for the world's most efficient fighting machine, the Roman army – he nonetheless exhibits a superstitious awe of individuals ready to lay down their lives for what to him would have seemed trifling religious niceties. It is possible therefore that he may genuinely have raised some objection to putting Jesus to death just to satisfy the demands of the Sadducean high priesthood. In this regard, and given the gospels' portrayal of a Jewish crowd positively baying for Jesus' blood when Pilate suggested he might be spared, many writers have remarked on the strange and seemingly unexplained change that seems to have happened from the effusive welcome that Jesus had reportedly been given on his arrival in Jerusalem just a few days before. One possible explanation is that Jesus was disowned by those who had welcomed him to Jerusalem because he had failed to sanction the abortive uprising against the Romans that arguably they had launched in his name. If the latter were the case, it would inevitably have been accompanied by disillusionment and bitterness against Jesus as a betrayer of those who had given their lives in his cause. But arguably the likelier explanation is that the second, blood-thirsty crowd was one carefully orchestrated by the Sadducees using their own paid employees. With an estimated twenty thousand Temple servants and eighteen thousand workmen on their payroll, they would scarcely have had difficulty in finding a mob to perform to their tune. This is further suggested by Josephus' bald statement, 'Upon an indictment *by leading members of our society*, Pilate sentenced him [Jesus] to the cross'.

Of the details of this crucifixion, all the gospels relate that Jesus was beaten as a preliminary and also that he was scourged, that is, lashed repeatedly with a pellet-studded whip (Matthew 27: 26; Mark 15: 15; John 19: 2). Apparently seriously weakened by this maltreatment, he reportedly had difficulty carrying his 'cross' to the crucifixion site (although this is generally thought to have been just the beam from which he would be suspended, it would have been quite heavy enough). This necessitated the aid of the bystander Simon of Cyrene. Once at the execution site Jesus was stripped of all his clothes, and although we are not directly told that nails were driven through his hands and feet, this may be assumed from John 20: 25.

Otherwise the gospel writers seem to have been concerned to spare their readers the more harrowing details of the procedure, no doubt because these were all too familiar at the time. Earlier employed by Scythians, Assyrians and Carthaginians – none of them the most squeamish of people – crucifixion was universally execrated as a form of punishment, even the Romans reserving it only for slaves and for foreign rebels. Again, because crucifixion was so abhorred, only the scantest of contemporary information about it has survived. Mostly this has been in the form of artistic representations, two of these crude graffiti, one from Pozzuoli, just outside Naples, the other from the Palatine Hill, near Rome, and two others tiny depictions on gems, one of these in the Pereire Collection in Paris.

Also, despite many thousands having been crucified during the Roman era – in 71 BC alone the Roman consul Crassus had six thousand rebels of the Spartacus uprising strung up along Italy's Via Appia – there has been a

Among the very few contemporary visual representations of crucifixion, a crude graffito showing the victim with knees apart, and appearing to have been hung facing the cross. From Pozzuoli, near Naples.

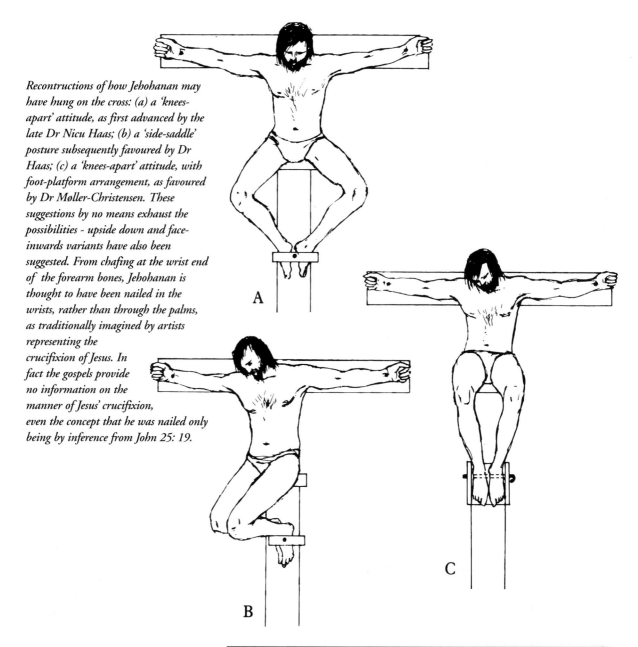

Recontructions of how Jehohanan may have hung on the cross: (a) a 'knees-apart' attitude, as first advanced by the late Dr Nicu Haas; (b) a 'side-saddle' posture subsequently favoured by Dr Haas; (c) a 'knees-apart' attitude, with foot-platform arrangement, as favoured by Dr Møller-Christensen. These suggestions by no means exhaust the possibilities - upside down and face-inwards variants have also been suggested. From chafing at the wrist end of the forearm bones, Jehohanan is thought to have been nailed in the wrists, rather than through the palms, as traditionally imagined by artists representing the crucifixion of Jesus. In fact the gospels provide no information on the manner of Jesus' crucifixion, even the concept that he was nailed only being by inference from John 25: 19.

A

B

C

The breaking of the legs of the crucified. The bones of Jehohanan's legs can be seen to have been broken by 'a single, strong blow' shortly before death, in precisely the manner recorded of the robbers crucified alongside Jesus (John 19: 31-2). A measure that would have prevented the crucified from raising himself in order to breathe (thus hastening death), this is a notable instance of archaeology confirming the gospel record.

Ankle-bones of a first-century Jew called Jehohanan, joined by a six-and-a-half-inch crucifixion nail. The only known victim of crucifixion so far scientifically excavated, Jehohanan's skeleton was found in an ossuary in an extensive Jewish cemetery of Jesus' time discovered in 1968 in the northern Jerusalem suburb of Giv'at ha-Mivtar. Forensic examination revealed that in life Jehohanan had been slightly disfigured by a cleft palate, and that he was crucified while in his mid-twenties. Traces of wood found either side of the ankle-bones have been variously explained as from the titulus or notice recording Jehohanan's crime, or from a foot-platform to which his feet were nailed.

marked dearth of identifiable skeletal remains for them. One of the reasons for this seems to have been a medical black market for crucifixion nails in antiquity, for they were thought to be effective against bee-stings, fevers and epilepsy, and if withdrawn from the body no easily identifiable trace was left on the skeleton. In 1968, however, following the discovery of an ancient Jewish cemetery at Giv'at ha-Mivtar in northern Jerusalem, several ossuaries or bone boxes came to light, one of which was found to contain an adult male skeleton whose two heel bones were securely joined together by a nail nearly six and a half inches long. The ossuary's inscription identified this individual as one 'Jehohanan', and it is evident from the skeletal remains that he was a gracefully built, cleft-palated male in his mid-twenties, who undoubtedly died of crucifixion.

The discovery has raised lively interest among both Christians and Jews, with no little controversy regarding the exact form the crucifixion took. The Israeli anatomist Dr Nicu Haas, who conducted the main forensic examination, favoured the legs having been forced into an awkward side-saddle position, but renowned Israeli archaeologist the late Dr Yigael Yadin thought otherwise, opting instead for the knees having been kept apart. According to Yadin, although the ossuary's inscription is difficult to decipher, it may well read: 'Jehohanan…the one hanged with his knees apart', and such a position certainly corresponds with the Pozzuoli graffito and the Pereire Collection gem. Another possible reconstruction has come from the Copenhagen Medical Museum specialist Dr Møller-Christensen who has deduced from traces of wood on both sides of Jehohanan's ankles that his feet had been forced into a crude wooden frame and were then locked in with a transverse nail.

Of course, whatever the exact method used, Jesus was not necessarily

Magical gem of the Roman period depicting a crucifixion, this time with the victim clearly suspended face outwards, but again with the legs wide apart. From a magical gem formerly in the Pereire Collection, Paris.

crucified the same way as Jehohanan, for crucifixion procedures are known to have varied, the disciple Peter, for instance, reputedly having been crucified upside down. But there is one feature of Dr Nicu Haas' observations on Jehohanan's skeleton which has a particular importance in suggesting that the gospels are, at least to some extent, eyewitness accounts. Dr Haas noted:

> The right tibia and the left calf bones (tibia and fibula) were all broken in their last third at the same level, but in a different manner: the right tibia had brutally been fractured, by comminution, into sharp slivers; the left tibia and fibula were broken by a simple, oblique, dentate-serrate line. Both types of fractures are characteristic in fresh bone. The fracture of the right tibial bone (the fibula being unavailable for study) was produced by a single, strong blow. This direct, deliberate blow may be attributed to the final 'coup de grâce'.

Essentially, Jehohanan had his legs savagely smashed, immediately recalling the breaking of the legs of Jesus' two crucifixion companions exclusively reported in the John gospel:

> ... to prevent the bodies remaining on the cross during the Sabbath ... the Jews asked Pilate to have the legs broken and the bodies taken away. Consequently the soldiers came and broke the legs of the first man who had been crucified with him and then of the other. When they came to Jesus they found he was already dead, and so instead of breaking his legs one of the soldiers pierced his side with a lance ... (John 19: 31-4)

The 'breaking of the legs' would seem to have been a procedure carried out only on Jewish crucifixion victims, for in other countries they would be left on the cross during the night, and it might take up to three days for them to expire. But in deference to the Mosaic prohibition on the leaving of a body on a cross after sundown, the Romans broke the legs of crucified Jews to hasten death, John's report thereby providing an authentic detail of which a Gentile writer, working from a distance, could not be expected to have been aware. Accordingly, whereas the old German theologians supposed the 'breaking of the legs' to have been an invention of the gospel writer in order to fulfil the Messianic prophecy of Psalm 34: 20, 'God rescues him ... Taking care of every bone ... God will not let one be broken', modern archaeology has proved them wrong, finding instead that it argues for the gospel's veracity. There is also medical support for the view that the John gospel's narrative content at least embodies other authentic, eyewitness detail, as in its writer's claim in respect of another crucifixion detail, the physiological effects of the lance reportedly thrust into Jesus' side:

… immediately there came out blood and water. This is the evidence of one who saw it – trustworthy evidence, and he knows he speaks the truth … (John 19: 34, 35)

According to some medical specialists, the 'water' would have been from fluid that had accumulated in lungs badly damaged from the beatings that Jesus suffered.

All the canonical gospels report as the final act of the crucifixion saga the arrival on the scene, after Jesus' death, of a hitherto unmentioned secret disciple, a 'rich man' called Joseph of Arimathea, who took charge of Jesus' body. Mystery surrounds the reasons why such a man, apparently influential enough to gain ready access to Pilate, should have emerged only at this moment, and also why not a single one of the associates of Jesus who might have been expected to have tried to organize some form of burial for him appears to have done so. Joseph, we are told, provided the grave linen and spices for the burial, and the tomb itself. Although a Jew would normally have been buried in his Sabbath-best clothes, Jesus had had all his clothes removed and shared out as part of the pickings by the execution squad, and Joseph is described as purchasing a length of linen in which to wrap the otherwise naked corpse.

Inevitably thoughts turn to the now notorious Turin Shroud, a length of linen in Turin Cathedral which bears seeming imprints of a naked, crucified body. Although the Shroud's history could be traced with certainty only back to the 1350s, the discovery in 1898 of its life-like photographic image when seen in negative revolutionized serious interest, so much so that evidence steadily mounted that it could be the very cloth purchased by Joseph of Arimathea – until 1988. In that year radiocarbon dating carried out by three separate laboratories showed the Shroud's fabric

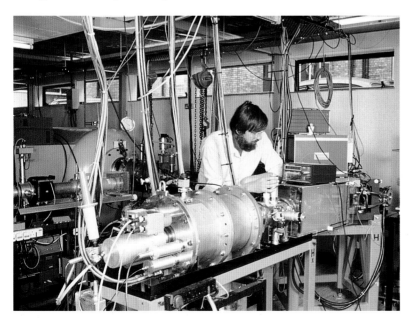

The radiocarbon dating laboratory at Oxford University, one of three which tested small samples of the Shroud's linen in 1988. According to the laboratories' instrumentation, the flax from which the Shroud was woven 'died' sometime between 1260 and 1390, thereby strongly suggesting it to be a mediaeval fake. However, no truly satisfactory explanation has yet been forthcoming for how such a convincingly photographic image could have been created so long before the age of photography. Despite widespread popular belief that the Shroud has been 'proved' a fake, carbon dating readings are not necessarily infallible, and some as yet undetermined anomaly to these remains an open possibility.

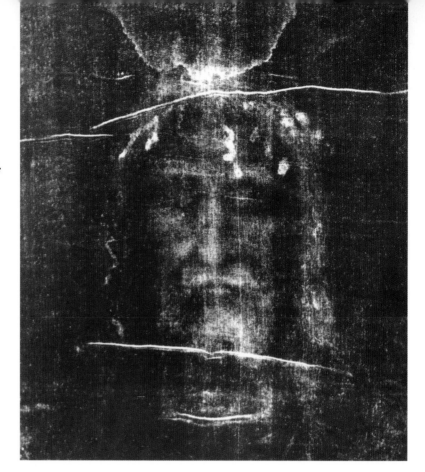

The famous negative of the facial image on the Turin Shroud, once widely reputed to be the cloth which wrapped Jesus in the tomb. Whenever the Shroud is photographed using black and white film, the ghostly imprint faintly visible on the cloth itself becomes transformed into this convincingly photographic likeness.

to have been made sometime between 1260 and 1390 AD, its mysterious image thereby being most likely the work of a mediaeval forger. Subsequently the Turin cloth has been the subject of a variety of absurd claims ranging from deliberate 'rigging' of the carbon dating to the proposition that it was a 'photograph' invented by none other than Leonardo da Vinci. Even so, its mystery remains very far from being resolved. Medically the Shroud's body image and apparent bloodstains are so convincing that dozens of well-respected specialists continue to contend that the cloth genuinely wrapped someone crucified in a manner identical to that recorded of Jesus. Historians can show that some form of cloth mysteriously imprinted with Jesus' likeness was recorded at least as far back as the sixth century – well over six centuries before the earliest date claimed by the carbon dating. And some highly talented professional artists have confessed themselves baffled how anyone, of any century, could have so convincingly 'forged' facial and body images of the Shroud's astonishing subtlety. Because of certain anomalies now emerging concerning radiocarbon dating's claimed margins of accuracy, the much-publicized scientific 'proof' of the Shroud's fraudulence may yet be in need of some serious revision.

But although the Shroud, if genuine, can provide the most powerful data on Jesus' 'way of the cross' – effectively taking on the rôle of a Fifth Gospel – it is by no means central to our understanding of Jesus. The same cannot be said, however, of the mystery surrounding what happened to his body within just a few hours of the time when he was first laid, to all appearances dead, in Joseph of Arimathea's brand new tomb.

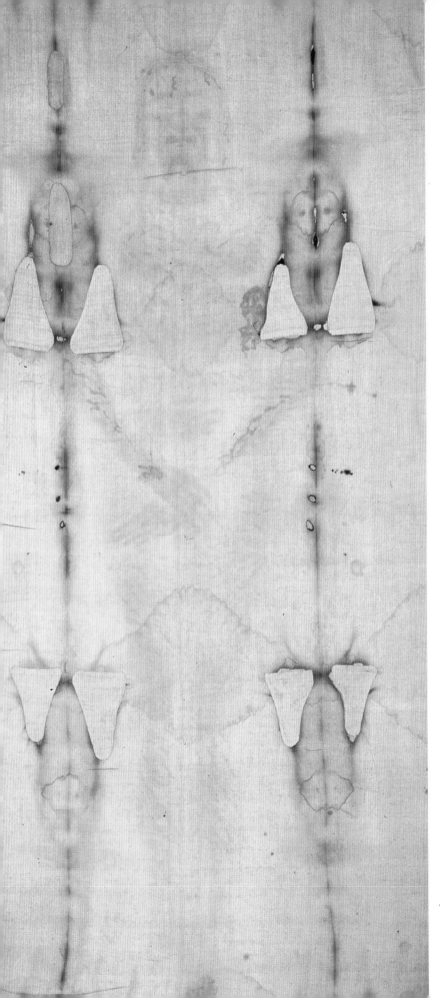

Image of the frontal half of the whole body image imprinted on the Shroud, seen as it appears to the naked eye. Nailing is notably indicated through the wrists, reminiscent of the crucifixion of Jehohanan. A flow of what seems to be blood from a wound in the chest readily corresponds with the action of the lance thrust into Jesus' side described in John 19: 34. The triangular shapes are patches from a fire which nearly destroyed the cloth in 1532.

10
DID JESUS REALLY RISE FROM THE DEAD?

According to the gospels, Joseph of Arimathea laid Jesus in his own new, rock-cut tomb 'in which no-one had yet been buried' (John 19: 41). This is described as having been in a garden, close to Golgotha (John 19: 41-2), and with a 'very big' stone rolled across the entrance-way (Matthew 27: 60; Mark 15: 46; 16: 3-4). More than sixty examples of such rolling-stone tombs can still be seen in and around Jerusalem. Their entrance boulders can weigh up to two tons, though if on level ground they can with a little effort be rolled aside by just one person. Although the John gospel's information that 'no-one had yet been buried' in the tomb might appear puzzling, in fact this is consistent with the evidence of Jewish rock-cut tombs from Jesus' time that have been excavated in recent years.

Thus, as was found, for instance, during the earlier-mentioned excavations at Giv'at ha-Mivtar, a single Jewish tomb might contain one or more benches or 'laying-out' places, together with as many as eight or more chambers cut into the rock (see overleaf) to accommodate ossuaries, the stone boxes in which the bones were gathered once the corpse had decomposed. Since each tomb-chamber might contain two or three ossuaries, and each ossuary several sets of bones, a single tomb could be used for thirty or

Opposite *Rolling-stone tomb in the environs of Jerusalem. This example is one of several tombs that feature a large 'rolling-stone' boulder which could be rolled across to seal their entrance-way. Such a boulder readily corresponds to the gospel account of the women visiting Jesus' tomb asking: 'Who will roll away the stone for us from the entrance to the tomb?' (Mark 16: 3). According to the Mark gospel, the stone used for Jesus' tomb was 'very big'. Surviving examples can sometimes weigh up to two tons, but if on level ground it is possible for them to be moved by just one person, albeit with effort.*

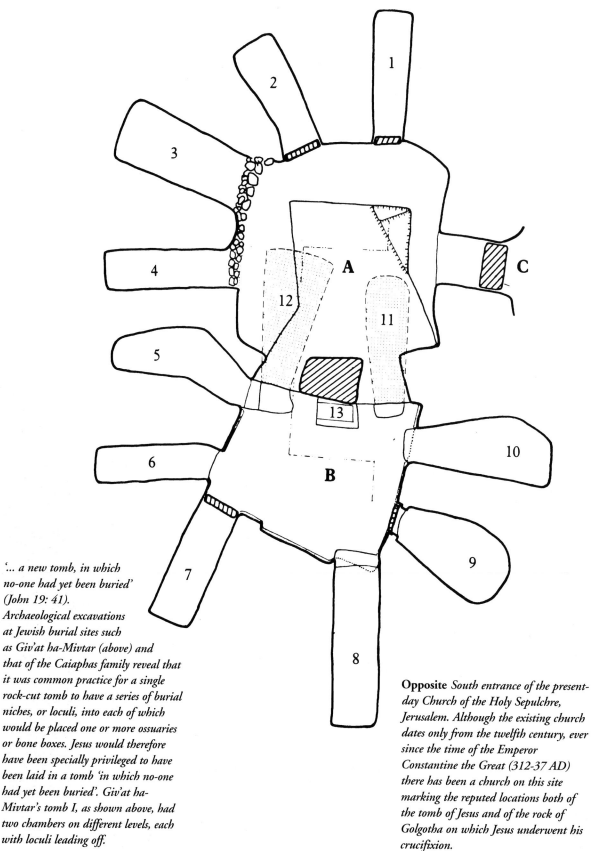

'... a new tomb, in which no-one had yet been buried' (John 19: 41). Archaeological excavations at Jewish burial sites such as Giv'at ha-Mivtar (above) and that of the Caiaphas family reveal that it was common practice for a single rock-cut tomb to have a series of burial niches, or loculi, into each of which would be placed one or more ossuaries or bone boxes. Jesus would therefore have been specially privileged to have been laid in a tomb 'in which no-one had yet been buried'. Giv'at ha-Mivtar's tomb I, as shown above, had two chambers on different levels, each with loculi leading off.

Opposite *South entrance of the present-day Church of the Holy Sepulchre, Jerusalem. Although the existing church dates only from the twelfth century, ever since the time of the Emperor Constantine the Great (312-37 AD) there has been a church on this site marking the reputed locations both of the tomb of Jesus and of the rock of Golgotha on which Jesus underwent his crucifixion.*

Plan of Jerusalem showing the relation of the present-day Church of the Holy Sepulchre to the nearby city walls. The so-called Third Wall was built by Herod Agrippa between 41 and 44 AD, shortly after Jesus' crucifixion. At the time of the crucifixion, however, the site was outside the city - or 'not far from the city' as Golgotha is described in John 19: 20. This therefore supports the authenticity of the Church of the Holy Sepulchre's location.

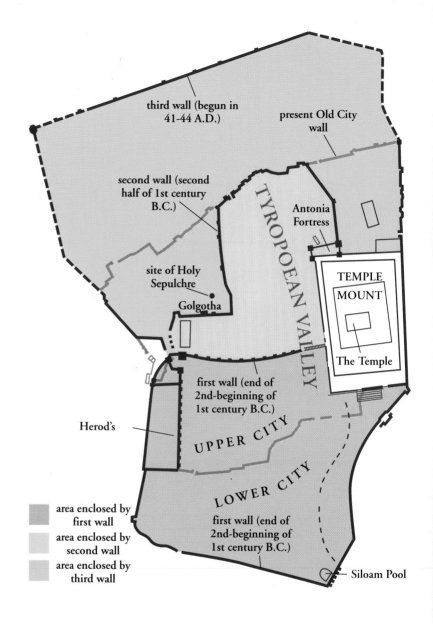

third wall (begun in 41-44 A.D.)

present Old City wall

second wall (second half of 1st century B.C.)

TYROPOEAN VALLEY

Antonia Fortress

site of Holy Sepulchre

Golgotha

TEMPLE MOUNT

The Temple

first wall (end of 2nd-beginning of 1st century B.C.)

Herod's

UPPER CITY

LOWER CITY

area enclosed by first wall

area enclosed by second wall

area enclosed by third wall

first wall (end of 2nd-beginning of 1st century B.C.)

Siloam Pool

Opposite *The nineteenth-century edicule within the Church of the Holy Sepulchre, enshrining what remains of the reputed tomb of Jesus. Constantine the Great's architects rather too enthusiastically cut away much of the hillside around the tomb in order to expose the interior chamber, thus even at that early time ruining the tomb's original appearance.*

more people over a period of decades. For a tomb to be one in which 'no-one had yet been buried' would therefore be at least worthy of comment. It also provides an element of authentic Jewish detail bearing in mind that, for the Romans and other Gentiles of Jesus's time, cremation was the norm.

But where was Jesus' tomb located in relation to present-day Jerusalem? Today the traditional site is marked by the mainly Crusader-built Church of the Holy Sepulchre, a bewildering rabbit-warren of an edifice, always under repair and teeming with tourists, with in its midst a rather ugly, many times rebuilt edicule, or 'little building', housing a carefully protected marble slab covering all that remains of the purported bench on which Jesus was laid out in death. This location has been identified as Jesus' burial place at least since the time when Helena, mother of the first Christian

Roman Emperor Constantine the Great, reputedly 'discovered' it back in the fourth century AD. As recounted by the near-contemporary church historian Socrates Scholasticus:

> Helena went to Jerusalem, to find what had been that city as desolate as 'a lodge in a garden of cucumbers'...after the Passion Christians paid great devotion to Christ's tomb, but those who hated Christianity covered the spot with a mound of earth, built a temple of Aphrodite on it, and set up her statue there, so that the place would not be forgotten. The device was successful for a long time – until, in fact, it became known to the Emperor's [i.e. Constantine the Great's] mother. She had the statue thrown down, the earth removed and the site cleared, and found three crosses in the tomb...With them was also found the *titulum* on which Pilate had written in various languages that the Christ crucified was the king of the Jews...

From one of those three crosses found by Helena came most of the pieces of the 'True Cross' venerated in numerous churches and cathedrals throughout the world. What purports to be the *titulus* can also still be seen in Rome's Basilica of Santa Croce in Gerusalemme, a puzzling piece of work with an inscription just decipherable as 'Jesus the Nazarene, King of the Jews', written in Aramaic, Greek and Latin (see John 19: 19). The authenticity of this has to be considered doubtful, likewise probably the pieces of the cross, though no-one can be sure.

But in view of the early attested marking of the spot with the Temple of Aphrodite (known to have been built by the Emperor Hadrian), there is a more than reasonable case for accepting the Church of the Holy Sepulchre as genuinely enshrining the one-time tomb in which Jesus' body was laid. Although according to the gospels Jesus' tomb was located outside Jerusalem's walls, by Helena's time these walls had been rebuilt, the reputed tomb being found inside them. There must, therefore, have been something very compelling about the location for Helena to have ignored the gospels' clear descriptions. As archaeologist Dr Kathleen Kenyon discovered in the 1960s, the Church of the Holy Sepulchre site *was* outside the city walls of Jesus' time, and would seem to have been within a quarry then being used for burials.

Frustratingly, however, Constantine the Great's engineers cut away the rock into which the tomb had been set, leaving it first free standing, and then before the end of the fourth century surrounded by a rotunda within a grandiose church. This church and the tomb alike subsequently became subjected to sometimes exhaustive Moslem attacks so that today almost every vestige of how it looked if and when Jesus was laid in it has been lost. This has prompted many Christian pilgrims to turn instead to the altogether more authentic-looking 'Garden Tomb', which General Gordon of Khartoum, on visiting Jerusalem in 1883, suggested might have been the true one used for Jesus. Located just a short walk north of Old City Jerusalem's Damascus Gate, this is today beautifully maintained as an inter-denominational place of prayer, though as even its guides admit there is very little evidence in favour of it having been the original.

But the real question is: what happened to Jesus' body as laid in the true tomb, wherever this was, and whatever it looked like? According to every available early source, Jesus died on the cross at the hands of the world's most efficient executioners, the Romans. Before his body was taken down from the cross the Roman governor Pontius Pilate reportedly sent a senior officer to ensure that he was genuinely dead (Mark 15: 45). The author of the John gospel observed that in order to leave nothing to chance a lance was plunged into his chest, whereupon blood and a watery fluid oozed out (John 19: 34). According to the Matthew gospel's author, a guard was even mounted and official seals affixed to the entrance stone in order to prevent any possibility of trickery (Matthew 27: 66).

Because the Matthew gospel alone tells the story of the guard, also of a 'violent earthquake' and of the 'angel of the Lord' rolling away the entrance stone, it is probably safest to regard these as pious embroideries by an author demonstrably over-fond of the miraculous. It is equally impossible to know quite what to make of the differing accounts of the young man or men encountered at the tomb (Mark 16: 5; Luke 24: 4; see the parallel passages featured earlier on p.27), except that the bench on which Jesus' body would have been laid, as still to be seen in surviving rolling-stone tombs, certainly would have provided sufficient space for individuals to be seated at both head and foot. But altogether more important is the agree-ment of all sources that just two days after Jesus had been laid in the tomb not only had his body mysteriously disappeared but people who had known him well began to have strange experiences of seeing him among them. Sometimes, distrusting their own senses, they reported seeing him pass through locked doors, yet he was able to talk and eat with them (Luke 24: 43). Reportedly he even felt like a living person to the touch (John 20: 27, 28). The convincingness of these encounters to those on the receiving end is powerfully conveyed by the speech attributed to Peter in the tenth chapter of Acts:

> Now I and those with me can witness to everything he did throughout the countryside of Judaea and in Jerusalem itself: and also to the fact that they killed him by hanging him on a tree, yet three days afterwards God raised him to life and allowed him to be seen, not by the whole people, but only by certain witnesses God had chosen beforehand. Now we are those witnesses – we have eaten and drunk with him after his resurrection from the dead … (Acts 10: 39-42)

As even 'Jesus-did-not-exist' exponent Professor G. A. Wells has acknow-ledged, this powerful belief caught on very soon after the events described,

Exterior (left) and interior views of the so-called 'Garden Tomb', which General Gordon of Khartoum suggested could have been the true tomb of Christ. Spared much of the historical destructions and accretions that have ruined what remains of the tomb within the Church of the Holy Sepulchre, the 'Garden Tomb' often appeals to Christian visitors to Jerusalem because it conforms to how they imagine Jesus' true tomb once looked. However, as even the 'Garden Tomb's custodians acknowledge, there is no serious evidence that it was the true location.

at least one attestor to the resurrection, the apostle Paul, being readily date-able. In Acts 18: 12 Paul is said to have appeared before the Achaean pro-consul Gallio while on his second mission, and since an inscription found at Delphi enables Gallio's administration to be accurately dated to 51-2 AD, simple back calculation establishes that Paul must have believed in Jesus' resurrection c. 40 AD, and according to some authorities, perhaps even as early as 36 AD. So what had happened to account for the fact that Paul and others held this belief? In this ostensibly simple question lies the central mystery of the Christian religion, and one for which there remains no uncontested rational answer.

The various accounts of the scene at the empty tomb on the first Easter morning are so full of inconsistencies that it is easy for sceptics to deride them. The writer of the John gospel describes Mary Magdalen arriving at the tomb alone, discovering the tomb to be empty and imparting the news to Peter and an unnamed 'other disciple, the one Jesus loved' (John 20: 2), generally identified as John. The Matthew author relates that Mary Magdalen was accompanied by 'Mary the mother of James and Joseph'. Mark adds a further companion, a woman called Salome, referred to in the Thomas gospel. Luke, who knows nothing of any Salome, speaks only of one 'Joanna' (presumably royal treasurer Chuza's wife – see p.87), together with other women who go off to tell the disciples what they have seen, though according to Mark, the women, 'frightened out of their wits… said nothing to a soul, for they were afraid' (Mark 16: 8).

Similar discrepancies occur in the reports of what was seen at the empty tomb. John's Mary Magdalen saw first two angels sitting in the tomb and then Jesus, whom she was not allowed to touch. Matthew's two Marys saw one seated angel, and then Jesus. Mark's three women saw a young man in a white robe, and Mary Magdalen alone saw Jesus. Luke's group of women saw two men in brilliant clothes who suddenly appeared at their side, but not Jesus himself, who was seen only by two disciples on the road to Emmaus. All four gospels describe Jesus subsequently appearing to the full group of disciples, but while Matthew and Mark set these appearances in Galilee, the Luke and John gospels suggest that the setting was Jerusalem. Luke also indirectly mentions an earlier appearance of Jesus to Simon Peter, one which seems to have gone unnoticed elsewhere in the gospels. But it is one of Paul's letters which gives the fullest information of all:

> … he [Jesus] appeared first to Cephas [Peter] and secondly to the Twelve. Next he appeared to more than five hundred of the brothers at the same time, most of whom are still alive, though some have died; then he appeared to James and then to all the apostles; and last of all he appeared to me too … (1 Corinthians 15: 5-8)

The documentation is an almost hopeless jumble of confusion, scarcely helped by the fact that the ever enigmatic Mary Magdalen, the only witness mentioned in every account except Paul's – for whom women didn't count – was obviously so unbalanced that she had needed to be cured by Jesus of 'seven devils'. The lack of a proper ending to the Mark gospel, as revealed by the *Sinaiticus* and *Vaticanus* manuscripts, merely adds to the problem. Yet had someone wholly invented the resurrection story one might have expected them to do so more convincingly than, for instance, representing women as the prime witnesses, when women's testimony carried a particularly low weight in Jewish Law. And in their own way the garblings and inconsistencies have the same quality as the memories of witnesses after a road accident, which are, after all, personal and often highly confused versions of the same true story.

Any number of theories have been advanced in an attempt to explain what really happened, but all may be reduced to permutations of six basic hypotheses:

1. The women went to the wrong tomb.
2. Unknown to the disciples, some independent person removed the body.
3. The disciples themselves removed the body and invented the whole story.
4. The disciples saw not the real Jesus, but hallucinations.
5. Jesus did not actually die on the cross, but was resuscitated, or in some other way survived.
6. Jesus really did rise from the grave.

Although it is impossible within a single chapter to do justice to these different hypotheses, quite clear is that the disciples and gospel writers anticipated that the first four theories would be proposed to explain the mystery. All the synoptic writers emphasize, for instance, how the women had carefully taken note of where Jesus was laid (Matthew 27: 61; Mark 15: 47; Luke 23: 55). The John gospel puts into the mind of Mary Magdalen the idea that the man she mistook for a gardener (in reality Jesus, as yet unrecognized) had for some reason taken the body away (John 20: 15). The writer of Matthew acknowledged that in his time there was a story in circulation that the disciples had stolen the body. He accused 'the Jews' of having bribed the guards posted at Jesus' tomb to say this. With regard to the possibility of hallucination, both the Luke and the John gospels emphasize the disciples' own incredulity at the solidity of what they were seeing, the Luke author, for instance, wonderingly reporting '…they offered him a piece of fish which he took and ate before their eyes' (Luke 24: 43). The John author noted the disciple Thomas' insistence that he was not prepared to believe unless he was able to put his fingers into the wound in Jesus' side, and recorded that Thomas was specifically allowed to do this.

In fact, quite aside from the gospel writers' evident anticipation of them, the first four hypotheses bear little serious scrutiny. Had there simply been a mistake over the location of the tomb, it would have been an easy

Jesus' resurrection appearance to Mary Magdalen, from a panel painting in the London National Gallery by the Italian Gothic artist Orcagna. Although according to the gospels Mary was one of the prime witnesses of Jesus rising from the dead, for Jews her testimony as a woman would have carried very low weight. However Mary was but one of more than five hundred who claimed to have experienced the resurrected Jesus, many of whom were prepared to die attesting the validity of this.

matter for any sceptic to go to the right location, show the body still there
and set the whole matter at rest. Had Jesus' body been taken away either by
a person unknown or by the disciples, we might surely have expected someone, sometime, to produce it. Such a hypothesis also fails to account for the
repeated attestations of Jesus being seen alive and well. With regard to the
possibility of hallucinations, it might of course be possible to envisage some
bizarre mass post-hypnotic suggestion that made Jesus seem to appear to
those so hypnotized, to seem to eat with them, and even to feel solid to
their touch. But this still totally fails to account for the reportedly very real
emptiness of Jesus' tomb.

Perhaps because the gospel writers do not take account of it, the fifth
hypothesis, that Jesus did not die on the cross, has been particularly
favoured by sceptics and sensationalists in recent years. In his *The Passover
Plot* the late Hugh J. Schonfield advanced the ingenious theory that the
sponge offered to Jesus on the cross (John 19: 29, 30) was soaked not in
vinegar but in a drug to induce the appearance of death. This was so that
he could be taken to the tomb by Joseph of Arimathea and there resuscitated, the lance thrust into Jesus' side being the unexpected eventuality
that caused the plot to misfire. According to Schonfield, the man seen by
Mary Magdalen was simply someone who had been deputed to help revive
Jesus, and the 'resurrection' was therefore nothing more than a case of
mistaken identity, Jesus' body having been quietly buried elsewhere.

Both before and after Schonfield all sorts of variants to this theory have
been offered. In D.H. Lawrence's short story 'The Man who Died', Jesus
was taken down too early from the cross, revived in the tomb, petrified his
followers, who assumed he was dead, 'resurrected', and then slipped away
to Egypt to enjoy conjugal relations with a priestess of Isis. The supposedly
factual *The Holy Blood and the Holy Grail* by Baigent, Leigh and Lincoln
represents Jesus' paramour as Mary Magdalen and their place of refuge as
the south of France, but it follows essentially the same plot, with Jesus
even going on to father a family. Within the last few years Dr Barbara
Thiering of the University of Sydney has resurrected the same idea in her
Jesus: The Man, as have the German writers Holger Kersten and Elmar
Gruber with their *The Jesus Conspiracy*. Thiering has based her arguments
on the idea that the gospels were all written in a code, so that virtually
everything in them has to be re-interpreted in the light of that code.
Kersten and Gruber have contended that the Vatican conspired with
radiocarbon dating scientists to ensure that the Turin Shroud was dated to
the Middle Ages so that its purported 'big secret', that it 'proves' that Jesus
was still alive when laid inside it, should not be allowed to destroy the
Christian faith. Despite the ingeniousness of such arguments, they merit
scant serious scrutiny.

The problem for all hypotheses of this kind, certainly those postulating
some form of resuscitation, was outlined more than a hundred years ago by
the controversial Tübingen lecturer David Strauss, one of those nineteenth-

century German theologians who in so many ways cast doubts on the gospel story. As Strauss wrote in his *New Life of Jesus*, published in 1865:

> It is impossible that a being who had stolen half dead out of the sepulchre, who crept about weak and ill, wanting medical treatment, who required bandaging, strengthening and indulgence ... could have given the disciples the impression that he was a Conqueror over death and the grave, the Prince of Life, an impression which lay at the bottom of their future ministry. Such a resuscitation ... could by no possibility have changed their sorrow into enthusiasm, have elevated their reverence into worship!

In support of this, and in full favour of the hypothesis that Jesus genuinely rose from the grave, is the sheer confidence about this that became exhibited by the previously denying and demoralized disciple Simon Peter. This is evident from his first post-crucifixion public speech to the inhabitants of Jerusalem and their fellow-Judaeans reported in the book of Acts:

> Men of Israel ... Jesus the Nazarene was a man commended to you by God ... This man ... you took and had crucified by men outside the Law. You killed him, but God raised him to life ... and all of us are witnesses to that. (Acts 2: 22-4, 32)

Peter went on to speak with similar passion on subsequently addressing non-Jews in Caesarea:

> Now I, and those with me, can witness to everything he [Jesus] did throughout the countryside of Judaea and in Jerusalem itself; and also to the fact that they killed him by hanging him on a tree, yet three days afterwards God raised him to life and allowed him to be seen, not by the whole people, but by certain witnesses God had chosen beforehand. Now we are those witnesses – we have eaten and drunk with him after his resurrection from the dead ... (Acts 10: 39-42)

Likewise meriting considerable weight as evidence is St Paul's clear and unequivocal statement in his letter to the Corinthians that the resurrected Jesus had been seen not only by himself, by Simon Peter, by the other disciples and by James but also by more than five hundred people at one time, most of whom he claimed to be still alive when he was setting his pen to papyrus. As pointed out by Dr Edwin M. Yamauchi, Associate Professor of History at Oxford, Ohio:

> What gives a special authority to ... [Paul's] list as historical evidence is the reference to most of the five hundred brethren being still alive. St Paul says in effect, 'If you do not believe me, you can ask them.'

Such a statement in an admitted genuine letter written within thirty years of the event is almost as strong evidence as one could hope to get for something that happened nearly two thousand years ago.

Overall then, while there are undeniable reporting flaws regarding Jesus' claimed resurrection, and at a time distance of nearly two thousand years knowledge of exactly what happened is beyond us, the evidence that something like it actually happened is rather better than sceptics care to admit. And quite incontrovertibly, belief in it spread like wildfire very soon after the crucifixion.

Thus the book of Acts mentions as one of the first new believers a Hellenistic Jew called Stephen. Although their ancestry and religion was Jewish, Hellenistic Jews lived in the fashionable Graeco-Roman style, and spoke the Greek language. From Josephus' information that Jesus' teaching 'attracted many Jews and many of the Greeks', Stephen's adherence need not be considered out of the ordinary. But whatever his background, he chose, just like Jesus had, to attack the material vanity of the Jerusalem Temple, harking back to the Isaiah text:

> With heaven my throne
> and earth my footstool,
> what house could you build me,
> what place could you make for my rest?
> Was not all this made by my hand?
>
> (Isaiah 66: 1, 2)

Stephen then went on fearlessly to accuse the Jerusalem Temple authorities of having, in executing Jesus, murdered the great prophet foretold by Moses. That same Jesus, he impassionedly declared, he could see there and then 'standing at God's right hand'. Without in this instance even pausing to refer their prisoner to the Roman governor, those whom Stephen had attacked peremptorily stoned him to death.

Stephen was but the first of many who would take up this same cause – including, as we shall see, previously reticent members of Jesus' own family. They would firmly profess Jesus as the Messiah or Christ predicted in the Jewish scriptures, and emphatically attest that he had come back to life again after having suffered the most public of deaths. What cannot be emphasized enough is that those who made such claims had absolutely no expectation of any material gain for their outspokenness. Their reward instead, as the following decades and centuries would demonstrate, was all too frequently to be faced with some form of violent death, from being stoned, to being torn to pieces by wild animals in a Roman arena, to being crucified in some yet more grotesque and painful manner.

The really unnerving feature is that time after time they accepted such terrors with an astonishing cheerfulness, totally confident that what they professed was truth, that death had been conquered, and that their eventual reward far outweighed whatever tortures ordinary mortals might try to inflict upon them in the meantime. And few of the men and women who took up this challenge would have counted themselves natural martyrs, or anything out of the ordinary. Although some were high-born, most were from every stratum of society, whether Jewish or Graeco-Roman.

We can only conclude, therefore, that whether these were among the first five hundred-plus direct witnesses, or whether they had merely come to know one or more of those witnesses at first or second hand, something very powerful had fired into them such resoluteness of belief. So, given such attestation, can the resurrection of Jesus be accepted as a real historical event? And was the one-time flesh-and-blood Jesus genuinely rather more than just an ordinary man? Whatever the answer, already born was a faith in such matters powerful enough to survive not only the early years of persecution, but even through to our own time.

11

A FAITH
IS BORN

A kindly Jewish rabbi from Cardiff once explained to me why most Jews have never accepted Jesus as their promised Messiah. He told me that according to the Hebrew prophets the true Messiah would bring in a kingdom of peace (e.g. Isaiah 11: 6-8). My response was to counter that the resurrected Jesus' first words to his disciples were 'Peace be with you' (Luke 24: 37; John 20: 19), also that Christians throughout nearly twenty centuries have believed Jesus' kingdom of peace to be in their hearts. But on a historical level, at least, the rabbi has to be accounted right.

For it is quite clear from the New Testament that from the very outset Jesus' followers were not even at peace with each other, let alone with the rest of the world, one serious cause of their dissension emanating from the self-styled apostle Paul, originally named Saul. As related in the book of Acts, Saul, a Hellenistic, or Greek-speaking, Jewish tentmaker from the Greek city of Tarsus in Asia Minor, had been approvingly present when the first martyr Stephen was stoned to death, and had subsequently made it his mission to hunt down other followers of Jesus on behalf of the Sadducean authorities.

Then, as described in one of the New Testament's best-known episodes,

Opposite *Head of an apostle often identified as Jesus' disciple Simon Peter, from a fresco of the mid-third century in the hypogeum of the Aurelii, Rome.*

at the height of Saul's persecuting he was dramatically stopped in his tracks on the Damascus road, and blinded for three days. As he subsequently related, he experienced the resurrected Jesus, he had his sight restored by a follower of Jesus called Ananias and was thereupon baptized as a Christian, taking the new 'Christian' name Paul.

Now while any other recruit to this new religion of Jesus might have been expected to take time to go and meet some of the original disciples, and to learn some background details of Jesus' life and teachings, Paul seems by nature to have been far too impatient for this. Even the strongly pro-Pauline Acts remarks that it was 'only a few days' before he began actively evangelizing for Jesus, and he himself described the process as even more swift:

> I did not stop to discuss this with any human being, nor did I go up to Jerusalem to see those who were already apostles before me, but I went off to Arabia at once, and later went straight back from there to Damascus. Even when after three years I went to Jerusalem to visit Cephas [Peter] and stayed with him for fifteen days, I did not see any of the other apostles. (Galatians 1: 16-19)

Paul therefore seems to have had little interest in Jesus' crucifixion as an actual and recent event, associated with flesh-and-blood individuals such as Pontius Pilate and the self-centred Jewish high priests – hence his failure even to mention these in his writings, as noted in an earlier chapter. Instead the experience of the resurrected Jesus was all that he felt he needed: '… the Good News I preached is not a human message that I was given by men, it is something I learned only through a revelation of Jesus Christ.'

Thus Paul saw Jesus' death on an other-worldly level of faith, a divine plan thought out 'before the aeons', whereby the 'powers that rule the world' crucified in ignorance a supernatural 'Lord of glory' (1 Corinthians 2: 8). And instead of referring to Jesus as 'the Christ', which would have been the correct translation of 'the Messiah' into Greek, he adopted the fashion of calling Jesus 'Christ' as if this were his proper name, ignoring its political connotations, likewise referring to him as the Son of God (Acts 9: 20). Furthermore, on the strength of his profound conversion experience, and being himself merely a Hellenistic Jew, he apparently decided that it should be perfectly permissible for Gentile converts to Jesus' teaching to discard the traditional requirements of the Jewish Law such as circumcision and prohibition of the eating of 'unclean' meats, requirements that Jews had laid down their lives to defend during the Maccabean revolt.

At this point we begin to find that Paul was by no means necessarily as universally revered a figure among members of the earliest Church as is often popularly supposed. When this idea was first put forward by the great Tübingen theologian Ferdinand Christian Baur back in the nineteenth century, it seemed daring at the time, yet it becomes obvious enough to anyone who reads Paul's letters not as religious documents but for their historical content that it must be true. Thus in Paul's letter to those whom he had converted in Galatia not long before, he mentioned certain others who had been there after him with 'a different version of the Good News' (Galatians 1: 6). In his first letter to the Corinthians, generally regarded as written about 57 AD, he noted regretfully:

> … there are serious differences among you. What I mean are all these slogans that you have, like 'I am for Paul', 'I am for Cephas [Peter]', 'I am for Christ'. (1 Corinthians 1: 11-12)

Although Paul studiously omitted to mention who his mysterious opponents are, he happened to let slip, in a typically exasperated remark in his second letter to the Corinthians,

> As far as I can tell, these arch-apostles have nothing more than I have. (2 Corinthians 2: 5)

Arch-apostles? From the well organized nature of these opponents, their close marking of Paul's activities and his obvious embarrassed reluctance to name them, modern scholars are in general agreement that these were Jesus' original fully Jewish followers who during Paul's lifetime remained based in Jerusalem. It is all too rarely appreciated just how little the surviving documentation tells us of the activities of these pioneering followers of Jesus – historically, a really serious loss – but Acts does give us the occasional important though tantalizing glimpse:

> The many miracles and signs worked through the apostles made a deep impression on everyone. The faithful all lived together and owned everything in common; they sold their goods and possessions and shared out the proceeds among themselves according to what each one needed. They went as a body to the Temple every day but met in their houses for the breaking of bread; they shared their food gladly and generously; they praised God and were looked up to by everyone. (Acts 2: 43-7)

In this brief description we get a picture of a group carrying out Jesus' teachings to the letter, and continuing to worship in the tradition of the old Jewish religion, just as Jesus himself had done. But, strangely, what we are not told is anything about this group's leadership. Acts makes it clear that there was a major controversy over whether uncircumcised Gentiles should receive baptism, with Jesus' disciple Simon Peter being sympathetic to a Roman centurion's eagerness to follow Jesus, and having a dream in which he apparently received divine sanction for the eating of 'unclean' foods. From Acts we also learn that Peter expounded this revelation at a council meeting in Jerusalem, that Paul became apostle to the uncircumcised, and that an individual called James (quoted as using the words 'I rule...') apparently agreed to less strictly orthodox rules being applied to pagan converts.

But there is an uncomfortable suggestion here that all is not being told quite straight, an impression which gains greater cogency from Paul's letter to the Galatians, in which Peter is described as initially eating with, and therefore expressing sympathy towards, uncircumcised Gentiles, but then receiving a visit from 'certain friends of James' who urged him to abandon his pro-Gentile stance. This Peter dutifully agreed to apparently for 'fear of the group that insisted on circumcision' (Galatians 2: 12), whereupon a clearly angry Paul tells us: 'When Cephas [Peter] came to Antioch ... I opposed him to his face, since he was manifestly in the wrong' (Galatians 2: 11).

Here considerable interest surrounds the identity of this mysterious James, who apparently had the authority to rule on matters of doctrine and adherence to traditional Jewish ways, even to the extent of overruling Peter. Why should the book of Acts be so reticent about him? Despite the popular supposition that Peter was first head of the Church, from a variety of sources it is apparent that this James was its first true leader. This is explicit in the Nag Hammadi 'Gospel of Thomas', which in Logion 12 represents Jesus naming 'James the Righteous' [an appellation to distinguish him from the disciple of the same name] as the disciples' leader after his own departure. It is equally explicit in the writings of the second-century Jewish author Hegesippus and the fourth-century Eusebius of Caesarea. The latter, who quoted from Hegesippus, unequivocally described James the Righteous as 'first to be elected to the episcopal throne of the Jerusalem Church'.

What is quite astonishing to discover, however, is that this James was none other than Jesus' brother. This is attested by Josephus who, describing with genuine sadness James' unjust execution at the hands of a Sadducean high priest in 62 AD, explicitly referred to him as 'the brother of Jesus called the Christ'. That this was no slip of Josephus' pen is firmly corroborated by Paul who remarked of a trip he had made to Jerusalem, 'I only saw James, the brother of the Lord' (Galatians 1: 20). It is also corroborated in the writings of Hegesippus and Eusebius. And in fact the same information checks out with the Mark gospel (which of course has no account of Jesus' 'virgin' birth) in a passage in which the people of Nazareth say of Jesus:

> This is the carpenter, surely, the son of Mary, the brother of James and Joset and Jude and Simon? His sisters too, are they not with us? (Mark 6: 3)

Although there are often attempts to explain away this passage on the grounds that 'brothers' can mean 'cousins' among Near Eastern peoples, the Josephus and other references provide every justification for believing that the use of the words 'brothers' and 'sisters' was intended to mean just that in this particular context.

So why was there such reluctance to acknowledge someone as important and interesting as Jesus' brother? Another sign of this reluctance is that although Paul, as earlier quoted from his letter to the Corinthians (1,15: 8), reported that Jesus had made a resurrection appearance to James, not one of the gospels has any report of this, the only other indication of it occurring in a tantalizingly cryptic extract from the lost 'Gospel of the Hebrews' that happened to be quoted in a later century by St Jerome:

> But the Lord, when he had given the shroud to the high priest's servant, went to James and appeared to him. For James had sworn that he would not eat bread from that hour when he had drunk the Lord's cup until he saw him rising from those who sleep… 'Bring', says the Lord, 'a table and bread'. He took bread and blessed it and broke it and gave it to James the Righteous, and said to him, 'My brother, eat your bread, for the Son of Man has risen from those who sleep'.

Family tree of Jesus, based on the assumption that the 'brothers and sisters' listed in Mark 6: 3, and mentioned elsewhere (John 7: 2; Acts 1: 14; 1 Corinthians 9: 5), were Jesus' immediate family. This is certainly how they were regarded by early authorities such as Tertullian and Hegesippus. Note how headship of the Jerusalem followers of Jesus passed to members of Jesus' family, his brother, James, then his cousin Simeon. A similar family tradition is to be noted among leadership of the Zealots.

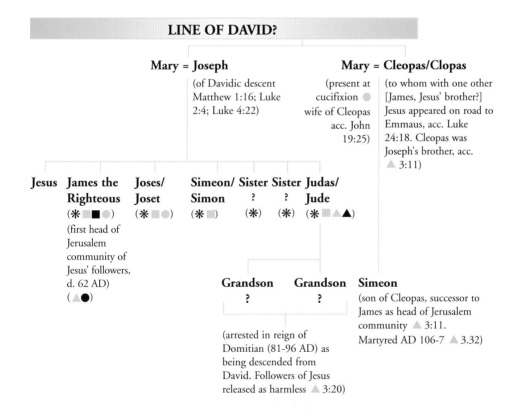

LINE OF DAVID?

Mary = Joseph
(of Davidic descent Matthew 1:16; Luke 2:4; Luke 4:22)

Mary = Cleopas/Clopas
(present at cucifixion ● wife of Cleopas acc. John 19:25)

(to whom with one other [James, Jesus' brother?] Jesus appeared on road to Emmaus, acc. Luke 24:18. Cleopas was Joseph's brother, acc. ▲ 3:11)

Jesus

James the Righteous
(✻ ■ ■ ●)
(first head of Jerusalem community of Jesus' followers, d. 62 AD)
(▲ ●)

Joses/ Joset
(✻ ■ ●)

Simeon/ Simon
(✻ ■)

Sister ?
(✻)

Sister ?
(✻)

Judas/ Jude
(✻ ■ ▲ ▲)

Grandson ?

Grandson ?

(arrested in reign of Domitian (81-96 AD) as being descended from David. Followers of Jesus released as harmless ▲ 3:20)

Simeon
(son of Cleopas, successor to James as head of Jerusalem community ▲ 3:11. Martyred AD 106-7 ▲ 3.32)

KEY

✻ Mark 6:3   ■ Matthew 13.55   ■ Galatians 1:19   ● Mark 15:40
● Josephus *Antiquities* 20:9.1 (200-3)   ▲ Hegesippus, as preserved in Eusebius'
History of the Church (references are to the Eusebius text)
▲ Jude 1

Whatever we may make of the 'Gospel of the Hebrews' passage, we seem to be faced with a straight, first-century clash of theologies, Paul's on the one hand, based on his other-wordly experience, and James' on the other, based on his fraternal knowledge of the human Jesus. And, despite the authority which should be due to the latter, it would seem to be Paul's that is all that has been allowed to come down to us. Or, in fairness, almost all.

For one of the most neglected of all New Testament documents is a letter traditionally attributed to this very James, brother of Jesus, and which would indeed appear to have been by him. Although this was dismissed by Martin Luther as 'a right strawy epistle', and tossed aside by the nineteenth-century German theologians as a work of the late second century, Dr John Robinson in his *Redating the New Testament* argued very cogently for James' authorship, and the most serious objection, that the Greek is too good for a Galilean Jew, has recently been almost totally undermined by the latest findings on the quality and quantity of Greek spoken in Jesus' Galilee (see p.63). As noted by the editors of today's Jerusalem Bible, the James letter, despite its good Greek, is full of hebraisms, it exhibits a close similarity to Jesus' Sermon on the Mount teachings and reveals its early composition by portraying Jesus' followers still worshipping within the Jewish religion. But particularly significant is its gentle but firm stance on the importance of Jesus' teaching on communal living, as distinct from Paul's stress on a Christ of faith. In James' words:

> Take the case, my brothers, of someone who has never done a single good act, but claims he has faith. Will that faith save him? If one of the brothers or one of the sisters is in need of clothes and has not enough food to live on, and one of you says to them: 'I wish you well; keep yourself warm and eat plenty' without giving them these bare necessities of life, then what good is that? Faith is like that: if good works do not go with it, it is quite dead. (James 2: 14-17)

That James was intensely devout (as indeed suggested by the 'Gospel of the Hebrews' reference), and actually led a very much more outwardly pious lifestyle than that of his self-confessedly gluttonous and wine-bibbing brother, is quite evident from the lost writings of the second-century historian Hegesippus, as preserved by the fourth-century church historian Eusebius.

> He [James] drank no wine or intoxicating liquor and ate no animal food; no razor came near to his head; he did not smear himself with oil, and took no baths. He alone was permitteed to enter the Holy Place [of the Jerusalem Temple] for his garments were not of wool, but of linen. He used to enter the Sanctuary alone, and was often found on his knees beseeching forgiveness for the people, so that his knees grew hard like a camel's from his continually bending them in worship of God.

Yet equally clear is that whatever reservations he may earlier have had about his brother (he was presumably one of the family members who had set out to take charge of Jesus, 'convinced he was out of his mind'; Mark 3: 21), James now firmly recognized Jesus as the great Messiah recorded by the prophets, who had died to save men's sins, and who had risen from the dead. Hegesippus continued:

> Representatives of the seven popular [Jewish religious] sects … asked him [James] what was meant by 'the door of Jesus' and he replied that Jesus was the Saviour. Some of them came to believe that Jesus was the Christ … those who did come to believe did so because of James. Since therefore many even of the ruling class believed, there was an uproar among the Jews and Scribes and Pharisees, who said there was a danger that the entire people would expect Jesus as the Christ.

Hegesippus went on to describe James making himself yet more explicit by proclaiming from the Temple parapet, possibly from the same spot on which trumpeters signalled the start and end of the Sabbath, that Jesus as the Son of Man was now 'sitting at the right hand of the Great Power' and would come again 'on the clouds of heaven'. That bold affirmation, which had already proved so fatal in the case of Stephen, again proved far too much for the Temple's controlling Sadducean priesthood who, like Caiaphas and his cronies before them, decided that James now had to be forever silenced. As described by Josephus, when Festus, a successor to Pontius Pilate, died in 62 AD, this left a short vacuum while Festus' appointed replacement, Albinus, journeyed from Rome, providing the then high priest, Ananus, with the opportunity he needed to arrange for James' death with the least likelihood of opposition. In Josephus' words:

> The younger Ananus … was headstrong in character and audacious in the extreme. He belonged to the sect of the Sadducees, who in judging offenders are cruel beyond any of the Jews, as I have already made clear. Being a man of this kind Ananus thought he had a convenient opportunity as Festus was dead and Albinus still on the way. So he assembled a council of judges and brought before it James, the brother of Jesus, known as Christ, and several others, on a charge of breaking the Law, and handed them over to be stoned.

Before 'the most fair-minded people in the City' had time to intervene, Ananus' lackeys hurled James from the Temple parapet, stoned him on seeing that he was still alive, then finally beat him over the head with a fuller's club. James, for his part, apparently asked for divine forgiveness for them to his dying breath, just as his brother had done before him.

It is clear then that even as early as the three decades immediately following Jesus' crucifixion there were serious divisions between different

Head of an apostle often identified as Jesus' disciple Simon Peter. Peter is believed to have been crucified in Rome during Nero's reign of terror, and a skeleton that some have argued to be Peter's was found during excavations beneath the high altar of St Peter's, Rome. These same excavations revealed a very early shrine seemingly built to Peter's memory.

groups of Jesus' followers, both Jews and Gentiles, as well as serious trouble from traditional Jewish groups who opposed them. Inspired by appealing side-aspects of Jesus' teaching, there was also in embryo stages a bewildering variety of fringe groups, loosely collectively termed Gnostics. Some of these would not properly emerge for a century or so, but among them were Docetists (pronounced Do-see-tists), who conceived of Jesus as being such a heavenly being that he must have merely appeared to be human; Montanists, who practised glossolalia or 'speaking with tongues'; Marcionites, who appointed women as priests and bishops; and Carpocratians who, according to their enemies at least, contended that every mortal sin needed to be experienced in order for the soul to reach heaven.

But alike for all varieties of the earliest Christians and for their conforming Jewish counterparts, it was the decade that we now know as 60-70 AD that was to prove the most terrible. When, whether by deliberate arson or otherwise, a huge part of Rome was destroyed by fire in 64 AD, it suited the Emperor Nero to blame the Christians, and it was in recording this that the Roman historian Tacitus made his famous reference to Jesus. In Tacitus' words:

> Nero fabricated scapegoats – and punished with every refinement the notoriously depraved Christians (as they were popularly called). Their originator, Christ, had been executed in Tiberius' reign by the governor of Judaea, Pontius Pilate. But in spite of this temporary setback the deadly superstition had broken out afresh, not only in Judaea (where the mischief had started), but even in Rome... First Nero had self-acknowledged Christians arrested. Then, on their information, large numbers of others were condemned – not so much for incendiarism as for their anti-social tendencies. Their deaths were made farcical. Dressed in wild animals' skins, they were torn to pieces by dogs, or crucified, or made into torches to be ignited after dark as substitutes for daylight. Nero provided his Gardens for the spectacle, and exhibited displays in the Circus, at which he mingled with the crowd...

The Galilean Simon Peter had reportedly made his way to Rome sometime before these atrocities, and it is more than a little testimony to the earliness of the New Testament books, particularly a historical one such as Acts, clearly a follow-up to the Luke gospel, that while reporting earlier episodes of his life they nowhere record his death. Only via later tradition do we learn he was probably among those whom Nero put to death during this terrible time, reputedly at his own request being crucified upside down through his feeling unworthy at being crucified exactly as Jesus had been. Paul for his part seems to have gone to Rome around 60 AD, finding, as Acts records, an already established community of 'brothers' to greet him (Acts 28: 15), but having the fortune to depart before the Neronian terror,

Most famous of Roman arenas, the Colosseum, Rome, inaugurated by Titus in 80 AD. Many early Christians are believed to have met their deaths here as entertainment for the Roman populace, though direct evidence of this is scanty.

only to find himself, as we learn from 2 Timothy, back there awaiting trial around 67 AD. Again, despite the New Testament incorporating so much of his life and letters, it has no record of the outcome of this, or the manner of his death – as if, as it were, the relevant books 'went to press' before this.

But whatever torments James, Peter, Paul and the Rome community of Christians went through, these were but curtain-raisers for what the rest of the 60-70 AD decade had in store. The gospels convey Jesus as warning his disciples explicitly enough of the sufferings they and their followers would have to undergo in his name: 'They will hand you over to be tortured and put to death, and you will be hated by all the nations on account of my name' (Matthew 24: 9). 'Men will seize you and persecute you; they will hand you over to the synagogues and to imprisonment, and bring you before kings and governors because of my name … You will be betrayed even by parents and brothers, relations and friends, and some of you will be put to death' (Luke 21: 12, 16). Nothing, however, could have been more specific or (at the time) more unbelievable than his dread prophecy of the Jerusalem Temple's destruction. In the words of the Matthew gospel,

> Jesus drew his [disciples'] attention to the Temple buildings. He said to them … 'You see all these? I tell you solemnly, not a single stone will be left on another: everything will be destroyed'. (Matthew 24: 1-2; also Mark 13: 1-4 and Luke 21: 5-7)

Those words, of course, related to the most terrible event ever to befall trouble-torn Jewry, the fall of Jerusalem and wholesale destruction of the Temple in 70 AD, following the revolt against the Romans that had broken out four years earlier. But, as touched on in an earlier chapter, did the gospel writers simply put the prophecy into the mouth of Jesus after the event? Or, if writing before the event, did they record an absolutely genuine prophecy on his part? In favour of the latter, it would surely have been almost irresistible for anyone writing afterwards not to make considerable capital out of this incredible prophecy having been so dramatically fulfilled. Yet not one of the gospel-writers alludes to it.

Whatever the answer, the actuality and sheer terror of Jerusalem's fall is a matter of absolutely firm record. This may be gauged historically, from chroniclers such as Josephus, and archaeologically from the almost complete erasure of the Herodian period edifices on the Temple Mount. Most vivid and indeed poignant of all, however, is a hitherto unmentioned discovery by Israeli archaeologist Nahman Avigad and his fellow-excavators in the house of the priestly Kathros family (see pp.107-8). Lifting up a fire-blackened piece of masonry they found beneath this a thick layer of charred wood, ashes and soot which accompanying pottery showed to date to around the first century AD, and which was dated even more exactly by a coin inscribed 'Year four of the Redemption of Zion' (that is, the fourth year of the Jewish Revolt), corresponding to our 69 AD. But the real chiller

Graphic evidence of the fall of Jerusalem: the arm and finger-bones of a young woman who died during the Romans' savage sack of the city in 70 AD. Found in the so-called 'Burnt House' associated with the Kathros family, her fingers can be seen frozen in the act of clutching at a step, and she seems to have been overcome by smoke when the Romans set fire to the house as part of their general destruction of the city.

was the unearthing, amidst all the debris, of the arm-bones of a young woman, her fingers still fixed in the last movement she made in life, clutching at a step. As the archaeologists deduced, this poor girl most likely suffocated as the fire burned around her. And that fire needed little identification, for Josephus had described it all too vividly in his account of Jerusalem's fall:

> They [the Romans] … blocked the narrow streets with corpses, deluging the whole city with gore … At dusk the slaughter ceased, but in the night the fire gained mastery, and on the 8th of Gorpaios [roughly our September] the sun rose over Jerusalem in flames …

The Matthew gospel records Jesus having forewarned his disciples of this time of troubles, advising them:

> 'When you see Jerusalem surrounded by armies, you must realize that she will soon be laid desolate. Then those in Judaea must escape to the mountains, those inside the city must leave it, and those in country districts must not take refuge in it'. (Luke: 21 20,21)

That some of his Jewish-born followers heeded this at around the time of Jerusalem's fall is attested by a Church tradition that a contingent of them headed for Pella on the east bank of the Jordan. These, later variously

Remains of the Jewish Christians' first-century church on Jerusalem's Mount Zion? Well-dressed Herodian stone blocks, thought to have been re-used from the rubble of the destroyed Jerusalem Temple, are seen here forming part of a so-called 'Tomb of David' on Mount Zion. According to Benedictine monk Bargil Pixner, this 'tomb' was actually a synagogue (see below), and was built by the Judaeo-Christian community of disciples when they returned to Jerusalem around 74 AD, four years after the Romans had destroyed the Temple and much of the surrounding city.

Drawing of eastern wall of the 'Tomb of David' showing in its lower portions the unevenly laid Herodian blocks that are thought to have formed part of the Judaeo-Christians' synagogue on Mount Zion. From a drawing by the French priest and archaeologist Louis Hugues Vincent (1872-1960).

to be labelled 'Nazarenes' and 'Judaeo-Christians', appear to have had as their gospels both an early Aramaic version of the Matthew gospel and the 'Gospel of the Hebrews', both long lost. As some evidence of their settlement in Pella, excavations in 1967 of Pella's ancient West Church revealed a sarcophagus beneath the apse, which judging from its Jewish style of decoration and Christian context may once have belonged to an early leader of this same community.

But according to the tenth-century patriarch Eutychius, who seems to have had access to early documents no longer extant, at least some of these Judaeo-Christians 'returned to Jerusalem in the fourth year of the Emperor Vespasian [i.e. 73 AD] and built there their church'. What may well be remains from this church have recently been identified by Benedictine monk Bargil Pixner in a dressed stone edifice erroneously labelled 'the Tomb of David' tucked amidst a complex of buildings next to the Dormition Church on Jerusalem's south-western hill today called Mount Zion. Comprising part of a later Church of the Apostles (thought to mark the house with the upper room where the apostles assembled after Jesus' ascension), this edifice has in the lower parts of its walls massive and beautifully dressed stones of exactly the type used for Herod's Temple. From the stones' chipped corners and different heights, they seem to have been rescued from the rubble of the Temple site (a salvage operation we might expect of the Temple-going Jerusalem Christians described in Acts 2: 43-7), and used for a synagogue-style building, in which regard a particularly tell-tale feature is

that this is oriented not to the Temple, as any true synagogue would have been, but to the tomb of Jesus as marked by the site of the Church of the Holy Sepulchre.

If this thinking is correct, this very early church would have been constructed on the orders of Simeon, son of Cleopas, who is recorded to have succeeded James, brother of Jesus, as head of Jerusalem's Judaeo-Christian community. Since Simeon's father, Cleopas (almost certainly the same Cleopas to whom Jesus appeared on the road to Emmaus, Luke 24: 13-35), was the brother of Jesus and James' father, Joseph, Simeon would have continued Jesus and James' own Davidic blood-line, there apparently having followed thirteen other 'Bishops' of Jerusalem, some also with this same blood-line.

In 132 AD, however, following another Jewish revolt, the Romans expelled all Jews, including Judaeo-Christians, from Jerusalem, and made it into a totally new Roman metropolis under the name Aelia Capitolina. Jesus and James' enemies, the Sadducees, had already been finished by their Temple's destruction after the First Revolt, but those mainly Pharisaic members of the Sanhedrin who survived now made Sepphoris in Galilee their new seat, largely because Sepphoris had escaped destruction since its strongly pro-Roman citizens refused to join the Revolt. Accordingly, it was from thoroughly Roman Sepphoris, ironically filled with pictorial works of art that flouted the old Jewish Law (see below), that the *Mishnah* began to be compiled around 200 AD.

Near perfection in human portraiture: a breathtakingly beautiful mosaic head of a girl, dating from the third century AD, uncovered by archaeologists excavating at Sepphoris in 1987. The Graeco-Roman artist who created this must virtually have rubbed shoulders with the Jews who compiled the Mishnah *at Sepphoris at around this time. For these latter such pictorial representation of a human likeness would have been strictly forbidden.*

Well before the Second Revolt, however, Jews and Christians had started what became their irretrievable drift apart, with Judaeo-Christians, who had previously continued to worship in traditional Jewish synagogues, being deterred from doing so, and eventually dwindling away, and Gentile Christians, despite occasional periods of persecution, steadily winning further converts throughout the Graeco-Roman world. It was of course somewhat easier for the latter in view of the intense wave of anti-Jewish feeling across the Roman Empire in the wake of the Revolt. And, as explained earlier, this was almost certainly why the gospels of Jesus that have survived were edited and adapted to a Gentile standpoint, with Jesus' association with the Jewish people deliberately down-played, and attention deflected from the activities of those Jewish Christians led by James and his successors.

From these tangled beginnings there therefore emerged what can now, for the first time, legitimately be labelled 'Christianity' as a distinct religion in its own right, rather than a mere branch of the old Jewish religion. Even Tacitus, who described the Rome Christians as 'notoriously depraved', acknowledged that the city's ordinary citizens had taken pity on their sufferings, and although under the emperors Domitian (81-96 AD), Decius (249-51 AD) and Diocletian (284-305 AD) there were fresh persecutions of a savagery rivalling those of Nero, more enlightened emperors such as Hadrian (117-38 AD) and Antoninus Pius (138-61 AD) allowed long periods of unofficial toleration. In Hadrian's reign, for instance, Rome's Christians enjoyed sufficient toleration to organize their religion under presbyters, bishops and deacons and even to build a proper shrine over the earth grave in which Jesus' disciple Peter was believed to have been laid. From this shrine's archaeological discovery within the last few decades, it is apparent that it originally formed part of a walled structure, complete with a courtyard for public assembly and in one corner a low doorway leading into what seems to have been a baptistry. There can be little doubt that it was a very early church building, and in this respect it, the Mount Zion synagogue and the 'St Peter's house' discovered at Capernaum jostle each other for priority as the earliest examples.

Christianity received a further boost when in October 312 AD a vigorous young Roman blue-blood called Constantine fought and won under the Christian 'Chi-Rho' monogram the battle of the Milvian Bridge, gaining for himself the Roman Empire and for Christianity not only toleration but what would soon become the status of an official religion. For many Christians who had all too recently suffered blinding and mutilations under Diocletian's persecutions this must have seemed like an answer to their prayers, and church building could now begin to flourish as never before.

But whatever Jesus may or may not have intended for the promulgation of his Good News, this new official status was not necessarily all blessing. With it came councils, such as Nicaea (325 AD), at which arbitrary decisions on doctrinal issues would be made which would split one

Christian faction from another even more than they had been back in the first century. It is true that some of these issues, such as the fixing of an arbitrary date for celebrating Jesus' birthday, were ultimately matters of very little real importance (future department store profits notwithstanding).

But others were altogether profound, in particular the deepest and most difficult issue of all: just who was Jesus? And just to what extent was he, and is he, God's Son? Was he some all-time divine entity, 'eternally begotten of the Father', who had always existed since the beginning of time, and had merely appeared human when he took on flesh sometime around 4 BC? Or was he an ordinary man of human parentage somehow specially chosen by God to convey his all-time message about how humans should behave to one another, a message so heartlessly returned by humankind signed in very real blood? These questions were potent enough causes of squabbling among the Nicaea delegates back in the year 325 AD. But they remain every bit as difficult and controversial to this very day.

Typifying Christianity's establishment as an official religion of the Roman Empire is this depiction of Jesus in a manner very reminiscent of the Roman god Apollo, but with the 'Chi-Rho' monogram clearly identifying him as Christ. Mosaic from a Roman villa at Hinton St Mary, Dorset, now in the British Museum, London.

12
THE REAL
JESUS

Today we live on the very eve of the third millennium of Jesus' birth. Indeed, if our historical assessments of the true date of his birth have any validity, we are already into that millennium, making whatever celebrations are planned for the early hours of 1 January 2000 AD somewhat mis-timed. But likewise making those celebrations more than a little hollow is the fact that the society we live in is arguably more pagan and less Christian than throughout most of those last two thousand years. Millions upon millions go about their daily lives without a moment's thought for Jesus, except perhaps to use his name as an expletive. They may happily exchange gifts on the day arbitrarily chosen as his birthday. They may send out dozens of so-called 'Christmas' cards to their friends. But it will not occur to them to enter a church unless for a wedding, a funeral, or out of historical curiosity. For them Jesus has long since been bypassed by the age of science and moral freedoms. Even if they accept that he lived, they will probably dismiss him as just some obscure preacher who died a long time ago and about whom tall stories of his rising from the dead got out of hand. For those who think thus, Jesus has long lost any interest or relevance, and two thousand years of Christianity, with all its accompanying paraphernalia of churches and art works, have been an expensive waste of time.

Opposite *'I gazed into the visions of the night. And I saw, coming on the clouds of heaven, one like the son of man…' (Daniel 7: 13). Jesus seen coming 'on the clouds of heaven', as in Daniel's prophecy, from a mosaic in the apse of the basilica of SS Cosmas and Damian, Rome.*

The easy option would be for us to conclude likewise. After all, we have seen that the gospels are not exactly infallible in the information they contain, and their reporting is by no means entirely of the direct eyewitness variety. We have established that the Matthew and Luke birth stories are more than a little inconsistent with each other. We have learned how at least some of the miracles might be explained by some form of hypnosis. Admittedly we found Jesus' teachings appealing, and were impressed by the intensity of belief in his resurrection on the part of those who witnessed this. But we might still question whether these can persuade us that he was, as defined in the Nicene creed : 'the only son of God, eternally begotten of the Father, God from God, Light from Light, true God from true God, begotten not made, of one being with the Father' through whom 'all things were made'. We know that the council of bishops at Nicaea who devised this formula entirely lacked our present-day scientific knowledge that 'all things made' took many millions of years to manifest into the form known as humankind, which makes their idea that Jesus was already around at the time of some cosmic 'Big Bang' seem all the more insubstantial and far-fetched.

But would the flesh-and-blood Jesus who tramped the byways of Galilee himself have necessarily expected or held to any belief that he was 'God from God' and 'eternally begotten, not made'? To get some perspective on this it may be helpful to take ourselves back to the times in which Christianity came into being, during which it was surprisingly easy for an ordinary man to be believed to be a god. At least as early as the reign of Tiberius, who was Jesus' contemporary, Roman emperors worked hard to cultivate a divine image, just as kings and pharaohs had done for centuries before them. It was commonplace for artists and sculptors to be commissioned to portray the emperor as Zeus/Jupiter or Heracles, and for the emperor's image on legionary standards to be worshipped by Roman armies. When Tiberius' nephew Germanicus died a beautiful cameo was made of him being received into the heavenly pantheon, with the former Emperor Augustus among the gods.

That such deification could be believed of more ordinary men, even practising Christians, is quite evident from the account in Acts of Paul and Barnabas healing a cripple in the Asia Minor town of Lystra, in Lycaonia:

A man sat there (in Lystra) who had never walked in his life, because his feet were crippled from birth; and as he listened to Paul preaching, he managed to catch his eye. Seeing that the man had the faith to be cured, Paul said in a loud voice, 'Get to your feet – stand up' and the cripple jumped up and began to walk. When the crowd saw what Paul had done they shouted in the language of Lycaonia, 'These people are gods who have come down to us disguised as men'. They addressed Barnabas as Zeus, and since Paul was the principal speaker, they called him Hermes. The priests of Zeus-outside-the-Gate, proposing that all the

One of the earliest depictions of Jesus as bearded and long-haired. As a Jew this would have been his likeliest mode of hairdressing, although the gospels do not mention a single detail of his human appearance, whether he was bearded or clean-shaven, tall or short, fat or thin, handsome or ugly. From a fourth-century ceiling fresco in the cemetery of Commodilla, Rome.

people should offer sacrifice with them, brought garlanded oxen to the gates. When the apostles Barnabas and Paul heard what was happening, they tore their clothes and rushed into the crowd shouting 'Friends, what do you think you are doing? We are only human beings like you ...' Even this speech, however, was scarcely enough to stop the crowd offering them sacrifice. (Acts 14: 8-18)

Even the Jewish world, surrounded and permeated as it was with Hellenism, was susceptible to such ideas. The story was told of Herod the Great's grandson, Herod Agrippa, who in the decade that Jesus was crucified was thrown into prison for suspected treachery against Tiberius. When on his first day of captivity an owl alighted on a branch above Agrippa's head, an old German prisoner told him it was a good omen: he would shortly be released and regain his royal status. But he also warned Agrippa that when he saw the bird again, he would die within five days. Just as predicted, Agrippa was released, and in 37 AD became King of the Jews, ruling over Herod the Great's former territories. At the height of his power, in 44 AD he attended in great style the quadrennial Roman games at Caesarea, appearing in dazzling robes of silver, which sparkled in the sunshine. Sycophants around him cried out that he was a god, not a man, and Agrippa, flattered, failed to reprove them. It was his fatal mistake. He looked up ... and there was the owl, flying towards him. Seized by sudden stomach pains he died in agony five days later, 'eaten away with worms', as noted with relish in Acts 12: 23. Whether or not this is just a good story, it is the clearest possible example of how easily pagans could and would acclaim a man as a god, and what a fatal blasphemy it was for a Jew even to think in these terms.

So, given all that we have learned, could Jesus have regarded himself as God? Ostensibly, no. In the Mark gospel, the most consistent in conveying Jesus' humanity, a man reportedly ran up to him and addressed him with the words 'Good master'. Jesus' response was a firm rebuke: 'Why do you call me good? No one is good but God alone' (Mark 10: 18). In the John gospel, the one with the most accent on Jesus' divinity, he is quoted as stating quite categorically, 'the Father is greater than I' (John 14: 28). If Jesus had really wanted people to believe he was on any sort of equal footing with God the Father, a convenient opportunity came when, as described in the Mark gospel, a scribe reportedly asked him: 'Which is the first of all the commandments?' But instead of introducing some new formula to link himself to God, or to a Trinity, Jesus unhesitatingly looked to his traditional Jewish roots, quoting the great *Shema Israel* ('Listen Israel'), the confession of faith which every practising Jew recites morning and evening every day of his life:

This is the first: Listen Israel, the Lord our God is the *one* Lord [italics mine], and you must love the Lord your God with all your heart, with all your soul, with all your mind, and with all your strength. (Mark 12: 29, 30)

What, then, about the idea that Jesus was God's son? Might he have believed this? For twenty centuries for unbelievers the centrality of such a title to Christianity has represented by far the biggest stumbling block about Jesus, from the Sadducean priests who interrogated him after his arrest (e.g. Mark 14: 61-4), to the Hindu Mahatma Gandhi (who declined to accept the 'God's son' appellation but otherwise revered him as 'one of the greatest teachers humanity has ever had'), to that large majority of present-day Westerners who never think of attending any Christian church.

In genuine deference to these unbelievers' difficulties, we have ourselves already seen that the gospel stories of Jesus' purportedly 'divine' birth feature only in the Matthew and Luke gospels, and then contradictorily. They also lack the convincing quality of much else of the gospel material, and are never alluded to again. Also noticeable is the fact that when described teaching his disciples Jesus is never represented as directly using the title 'Son of God' of himself, consistently preferring instead the enigmatic, and far more humble-sounding, 'Son of Man'. Features such as these have encouraged theologians of the old German stable to downgrade Jesus' perception of himself so that, for example, the distinguished New Testament scholar Helmut Koester, Professor of New Testament Studies at Harvard Divinity School, has concluded:

> It is a simple historical fact that Jesus was an Israelite from Galilee and that he understood himself to be nothing else but a prophet in Israel and for Israel.

But despite Professor Koester, it is important that we ask ourselves what exactly Jesus meant when he used the term 'Son of Man'? In the New Testament this is to be found, with just one exception (Acts 7: 56), solely in the gospels and solely from the reported words of Jesus himself when he was speaking of himself. And when we look into the Old Testament for his source of it, we find this unmistakably in Daniel's great prophecy:

> I gazed into the visions of the night,
> And I saw, coming on the clouds of heaven,
> one *like a son of man* [italics mine].
> He came to the one of great age
> And was led into his presence.
> On him was conferred sovereignty,
> glory and kingship,
> and men of all peoples, nations and languages became
> his servants.
> His sovereignty is an eternal sovereignty
> which shall never pass away ...
>
> (Daniel 7: 13-14)

'Son of God' in the Dead Sea Scrolls. Among the most interesting of the 15,000 scroll fragments found in the Dead Sea Scrolls' Cave Four is this one, designated 4Q246. As translated by the Roman Catholic scholar Joseph Fitzmyer, part of this reads: '... all shall serve [him and he] shall be called [son of] the [gr]eat God, and by his name shall he be named. He shall be hailed the Son of God, and they shall call him Son of the Most High. As comets [flash] to the sight, so shall their kingdom...'. Although this cannot be regarded as a reference specifically to Jesus, it clearly shows that some Jews of Jesus' time expected their great Messiah to come to carry the title 'Son of God'.

Now as the gospels make clear, Jesus was very careful to stress the very earthly sufferings he would have to undergo when he spoke of himself as the Son of Man (e.g. Matthew 17: 22, 23). But there can also be absolutely no doubt that he quite deliberately and pointedly identified himself with this exalted heavenly being 'seen' by Daniel, a being specially appointed by God (the one 'of great age'), to rule as Messiah/King an eternal and universal kingdom.

Also clear is that he accepted that with this same being went the title 'Son of God'. It is particularly notable from the Mark gospel that early in Jesus' ministry madmen reportedly acclaimed him as this, only for him sternly to warn them 'not to make him known' (Mark 3: 12), which we may interpret as a tacit acknowledgement that this is nevertheless what he knew himself to be. But then came the dread moment when he was seized and put on trial for his life before the Sadducean priesthood, with Caiaphas coldly and calculatingly putting to him: 'Are you the Christ, the Son of the Blessed One?'

Fascinatingly, Jesus this time neither equivocated, nor tried any psychologists' tricks, like answering a question with a question. Instead, he forthrightly responded:

I am, and you will see the Son of Man seated at the right hand of the Power and coming with the clouds of heaven. (Mark 14: 62)

That he was there and then, perhaps in one of the rooms of the Palatial Mansion excavated by Nahman Avigad, identifying himself with the God-appointed universal king of Daniel's prophecy is as unmistakable to us today as it was then to the high priest Caiaphas whose more temporal power had brought him there. As will be recalled, both the first Christian martyr, Stephen, and Jesus' brother, James, would later make affirmations about Jesus in almost identical circumstances, with almost identical words, and with similarly fatal results. Further underlining that Jesus really did see himself as God's son (any human paternity by Joseph notwithstanding) and as the rightful heir to God's universal kingdom, is a revealing parable quoted of him that is far too characteristic to have been invented by anyone else. The parable of the wicked husbandmen, or tenant farmers, this appears not only in all three synoptic gospels (Mark 12: 1-12; Matthew 21: 33-46; Luke 20: 9-19) but also in a particularly explicit and primitive form in the Nag Hammadi 'Gospel of Thomas':

Jesus seen coming 'on the clouds of heaven', as in Daniel's prophecy: 'I gazed into the visions of the night. And I saw, coming on the clouds of heaven, one like the son of man…' (Daniel 7:13)

> He [Jesus] said, 'There was a good man who owned a vineyard. He leased it to tenant farmers so that they might work it and he might collect the produce from them. He sent his servant so that the tenants might give him the produce of the vineyard. They seized his servant and beat him, all but killing him. The servant went back and told his master. The master said, 'Perhaps [they] did not recognize [him]'. He sent another servant. The tenants beat this one as well. Then the owner sent his son and said, 'Perhaps they will show respect to my son.' Because the tenants knew that it was he who was the heir to the vineyard, they seized him and killed him. Let him who has ears hear…

The meaning of this parable is of course quite unmistakable. The 'good' vineyard owner is God, the vineyard his kingdom and his tenant farmers mankind/the house of Israel. The servants are the Old Testament prophets, some of whom were indeed badly treated in their time. But quite distinct from these, and suffering a far worse fate, is the vineyard owner's son. Jesus could hardly have spelled out more plainly his role in a future drama that he would play out with his own life, or that, as 'the son', his relationship with God and his right to inherit his Father's kingdom was unique and different from that of anyone who had gone before. Most eerily and disturbingly, here we also see him, to all appearances a flesh-and-blood Galilean of the first century AD, calmly explaining in advance the excruciating death that with our hindsight we know he would undergo, as matter-of-factly as if he were watching it all through a window.

Now it is at this point that all our previous, modern-minded complacency that Jesus was probably just some God-inspired teacher necessarily receives its severest jolt. If this man could so clearly and dispassionately look into the future – and not only his own future, for we have earlier suggested the genuineness of his 'destruction of the Temple' prophecies – did the past, the time before his own human birth, likewise have no barriers for him? Was this how, during his so-called 'Transfiguration', a dumbfounded trio of his disciples saw him in the company of Moses, who died at least as early as 1200 BC, and Elijah, who died back in the ninth century BC (Matthew 17: 1-13; Mark 9: 2-13; Luke 9: 28-36)? Did space likewise hold no normal bounds for him, hence his reported walking on water, and his sudden appearances in a variety of places, including passing through closed doors, after his resurrection?

For the sceptical-minded reader it might seem unacceptable, in an otherwise objective book, now to be apparently accepting at face value such matters supernatural. But it is only the truth of this sheer bounds-of-time-and-space-defying power, verberating and reverberating among the far from simple peoples of first-century Galilee and Judaea, that can explain the sudden confident abandonment of any fear of death that was taken on by men such as Simon Peter, and Stephen and James, and that gave birth to Christianity. Likewise, and no less importantly, only the equally clear and fearful recognition of this same power on the part of the hard-hearted men who controlled the Temple can explain their so malevolent and repeated concern to snuff it out whenever it showed itself to them. As will be recalled from the earlier-quoted parable, the tenant farmers (with whom we may particularly identify the Temple priesthood) 'knew he [the vineyard owner's son, and therefore Jesus] was the heir to the vineyard' and determined to kill him. Likewise evident, particularly from Mark's gospel, is that those who were reputedly possessed by devils were quickest to recognize Jesus as 'Son of God'.

This clear recognition of the power of good by the power of evil, and the perennial and seemingly insatiable anxiety of the latter to stamp out the former, is supremely important because, as many a committed Christian of today can corroborate, it is very real and remains every bit as active as it was in Jesus' time. As Father Thomas Keating has expressed it in his book *The Mystery of Christ*:

> … union with Christ is not some kind of spiritual happy hour. It is a war with the powers of evil that killed Jesus and that might kill us, too, if we get in their way. Because we live in the human condition, the divine light is constantly being challenged by the repressive and regressive forces within us as individuals and within society, neither of which wants to hear about love, certainly not about self-giving love.

Speaking personally, one of my most painful and yet illuminating experiences, having as a writer expressed my beliefs in Jesus in the 1984 version of this book and also in the otherwise so discredited Turin Shroud, has been to be most deviously targeted in efforts to undermine these beliefs by certain plausible-sounding and publicity-seeking people with absolutely no concern for truth. The illuminating aspect is that for modern-day people to be so motivated can only mean that they actually do recognize truth, but like Caiaphas, see it as too threatening to their own quite different priorities for it to be allowed to live.

This is but one reason why, although I regard my brand of Christianity as one still fettered by my historical training and by what was once a very strong agnosticism, I can conclude with now much greater conviction than in 1984 not only that there was a very real flesh-and-blood Jesus of Nazareth who walked the byways of Galilee two thousand years ago and was very publicly crucified by the conniving of Caiaphas and his cronies, but also that in a very real sense he lives on as Lord of all humankind, and will do so throughout eternity.

As we noted in the last chapter, Jesus' brother James spoke of Jesus as 'the door', the important supplement to that particular imagery being that in each of our lives that door is always open, and we have but to walk through to find our past failings forgiven and our daily earthly cares as nothing.

Of course, Christians and non-Christians alike will always squabble over issues such as whether Jesus was born by some form of divine insemination of his mother Mary, whether he forms part of a Trinity, whether he was around from the beginning of Creation, whether he really died when he was crucified, and much else. As has been beautifully expressed by Birmingham lecturer Frances Young:

> ... there are as many different responses to Jesus Christ as there are different fingerprints... Attempts to produce creeds are inevitably divisive or compromising... What we need is not new creeds but a new openness.

Which is why ultimately all that is really important is that, unlike any human being, however saintly, throughout history, Jesus still *is*. In a way still beyond our human understanding, two thousand years ago something of God was made flesh in him, and shone through him and spoke through him, so that the sick were healed and miracles happened. And because he was such a perfect vessel of God, on death he did not die as other humankind but passed through that so illusory barrier to become the open door to the divine, and to the eternal values of truth and love.

This is the real Jesus, and the free choice (and it is one that does have the bounds of our individual spans of mortality) is whether we continue to live as if Caiaphas really succeeded in silencing Jesus two thousand years ago – or we boldly go through that door to find him still very much alive...

13

REFERENCES, BIBLIOGRAPHY AND INDEX

The following notes and bibliography are intended for readers wishing to explore further the issues raised in *Jesus: The Evidence*. In the interests of simplicity, sources appear in the notes only in an abbreviated form, except in the case of very specialized publications. Full publishing details will be found in the bibliography.

REFERENCES

1

GETTING BACK TO THE BASICS

p.12   **Dr John Covel:** See the extracts from Dr Covel's diaries in *Early Voyages* by J.T. Brent.

p.12   **Hon. Robert Curzon:** The quotation derives from his *Visit to the Monasteries*, p.366.

p.12   **Constantin Tischendorf:** For an excellent account of the discovery of *Sinaiticus*, and that of other early biblical manuscripts, see Deuel's *Testaments of Time*, also Tischendorf's own account, *Codex Sinaiticus: Tischendorf's Story and Argument Related by Himself.*

p.14   **Tischendorf's alleged theft of Sinaiticus:** The monks of Sinai still regard Tischendorf as having stolen their manuscript, and display a letter in which Tischendorf acknowledges that he has the manuscript merely on loan (see G.H. Forsyth, 'Island of Faith', p.91). But this letter was written before the monastery had accepted a substantial payment from Tsar Nicholas, a payment negotiated by Tischendorf, apparently for the purchase of *Sinaiticus*. For the announcement of the British acquisition of *Sinaiticus*, see *The Times*, 21 December 1933, p.15.

pp.18-19   **Oxyrhynchus excavations:** The quotation from Grenfell derives from his article 'The Oldest Record ...', p.1030. For details of the other manuscript fragments discovered by Grenfell and Hunt, see their multi-volume *The Oxyrhynchus Papyri* published by the Egypt Exploration Fund. Their work was carried on by others after their deaths.

p.19   **Nag Hammadi discovery:** The manuscripts were almost certainly originally hidden by someone from the nearby monastery of St Pachomius. For background on the whole story, and an appraisal of the manuscripts themselves, see Elaine Pagels, *The Gnostic Gospels*. Full translations of the manuscripts are to be found in James M. Robinson, *The Nag Hammadi Library*, from which the 'Gospel of Thomas' and other extracts quoted in this book are derived.

p.20   **Egerton Papyrus 2:** A full translation and definitive appraisal is to be found in Bell and Skeat, *Fragments of an Unknown Gospel*.

p.21   **Chester Beatty Collection:** News of the Chester Beatty acquisition was announced in an article by Sir Frederic George Kenyon, *The Times*, 19 November 1931, p.13. See also Kenyon's *The Chester Beatty Biblical Papyri* for a definitive appraisal. The exact location where the papyri were found remains unknown.

p.21   **Rylands Papyrus:** See C.H. Roberts, *An Unpublished Fragment of the Fourth Gospel*.

p.21   **Quotation from Bruce Metzger:** This derives from his 'Recently published Greek Papyri of the New Testament', *Biblical Archaeologist*, 10, 2 May 1947, p.38.

pp.22-3   **Magdalen Papyrus MS.Gr.17:** See Matthew D'Ancona, 'Eyewitness to Christ', *The Times*, 24 December 1994.

p.22   **Colin Roberts on the Magdalen Papyrus:** See Colin Roberts, 'An Early Papyrus of the First Gospel', *Harvard Theological Review*, 46, 1953, pp.233-7.

pp.22-3   **Dr Thiede on the Magdalen Papyrus:** See Carsten Peter Thiede, 'Papyrus Magdalen Greek 17 (Gregory-Aland 𝔭64): A Reappraisal', *Zeitschrift für Papyrologie und Epigraphik,* 105 (1995), pp.13-20.

2

HOW MUCH CAN THE GOSPELS BE TRUSTED?

p.26   **Manuscript punctuation, dating, etc.:** For a lucid, modern summary of the technical details, see Metzger, *Manuscripts of the Greek Bible.*

p.27   **Parallel passage technique:** For examples of this technique as applied to the synoptic gospels, see Throckmorton, *Gospel Parallels.*

p.27   **Reimarus' 'On the Aims of Jesus …':** The original German title of Reimarus' work was *Von dem Zwecke Jesu und seiner Jünger.* This was the last of the so-called Wolfenbüttel Fragments, published by G.E. Lessing after Reimarus' death (see Lessing in bibliography).

pp.27-8 **Strauss' 'The Life of Jesus …':** The original German title of Strauss's work was *Das Leben Jesu …* The first English-language version, translated by George Eliot, was published in 1846.

p.28   **F.C. Baur:** Although Baur's output was prodigious, only two of his works have been translated into English, *Paul the Apostle of Jesus Christ* (1873-5) and *The Church History of the First Three Centuries* (1878-9). For an excellent appraisal of his signifcance, see Stephen Neill, *The Interpretation of the New Testament,* pp.19-28.

p.28   **Mark as secretary or interpreter for Peter:** According to the second-century bishop Papias, as quoted in Eusebius, *History of the Church,* book 3: 'This too the presbyter used to say: "Mark, who had been Peter's interpreter, wrote down carefully, but not in order, all that he remembered of the Lord's sayings and doings. For he had not heard the Lord, or been one of his followers, but later, as I said, one of Peter's …"' Eusebius, *History,* translated by Williamson, p.152.

p.29   **John gospel written at Ephesus:** This is attested by, among others, the early church father Irenaeus (c.130-c.200 AD).

p.29   **Wrede:** The original German title of Wrede's work was *Das Messiasgeheimnis in den Evangelien,* published at Göttingen in 1901. It has never been translated into English, but for a summary of its content, see Albert Schweitzer, *The Quest of the Historical Jesus,* pp.328 ff.

pp.29-30 **Schweitzer:** The original German title of Schweitzer's book was *Von Reimarus zu Wrede,* published in 1905. The quotation derives from the English-language edition, p.396.

p.30   **Bultmann:** For Bultmann's own elucidation of the principles of 'form criticism', see his *Die Geschichte der synoptischen Tradition,* 1921, published in English as *The History of the Synoptic Tradition,* 1963.

p.31   **Quotation from Bultmann:** This derives from his *Jesus and the Word,* p.14.

p.31   **Dr Vermes on the Bultmann school:** The comment derives from Vermes, "Quest for the Historical Jesus"', *Jewish Chronicle Literary Supplement,* 12 December 1969.

p.32   **Don Cupitt:** Don Cupitt's remarks on the *zakkau/dakkau* misreading, to which I am indebted, derive from Cupitt & Armstrong, *Who was Jesus?,* pp.52, 53.

p.34   **Manual of Discipline:** The quotation derives from Vermes' *The Dead Sea Scrolls in English,* p.93.

pp.34-5   **Early Aramaic element in the John gospel:** According to C.F. Burney, speaking of himself: '...the writer turned seriously to tackle the question of the original language of the Fourth Gospel; and quickly convincing himself that the theory of an original Aramaic document was no chimera, but a fact which was capable of the fullest verification, set himself to collect and classify the evidence in a form which he trusts may justify the reasonableness of his opinion not merely to other Aramaic scholars, but to all New Testament scholars who will take the pains to follow out his arguments' (Burney, *The Aramaic Origin of the Fourth Gospel,* p.30). Olmstead somewhat arbitrarily separated the narrative and discourse elements of the gospel, arguing that the former represented the earliest and most authentic source of biographical information on Jesus. Variants of the same argument have subsequently been adopted by Professor Charles H. Dodd in his *Historical Tradition in the Fourth Gospel* (see especially p.120), and by Dr John A.T. Robinson in his *Redating the New Testament.*

pp.34-5   **The Gabbatha or Pavement:** For the arguments identifying the Sion Convent pavement with that referred to by the writer of the John gospel, see Fr L.H. Vincent, 'Le lithostrotos évangelique', also P. Benoit, 'Prétoire, Lothostroton et Gabbatha'.

p.35   **Quotation from Papias:** See Eusebius, op.cit., p.153.

p.37   **Professor Brandon and pro-Roman slant of the Mark gospel:** See Professor Brandon, *The Fall of Jerusalem and the Christian Church.*

pp.37-8   **Kümmel dating of the gospels:** See his *Introduction to the New Testament.*

p.39   **Quotation from Nicholas Sherwin-White:** This derives from p.191 of his *Roman Society and Roman Law in the New Testament.*

3
CAN WE BE SURE OF ANYTHING ABOUT JESUS' BIRTH?

pp.41-2 **John Allegro and Professor G.A. Wells:** For details of the works of these writers, see bibliography. John Allegro was forcefully refuted in *The Times,* 26 May 1970, and an acerbic review of Wells, *Did Jesus Exist?,* written by Dr John Robinson, appeared in the October 1976 *Journal of Theological Studies,* pp.447-9.

p.42 **Tacitus:** The reference to 'Christ' occurs in his *Annals of Imperial Rome,* book 15, 44. See Penguin translation by Michael Grant, p.354.

p.42 **Suetonius:** The full reference reads: 'Because the Jews at Rome caused continuous disturbances at the instigation of Chrestus, he [Claudius] expelled them from the city.' *The Twelve Caesars,* Penguin, translated by Robert Graves, p.197.

p.42 **Pliny:** The reference to Christians derives from his Letters, X, 96-7. For the best English translation, see B. Radice, *The Letters of the Younger Pliny* (Penguin, Harmondsworth, 1963), pp. 293-5.

pp.43-4 **Josephus on Jesus:** The passage describing Jesus as a 'wise man' occurs in *Antiquities* XX 3, 3 (63-4). The reference to James as brother of Jesus derives from *Antiquities* XX, 9, I (200-3). For a definitive appraisal of these passages, and the extent to which they have suffered alteration, see Excursus II 'Josephus on Jesus and James' in Schürer's *History of the Jewish People,* pp.428-41.

p.44 **Origen on Josephus and Jesus:** See his *Comm. in Matthaeum,* 10, 17 (referring to Matthew 13: 55); also *Contra Celsum,* 1, 47. Origen provides crucial corroboration that Josephus did refer to Jesus, but did not believe that he was the Messiah, or Christ.

p.44 **Agapius on Josephus:** See Shlomo Pines' *An Arabic Version of the Testimonium Flavianum and its Implications.*

p.45 **Quotations from 'Baraitha' and 'Tosefta':** These derive as follows:
1. Baraitha, *Babylonian Talmud,* Sanhedrin 43a.
2. *Ibid.*
3. Tosefta, *Hullin (Profane Things),* II, 22, 23.
4. Tosefta, *Hullin* II, 24.
For the fullest discussion of these extracts, see Rabbi Goldstein, *Jesus in the Jewish Tradition,* especially pp.22-51.

p.47 **Census of Quirinius:** For a definitive appraisal of the Luke gospel's deficiencies concerning this census, see Excursus I, 'The Census of

Quirinius', in Schürer's *History of the Jewish People* (1973 edition), pp.400-27.

p.48   **Kepler:** Kepler's original book describing his astronomical findings was *De Jesus Christi Salvatoris Nostri Vero Anno Natalitio,* published in 1606.

p.48   **Clark, Parkinson and Stephenson:** See bibliography.

4

WHAT OF JESUS' UPBRINGING?

p.52   **Jesus' education:** The Luke gospel story of Jesus astonishing the doctors in the Temple (Luke 2: 41-50) should be regarded with some caution, for Josephus tells a very similar story of himself at the age of fourteen. But there is no reason to believe Jesus was not well educated. As theologian C.F.D. Moule remarked: 'It seems fair to assume that, broadly speaking, the average Jew was better educated than the average Gentile, if only because Jewish family life was the soundest in the empire, and also the education which Jewish children received in the synagogue school was, within its limits, more conscientious and thorough than the teaching given by Gentile schoolmasters who had not necessarily the intensity of vocation belonging to a devout teacher of the Torah' (C.F.D. Moule, *The Birth of the New Testament,* p.157).

p.52   **Pantera, Panthera:** For a full discussion, with sources, see Goldstein, *Jesus in the Jewish Tradition,* pp.35-9.

p.52   **Origen's reference to Panthera:** As quoted by Origen, this reads: 'Mary was turned out by her husband, a carpenter by profession, after she had been convicted of unfaithfulness. Cast off by her spouse, and wandering about in disgrace, she then in obscurity gave birth to Jesus by a certain soldier Panthera' (Origen, *Contra Celsum,* refutation 1, 28).

p.52   **Panthera tombstone:** For a full appraisal, see A. Deissmann, *Light from the Ancient East,* pp.74, 75.

p.53   **Relatives of Jesus arrested for their descent from King David:** See Eusebius, *History,* III, 20, translated by Williamson, pp.126, 127.

p.53   **Gospel references to Nazareth:** In the Mark gospel, already noted as most likely the earliest, specific reference to Nazareth occurs only in chapter 1, verse 9. In four later passages (Mark 1: 24; 10: 47; 14: 67 and 16: 6) the original Greek refers to Jesus as 'the Nazarene'.

p.53   **Quotation from Rabbi Goldstein:** See his *Jesus in the Jewish Tradition,* p.24.

pp.54-5   **Jesus the countryman:** For Dr Geza Vermes' remarks on Jesus as a countryman, see his *Jesus the Jew*, pp.48, 49.

p.55   **References to 'Eleazar', 'Lazar' and 'Laze':** For a description of a Jewish ossuary bearing the name 'Eliazar', see *Gli scavi del 'Dominus Flevit'*, I, *Tipographia dei P. Franciscani*, (Jerusalem, 1958), p.92. For examples of 'Lazar' and 'Laze' at Beth She'arim, see M. Schwabe and B. Lifshitz, *Beth She'arim* II, no.177, p.73; no.93, p.34.

p.56-7   **Sepphoris:** For excellent background to James F. Strange's excavations, see Richard A.Batey, *Jesus and the Forgotten City.*

p.59   **Herod the Great's Caesarea:** For a useful introduction, see Kenneth G. Holum, Robert Hohlfelder, Robert J.Bull and Avner Raban, *King Herod's Dream: Caesarea by the Sea;* also Barbara Burrell, Kathryn Gleason and Ehud Netzer, 'Uncovering Herod's Seaside Palace', *Biblical Archaeology Review,* 19, 3, May/June 1993, p.50 ff.

p.61   **Quotation from Shirley Jackson Chase:** See Chase, *Jesus: A New Biography,* pp.205 ff.; also 'Jesus and Sepphoris', *Journal of Biblical Literature,* 45 (1926) p.18.

pp.62-3   **Hypocrite:** For useful discussion of this, and sources, see Richard A. Batey, 'Sepphoris: An Urban Portrait of Jesus', *Biblical Archaeology Review,* 18, 3, May/June 1992, pp.59 ff.

p.63   **Professor Fitzmyer on Jesus' knowledge of Greek:** See Joseph A. Fitzmyer, 'Did Jesus Speak Greek?', *Biblical Archaeology Review,* 18, 5, Sept/Oct 1992, p.58 ff.

5

HOW DID HE ACQUIRE HIS SENSE OF MISSION?

p.66   **Quotation from Josephus on John the Baptist:** This derives from *Antiquities* 18, pp.116-19.

p.66   **W.F. Albright on Aenon near Salim:** This quotation derives from Albright, *The Archaeology of Palestine,* p.247.

p.67   **Nudity during baptism:** This was prescribed in Hippolytus' *Apostolic Tradition* XXI, 3, 5, 11, and was required by the Pharisees in their baptism of proselytes and immersion for purification (*Mikwa'ot* 8 and 9; *B. Yebamot* 47b). It is implicit in Paul's reference to 'complete stripping' in Colossians 2: 11. In the earliest Christian art, where Jesus' baptism is a common theme, he is invariably represented as quite naked.

p.67   **'Son of God'**: James Mackey, in his *Jesus the Man and the Myth* has pointed out that any Jew '… if unusually faithful to the will of God in this world, could claim to be Son of God in that sense, and have that claim allowed. In the Judaea royal ritual the king was declared son of God on his enthronement' (p.65). For the association of this title with the royal ritual, see 2 Samuel 7 and Psalm 2.

p.68   **Nabi/Nabi'im**: Dr Geza Vermes has pointed out that a technically more correct rendition of the plural is *nebi'im. Nabi'im* has however been adopted in order to avoid confusion.

p.68   **King David's adultery**: For biblical references see 2 Samuel, chapters 11 and 12.

p.69   **Feeding of the five thousand**: For Dr John Robinson's observations on this passage, see his *Can we trust the New Testament?*, p.92.

p.69   **That Mark drew on two separate accounts of the feeding of the five thousand**: The Mark gospel author quotes two separate accounts of the feeding of large crowds, one of five thousand (6: 30-44), the other of four thousand (8: 1-10). As pointed out by Dr Vincent Taylor in *The Gospel According to St Mark* (London, 1966), it seems unlikely that these were two separate incidents, particularly since in the second the disciples ask: 'Where could anyone get bread to feed these people in a deserted place like this?', thus apparently ignorant of the first occasion, which they were reported to have witnessed. The sensible explanation is that Mark was working from two slightly different written versions of a single incident. Had his sources been verbal, he would have been more likely to recognize their common origin.

p.71   **Jesus as guerrilla leader**: See S.G.F. Brandon, *Jesus and the Zealots*, Hyam Maccoby, *Revolution in Judaea*, and Joel Carmichael, *The Death of Jesus*.

p.72   **Josephus on the Essenes**: The reference to Essene attitudes to possessions, weapons, footwear, etc. derives from his *Jewish War*, p.133.

p.73   **'Abba'**: There are considerable scholarly differences about the significance of Jesus' use of this word. Some have argued it to be the equivalent of our 'Daddy'. Jewish scholars such as Vermes, however, point out that it could be used both formally and as an expression of familiarity. It is to be noted that when Jesus began the so-called 'Lord's Prayer' (Matthew 6: 9-13) with the words 'Our Father in heaven', he was following the pattern of Pharisee prayer which still forms part of the Jewish Daily Prayer Book.

p.73 **'Abba' addressed to God by Honi the Circle Drawer's grandson:** See Vermes, *Jesus the Jew*, p.211.

p.73 **Tetragrammaton:** For an introduction to the use of this in early manuscripts, see Metzger, *Manuscripts of the Greek Bible*, pp.33-5.

p.73 **Quotation from Prof. Alan Millard:** This derives from a letter by Professor Millard, 'Helping to Imagine Jesus' Synagogue' published in *Biblical Archaeology Review*, May/June 1992, p.14.

6

FISHER OF MEN – AND WOMEN

pp.77-8 **Capernaum:** For a useful introductory article with sources, see John C.H. Laughlin, 'Capernaum from Jesus' Time and After', *Biblical Archaeology Review*, 19, 5, Sept/Oct 1993, p.54 ff.

pp.79-81 **Galilee boat:** See Shelley Wachsmann, 'The Galilee Boat – 2,000-year-old hull recovered intact', *Biblical Archaeology Review*, 14, 5, Sept/Oct 1988, pp.18 ff.

pp.82-4 **Fishing on the Sea of Galilee in Jesus' time:** See Mendel Nun, 'Cast your net upon the waters: Fish and Fishermen in Jesus' time', *Biblical Archaeology Review*, 19, 6, Nov/Dec 1993, pp.46 ff.

pp.87-8 **Quotation from the 'Gospel of Philip':** See J.M. Robinson, *The Nag Hammadi Library*, p.138.

7

MAN OF MAGIC

pp.91-3 **Jesus' reputation as a healer/sorcerer among Jews:** That Jesus' 'miracles' remained in Jewish folk-memory following the crucifixion is indicated by several Talmudic passages describing cures performed long after his death by means of charms inscribed with his name. See Tosefta, *Hullin* II, 22; *B.Av.Zar.* 27b; *Y.Av.Zar.* II, 40d; *Y.Sabb*, XIV, 14d.

p.93 **Quotation from Canon Anthony Harvey:** This derives from his *Jesus and the Constraints of History*, p.110.

pp.93-4 **Excavations at the Sheep Pool:** For an excellent, detailed account of these, and the literature surrounding the site, see Jack Finegan, *The Archaeology of the New Testament*, pp.142-7. See also J. Jeremias, 'The Rediscovery of Bethesda'. The names Bethzatha/Bezehta/Bethesda, etc., all appear to denote the same site.

p.94 **Quotation from the Bordeaux pilgrim:** This is a translation of the

Latin original published in P. Geyer, *Corpus Scriptorum Ecclesiasticorum Latinorum,* vol. 39 (Vienna, 1889), p.21.

p.94 **Emotional stress as a causative factor in hysterical illnesses:** For a medical appraisal of this, and discussion of the efficacy of hypnosis in the treatment of, for instance, stress-induced skin disorders, see Gordon Ambrose and George Newbold, *Handbook of Medical Hypnosis,* especially chapter 13.

pp.95-7 **Ichthyosis case:** For the detailed medical account of the successful use of hypnosis in this case, see Dr A.A. Mason, 'A Case of Congenital Ichthyosiform Erythrodermia of Brocq treated by Hypnosis', *British Medical Journal,* 23 Aug 1952, pp.422, 423.

p.97 **Professor Lionel Haward and ancient Egyptian use of hypnosis:** See Professor Haward's lecture 'Hypnosis in the service of research', p.2, also F.L. Griffith and H. Thompson, *The Demotic Magical Papyrus of London and Leiden.* According to Professor Haward, this describes self-hypnosis using a light source. British Museum Egyptologists have expressed some doubts over this interpretation, but the controlled induction of a trance-like state, whatever label may be given to it, originates way back in pre-history.

pp.98-9 **Quotation from Professor Oesterreich:** This derives from the English-language edition of his *Possession, Demoniacal and Other,* p.5.

p.99 **Christopher Neil-Smith:** See his *The Exorcist and the Possessed.*

p.99 **West Yorkshire 'possession' case:** For accounts of the trial associated with this, see *The Times,* 22 to 24 April 1975; also *The Yorkshire Post* of the same dates.

pp.99-100 **Multiple personality cases:** There is a growing literature on this subject. Chris Sizemore has written her autobiography under the title *Eve* (see bibliography, Sizemore and Pittillo). US author Daniel Keyes has written an account of the Billy Milligan case in *The Minds of Billy Milligan.* Flora Rheta Schreiber has graphically recreated the problems of a pseudonymous East Coast American art student in *Sybil* (first published in the UK by Allen Lane, 1974).

8

THE ROAD TO JERUSALEM

pp.106-8 **Nahman Avigad's excavations in Old City Jerusalem's Jewish Quarter:** See Nahman Avigad, *Discovering Jerusalem*; Nahman Avigad, *The Herodian Quarter in Jerusalem – Wohl Archaeological Museum;* also a useful introductory aricle by Nitza Rosovsky, 'A Thousand Years of History in Jerusalem's Jewish Quarter', *Biblical Archaeology Review*, 18, 3, May/June 1992, pp.22 ff.

p.108   **Martin Goodman:** See bibliography.

pp.108-9   **Discovery of the Caiaphas Ossuary:** See Zvi Greenhut, 'Burial Cave of the Caiaphas Family', *Biblical Archaeology Review*, 18, 5, Sept/Oct 1992, p.29; also Ronny Reich, 'Caiaphas' name inscribed on Bone Boxes', ibid., pp.38 ff.

pp.109-11   **Reconstruction of Herod's Temple by the Ritmeyers:** See Kathleen & Leen Ritmeyer, 'Reconstructing Herod's Temple Mount in Jerusalem', *Biblical Archaeology Review*, 15, 6, Nov/Dec 1989, pp.23 ff.

p.109   **Alec Garrard's reconstruction of Herod's Temple:** See Kathleen Ritmeyer, 'Herod's Temple in East Anglia', *Biblical Archaeology Review*, 19, 5, Sept/Oct. 1993, pp.62 ff.

pp.111-13   **Temple death penalty notices:** The inscription on these notices reads: 'Let no foreigner enter within the screen and enclosure surrounding the Sanctuary. Whoever is taken doing so will be the cause that death overtakes him.' (Deissmann, *Light from the Ancient East*, p.80).

pp.112-14   **Jesus' entry into Jerusalem:** The interpretation of Jesus' actions in this instance is derived from Canon Anthony Harvey's *Jesus and the Constraints of History*. It is to be acknowledged, however, that this interpretation is regarded with some scepticism by Dr Vermes.

9

THE ROAD TO THE CROSS

p.119   **Pilate dedicatory inscription:** For a full discussion of the inscription, see Carla Brusa Gerra, *Scavi di Caesarea Maritima*, pp.217-20.

p.120   **Solar calendar theory:** See A. Jaubert, *The Date of the Last Supper*.

p.123   **Gethsemane – Jesus' arrest not in a Garden:** See Joan E. Taylor, 'The Garden of Gethsemane: Not the Place of Jesus' Arrest', *Biblical Archaeology Review*, 21, 4, July/Aug 1995, p.26.

p.123   **Josephus on the Essenes' 'weapons to keep off bandits':** See *The Jewish War*, p.133.

p.124   **Dr Frederick Zugibe on haematidrosis:** See his *The Cross and the Shroud*, pp.2-13.

pp.125-8   **Trial of Jesus:** For a Jewish interpretation of this, see Paul Winter's *On the Trial of Jesus*. Classical historians have similarly suggested that the trial was a mere clandestine interrogation by Temple officials. Pilate's actions the next day are also regarded as makeshift and informal. See the report on a Cambridge lecture by F.G.B. Millar in *The Times,* 30 July 1971, p.3.

p.126   **High priest's tearing of his robes:** This appears to be a contemporary gesture of despair; see also Acts 14: 14. The rending of the veil of the Temple at Jesus' death (Mark 15: 38) seems to have been injected into the gospel story as a sign of God's despair at the Jewish establishment's rejection of Jesus.

p.126   **Chief priests' power of the death penalty:** Worth noting are the words Josephus attributes to the Roman commander Titus on his reproving those who participated in the First Jewish Revolt of 66-70 AD: 'You disgusting people! Didn't you put up that balustrade [on the Temple] to guard your Holy House? Didn't you at intervals along it place slabs inscribed in Greek characters and our own forbidding anyone to go beyond the parapet? And didn't we give you leave to execute anyone who did go beyond it, even if he was a Roman?' (Josephus, *Jewish War,* book 6, 136, translation by Williamson, p.347).

p.127   **Josephus on passive resistance:** The quotations derive from *The Jewish War,* Williamson translation, pp.138-9.

p.131   **Crucifixion victim discovered at Giv'at ha-Mivtar:** See N. Haas, 'Anthrolopological observations on the Skeletal Remains from Giv'at ha- Mivtar', *Israel Exploration Journal,* 20, 1970, pp.38-59.

p.131   **Dr Yigael Yadin:** For his comments on the Giv'at ha-Mivtar crucifixion remains, see his article 'Epigraphy and Crucifixion'.

p.131   **Dr Møller-Christensen's reconstruction:** See his article, 'Skeletal Remains …'.

pp.133-4 **The Turin Shroud:** For the definitive report of the radiocarbon dating, see P.E. Damon et al., 'Radiocarbon dating of the shroud of Turin', *Nature,* v.337, no.6028, 16 February 1989, pp.611-15. Recent attempts to attribute the Shroud to Leonardo da Vinci (Lynn Picknett & Clive Prince, *The Turin Shroud: In whose image?,* Bloomsbury, London, 1994) have been as unconvincing and unworthy as those attempting to show that the carbon dating was deliberately rigged (Holger Kersten & Elmar Gruber, *The Jesus Conspiracy,* Element, Shaftesbury, Dorset, 1994). Whatever the Shroud's true date – and radiocarbon dating's infallibility is by no means guaranteed – the Shroud's unmistakably photographic image remains far from satisfactorily explained.

10

DID JESUS REALLY RISE FROM THE DEAD?

pp.137-8   **Rolling-stone tombs:** For a complete description of 61 rolling-stone tombs, and accompanying discussion of the tomb of Jesus, see Eugenia L. Nitowski, *Reconstructing the Tomb of Christ from Archaeological and Literary Sources* (unpublished doctoral dissertation, University of Notre Dame, 1979).

pp.140-2   **Argument for Jerusalem's Church of the Holy Sepulchre marking the true site of Jesus' tomb:** The definitive report on the excavations carried out at the Church of the Holy Sepulchre is Virgilio C. Corbo, *Il Santo Sepolcro di Gerusalemme.* But for an excellent English-language general introduction, see Dan Bahat, 'Does the Holy Sepulchre Church mark the burial of Jesus?', *Biblical Archaeology Review,* 12, 3, May/June 1986, pp.26 ff.

p.142   **Quotation from Socrates Scholasticus:** This derives from his *History of the Church,* I, 17, English translation by A.C. Zenos, *Nicene and Post-Nicene Christian Fathers,* ser.2, vol.2, (Oxford, 1890).

p.142   **Kathleen Kenyon's excavations:** See her *Jerusalem, Excavating 3,000 Years of History.*

p.146   **The Gallio inscription:** For a full discussion of this, see Deissmann's *St Paul, A Study in Social and Religious History,* Appendix I, pp.244 ff.

p.151   **Strauss'** *A New Life of Jesus:* This was Strauss' second treatise on Jesus, originally published in German under the title *Das Leben Jesu für das deutsche Volk bearbeitet.* The quotation derives from the English ed., vol.I, p.412, published in 1879.

11

A FAITH IS BORN

p.158   **'Gospel of Thomas' reference to James:** 'The disciples said to Jesus, "We know that you will depart from us. Who will be our leader?" Jesus said to them, "Wherever you are, you are to go to James the Righteous ..."', J.M. Robinson, *Nag Hammadi Library,* p.119.

p.158   **'Gospel of the Hebrews' reference to Jesus appearing to James:** This is quoted in *St Jerome, De Viris Illustribus,* chapter 2.

pp.160-1   **Hegesippus' references to James:** An extensive extract from Hegesippus' writings on James has been preserved in Eusebius' *History of the Church,* book 2, chapter 23. See Penguin ed., translation by Williamson, pp.99-102.

p.161   **Josephus' reference to James:** This derives from his *Antiquities,* XX, 9, 1.

p.162   **Tacitus:** This reference is from Tacitus, *Annals,* book 15, 44.

p.162   **The fate of Peter:** For authoritative discussion of Peter's likely fate, see John Evangelist Walsh, *The Bones of Peter.*

p.165   **Young woman killed in the house of Kathros:** See Nitza Rosovsky, 'A Thousand Years of History ...', p.30.

p.165   **Quotation from Josephus:** From Josephus, *The Jewish War* (VI, 8, 4), translation by G.A. Williamson, p.370.

p.166   **Sarcophagus at Pella:** See Robert Houston Smith, 'A Sarcophagus from Pella', *Archaeology,* 26, pp.250-7.

pp.166-7 **Early Judaeo-Christian Church in Jerusalem:** See Bargil Pixner, 'Church of the Apostles found on Mount Zion', *Biblical Archaeology Review,* 16, 3, May/June 1990, pp.16 ff.

p.167   **Sepphoris pictorial works of art:** See anon., 'Mosaic masterpiece dazzles Sepphoris volunteers', *Biblical Archaeology Review,* 14, 1, Jan/Feb 1988, pp.30-33.

12
THE REAL JESUS

p.175   **Gandhi on Jesus:** 'To me he was one of the greatest teachers humanity has ever had. To his believers he was God's only begotten son. Could the fact that I do or do not accept this belief have any more or less influence in my life? Is all the grandeur of his teaching and his doctrine to be forbidden to me? I cannot believe so ... My interpretation ... is that Jesus' own life is the key to his nearness to God; that he expressed, as no other could, the spirit and will of God. It is in this sense that I see and recognize him as the son of God.' From Gandhi's *What Jesus means to me,* compiled by R.K. Prabhu (Navajivan Publishing House, Ahmadabad, 1959), pp.9 and 10.

p.175   **Quotation from Helmut Koester:** This is from Koester's 'Historic mistakes haunt the relationship of Chritianity and Judaism', *Biblical Archaeology Review,* 21, 2, Mar/Apr, 1995, p.26.

p.177   **Quotation from Nag Hammadi 'Gospel of Thomas':** This is Logion 65, as published in J.M. Robinson's *The Nag Hammadi Library,* pp.125-6.

p.178   **Quotation from Thomas Keating:** This is from his *The Mystery of Christ* (Amity, New York, 1987), p.17.

p.179   **Quotation from Frances Young:** This derives from her article, 'A Cloud of Witnesses', published in *The Myth of God Incarnate,* ed. John Hick, p.38.

BIBLIOGRAPHY

ALBRIGHT, W.F., *The Archaeology of Palestine* (Penguin Books, Harmondsworth, revised ed., 1956)

ALLEGRO, J., *The Sacred Mushroom and the Cross* (Hodder & Stoughton, London, 1970)

AMBROSE, G., & NEWBOLD, G., *A Handbook of Medical Hypnosis* (Bailliere Tindall & Cassell, London, 1968)

AVIGAD, N., *Discovering Jerusalem* (Thomas Nelson, Nashville TN, 1983)
The Herodian Quarter in Jerusalem – Wohl Archaeological Museum (Keter Publishing House, Jerusalem, 1989)

AVI-YONAH, M., 'A list of Priestly Courses from Caesarea' (*Israel Exploration Journal*, 12, 1962, pp.137-9)

BAHAT, D., 'Does the Holy Sepulchre mark the burial of Jesus?' (*Biblical Archaeology Review*, 12, 3, May/June 1986, pp.26 ff.)

BATEY, R., *Jesus and the Forgotten City* (Baker Book House, Grand Rapids, 1991)
'Sepphoris: An urban portrait of Jesus' (*Biblical Archaeology Review*, 18, 3 May/June, 1992)

BELL, H.I., & SKEAT, T.C., *Fragments of an unknown Gospel* (British Museum, London, 1935)

BENOIT, P., 'Prétoire, Lithostroton et Gabbatha' (*Revue Biblique*, 59, Paris, 1952, pp.531-50)

BOURGUET, P.DU, *Early Christian Art* (Weidenfeld, London, 1971)

BRANDON, S.G.F., *The Fall of Jerusalem and the Christian Church* (SPCK, London, 1951)
'Saint Paul, the problem figure of Christianity' (*History Today*, Oct 1961)
Jesus and the Zealots (Manchester University Press, 1967)
The Trial of Jesus of Nazareth (Batsford, London, 1968)

BRENT, J.T. (ed.), 'Extracts from the Diaries of Dr John Covel 1670-1679', *Early Voyages and Travels in the Levant* (*Hakluyt Society*, 87, 1893, pp.101-287)

BULTMANN, R., *Jesus and the Word* (Scribner, New York, 1958)
The History of the Synoptic Tradition (Oxford University Press, 1963)

BURNEY, C. F., *The Aramaic Origin of the Fourth Gospel* (Clarendon Press, Oxford, 1922)

BURRELL, B., GLEASON, K., & NETZER, E., 'Uncovering Herod's Seaside Palace' (*Biblical Archaeology Review*, 19, 3, May/June 1993, pp.50 ff.)

CARMICHAEL, J., *The Death of Jesus* (Victor Gollancz, London, 1963)

CASE, S.J., *Jesus, A New Biography* (University of Chicago Press, 1927)
'Jesus and Sepphoris' (*Journal of Biblical Literature*, 45, 1926)

CLARK, D., PARKINSON, J., & STEPHENSON, R., 'An Astronomical Re-Appraisal of the Star of Bethlehem. A Nova in 5 BC' (*Quarterly Journal of the Royal Astronomical Society*, 18, 1977, p.443)

CORBO, V., *Il Santo Sepolcro di Gerusalemme, Aspetti arceologici dalle origini al periodo crociato* (parts I-III, Franciscan Printing Press, Jerusalem, 1981-2)

CUPITT, D., & ARMSTRONG, P., *Who was Jesus?* (BBC, London, 1977)

CUPITT, D., *The Debate about Christ* (SCM, London, 1979)

CURZON, R., *A Visit to the Monasteries in the Levant* (reprint with introduction by D.G. Hogarth; Humphrey Milford, London, 1916)

DAMON, P.E., et al., 'Radiocarbon dating of the Shroud of Turin' (*Nature*, v.337, no.6028, 16 Feb 1989, pp.611-15)

DEISSMANN, A., *St Paul, A Study in Social and Religious History* (translation by L.R.M. Strachan; Hodder & Stoughton, London, 1912)

Light from the Ancient East, The New Testament illustrated by recently discovered Texts of the Graeco-Roman World (Hodder & Stoughton, London, 1927)

DEUEL, L., *Testaments of Time. The Search for Lost Manuscripts and Records* (Secker & Warburg, London, 1966)

DODD, C.H., *Historical Tradition in the Fourth Gospel* (Cambridge University Press, 1963)

EISENMAN, R., & WISE, M., *The Dead Sea Scrolls Uncovered* (Element, Shaftesbury, Dorset, 1992)

EUSEBIUS OF CAESAREA, *The History of the Church from Christ to Constantine* (translation by G. A. Williamson; Penguin Books, Harmondsworth, 1965)

FARMER, W. R., *The Synoptic Problem* (Macmillan, London & New York, 1964)

FARRAR, F.W., *The Life of Christ as represented in Art* (A. & C. Black, London, 1901)

FINEGAN, J., *The Archaeology of the New Testament* (Princeton University Press, 1969)

FITZMYER, J.A., 'Did Jesus speak Greek?' (*Biblical Archaeology Review*, 18, 5, Sept/Oct 1992, pp.58 ff.)

FORSYTH, G.H., 'Island of Faith in the Sinai Wilderness' (*National Geographic Magazine,* 125, Jan 1964)

GERRA, C.B., 'Le Inscrizioni', *Scavi di Caesarea Maritima* ('L'Erma' di Bret-schneider, Rome, 1966)

GOLDSTEIN, M., *Jesus in the Jewish Tradition* (Macmillan, New York, 1950)

GOODMAN, M., *The Ruling Class of Judea: The Origins of the Jewish Revolt against Rome* (Cambridge University Press, 1993)

GREENHUT, Z., 'Burial Cave of the Caiaphas Family' (*Biblical Archaeology Review*, 18, 5, Sept/Oct 1992, pp.29 ff.)

GRENFELL, B.P., 'The Oldest Record of Christ. The First Complete Account of the "Sayings of Our Lord"' (Introduction by F.G. Kenyon; *McClure's*, II, 1897, pp.1022-30)

GRENFELL, B.P., & HUNT, A.S., et al., *The Oxyrhynchus Papyri,* vols 1-25 (Egypt Exploration Fund, Graeco-Roman Branch, London, 1898-1959)

GRIFFITH, F.L., & THOMPSON, H., *The Demotic Magical Papyrus of London and Leiden* (Clarendon Press, Oxford, 1921)

GUILDING, A., *The Fourth Gospel and Jewish Worship* (Oxford University Press, 1960)

HAAS, N., 'Anthropological Observations on the Skeletal Remains from Giv'at ha-Mivtar' (*Israel Exploration Journal,* 20, 1970, pp.38-59)

HARVEY, A.E., *Jesus and the Constraints of History,* The Bampton Lectures 1980 (Duckworth, London, 1982)

HAWARD, L.R.C., 'Hypnosis in the Service of Research' (Inaugural Lecture delivered at the University of Surrey, 14 Feb 1979)

HICK, J. (ed.), *The Myth of God Incarnate* (SCM, London, 1977)

HOLUM, K.G., HOHLFELDER, R., BULL, R.J., & RABAN, A., *King Herod's Dream: Caesarea by the Sea* (Norton, New York, 1988)

JAUBERT, A., *The Date of the Last Supper* (translated from French; Alba House, New York, 1965)

JEREMIAS, J., 'The rediscovery of Bethesda', *New Testament Archaeology Monographs,* I (Southern Baptist Theological Seminary, Louisville, KT, 1966)

JONES, A.H.M., *The Herods of Judaea* (Oxford University Press, 1938)

JOSEPHUS, *The Jewish War* (translated by G.A. Williamson, rev. E. Mary Smallwood: Penguin, Harmondsworth, 1981)

The Antiquities of the Jews (translated by H. Thackeray, Loeb Classical Library, 6 vols, London, 1930-65)

KEE, A., *Constantine versus Christ* (SCM, London, 1982)

KENYON, F.G., 'The Text of the Bible, A New Discovery' (*The Times,* 19 Nov 1931, p.13)

The Chester Beatty Biblical Papyri, 8 vols (E. Walker, London, 1933-41)

KENYON, K., *Jerusalem: Excavating 3,000 years of History* (Thames & Hudson, London, 1967)

KHAN, M.F., *Deliverance from the Cross* (The London Mosque, London, 1978)

KLAUSNER, J ., *Jesus of Nazareth* (Allen & Unwin, London, 1925)

KOPP, C., *The Holy Places of the Gospels* (translated from German by Ronald Walls; Nelson, London, 1963)

KÜMMEL,W.G., *Introduction to the New Testament* (English translation by A.J. Mattill; London, 1970)

LAUGHLIN, J.C.H., 'Capernaum from Jesus' Time and After' (*Biblical Archaeology Review,* 19, 5, Sept/Oct 1993, pp.54 ff.)

LESSING, G.E. (ed.), *Von dem Zwecke Jesu und seiner Jünger* (G.E. Lessing, Brunswick, 1778)

MACCOBY, H., *Revolution in Judaea, Jesus and the Jewish Resistance* (Ocean Books, London, 1973)

The Sacred Executioner, Human Sacrifice and the Legacy of Guilt (Thames & Hudson, London, 1982)

MACKEY, J.P., *Jesus, the Man and the Myth* (SCM, London, 1979)

MASON, A.A., 'A Case of Congenital Ichthyosiform Erythrodermia of Brocq treated by Hypnosis' (*British Medical Journal,* 23 Aug 1952, pp. 422, 423)

METZGER, B., 'Recently published Greek Papyri of the New Testament' (*Biblical Archaeologist,* 10, 2 May 1947)

Manuscripts of the Greek Bible, An Introduction to Palaeography (Oxford University Press, 1981)

MITCHELL, T.C., *The Bible in the British Museum* (British Museum Press, London, 1988)

MØLLER-CHRISTENSEN, V., 'Skeletal Remains from Giv' at ha-Mivtar' (*Israel Exploration Journal,* 26, 1976, pp.35-8)

MONTEFIORE, H., 'Jesus, the Revelation of God' (*Christ for Us Today,* pp.108-10)

MOULE, C.F.D., *The Birth of the New Testament* (A. & C. Black, London, 1962)

NEILL, S., *The Interpretation of the New Testament 1861-1961* (Oxford University Press, 1964)

NEIL-SMITH, C., *The Exorcist and the Possessed* (James Pike, St Ives, 1974)

NICKELL, J., *Inquest on the Shroud of Turin* (Prometheus, New York, 1983)

NUN, M., 'Cast your Net upon the Waters: Fish and Fishermen in Jesus' Time' (*Biblical Archaeology Review,* 19, 6, Nov/Dec 1993, pp.46 ff.)

OESTERREICH, T.K., *Possession, Demoniacal and Other* (Kegan Paul, London, 1930)

OLMSTEAD, A.T., *Jesus in the Light of History* (Scribner, New York, 1942)

PAGELS, E., *The Gnostic Gospels* (Weidenfeld & Nicolson, London, 1980)

PINES, S., *An Arabic Version of the Testimonium Flavianum and its Implications* (The Israel Academy of Science and Humanities, Jerusalem, 1971)

PIXNER, B., 'Church of the Apostles found on Mount Zion' (*Biblical Archaeology Review,* 16, 3, May/June 1990, pp.16 ff.)

RITMEYER, K., 'Herod's Temple in East Anglia' (*Biblical Archaeology Review,* 19, 5, Sept/Oct 1993, pp.62 ff.)

RITMEYER, K. & L., 'Reconstructing Herod's Temple Mount in Jerusalem' (*Biblical Archaeology Review*, 15, 6, Nov/Dec 1989, pp.23 ff.)

ROBERTS, C.H., *An unpublished Fragment of the Fourth Gospel* (Manchester University Press, 1935)

'An Early Papyrus of the First Gospel' (*Harvard Theological Review*, 46, 1953, pp.233-7)

ROBINSON, J.A.T., *Honest to God* (SCM, London, 1963)

The Human Face of God (SCM, London, 1972)

Redating the New Testament (SCM, London, 1976)

Can we trust the New Testament? (Mowbray, London, 1977)

ROBINSON, J.M. (ed.), *The Nag Hammadi Library* (Harper & Row, New York, 1977)

ROSOVSKY, N., 'A Thousand years of History in Jerusalem's Jewish Quarter' (*Biblical Archaeology Review*, 18, 3, May/June 1992, pp.22 ff.)

SCHOLEM, G., *Major Trends in Jewish Mysticism* (Schocken Books, New York, 1941)

The Messianic Idea in Judaism (Schocken Books, New York, 1971)

SCHONFIELD, H.J., *The Authentic New Testament* (Dennis Dobson, London, 1956)

The Passover Plot (Hutchinson, London, 1965)

Those Incredible Christians, A New Look at the Early Church (Hutchinson, London, 1968)

SCHREIBER, F.R., *Sybil* (Allen Lane, London, 1974)

SCHÜRER, E., *History of the Jewish People in the Age of Jesus Christ* (rev. ed. with new material by G. Vermes and F. Millar; T. & T. Clark, Edinburgh, 1973)

SCHWEITZER, A., *The Quest of the Historical Jesus, A Critical Study of its Progress from Reimarus to Wrede* (translated by W. Montgomery; A. & C. Black, London, 1910)

SHERWIN-WHITE, A.N., *Roman Society and Roman Law in the New Testament* (Clarendon Press, Oxford, 1963)

SIZEMORE, C., & PITTILLO, E.S., *Eve* (Victor Gollancz, London, 1978)

SMITH, J.H., *Constantine the Great* (Hamish Hamilton, London, 1971)

SMITH, M., *Jesus the Magician* (Victor Gollancz, London, 1978)

SMITH, R.H., 'A Sarcophagus from Pella', *Archaeology*, 26, pp.250-57

STRAUSS, D.F., *The Life of Jesus Critically Examined* (translated by G. Eliot; Chapman, London, 1846)

New Life of Jesus (Williams & Norgate, London, 1865)

STREETER, B.H., *The Four Gospels, A Study of Origins* (Macmillan, London, 1927)

SUETONIUS, *The Twelve Caesars* (translated by R. Graves; Penguin Books, Harmondsworth, 1957)

TACITUS, *The Annals of Imperial Rome* (translated by M. Grant; Penguin Books, Harmondsworth, 1956)

TAYLOR, J.E., 'The Garden of Gethsemane: Not the place of Jesus' arrest' (*Biblical Archaeology Review,* 21, 4, July/Aug 1995, pp.26 ff.)

THIEDE, C.P., 'Papyrus Magdalen Greek 17 (Gregory-Aland $\mathfrak{p}$.[64]): A Reappraisal', (*Zeitschrift für Papyrologie und Epigraphik,* 105, 1995, pp.13-20)

THROCKMORTON, B.H.(Jr.), *Gospel Parallels: A Synopsis of the First Three Gospels* (Thomas Nelson Inc., New York, 1971)

TISCHENDORF, C. VON, *Codex Sinaiticus, Tischendorf's Story and Argument related by Himself* (Lutterworth Press, London, 1935)

TOYNBEE, A. (ed.), *The Crucible of Christianity* (Thames & Hudson, London, 1969)

TZAFERIS, V., 'Jewish Tombs at and near Giv'at ha-Mivtar' (*Israel Exploration Journal,* 20, 1970, pp.18-32)

VERMES, G., *The Dead Sea Scrolls in English* (Penguin Books, Harmondsworth, 1962)

'Quest for the Historical Jesus' (*Jewish Chronicle Literary Supplement,* 12 Dec 1969)

Jesus the Jew: A Historian's reading of the Gospels (Collins, London, 1973; Fontana, London, 1976: quotations from Fontana ed.)

VINCENT, L.H., 'Le lithostrotos évangélique' (*Revue Biblique,* Paris, 59, 1952, pp.5I3-30)

WACHSMANN, S., 'The Galilee Boat - 2,000-year-old Hull recovered Intact' (*Biblical Archaeology Review,* 14, 5, Sept/Oct 1988, pp.18 ff.)

WALSH, J., *The Bones of St Peter* (Victor Gollancz, London, 1983)

WARNER, M., *Alone of all her Sex: The Myth and Cult of the Virgin Mary* (Weidenfeld & Nicolson, London, 1976)

WELLS, G.A., *The Jesus of the Early Christians* (Pemberton, London, 1971)

The Historical Evidence for Jesus (Prometheus, New York, 1982)

WILSON, I ., *The Turin Shroud* (Victor Gollancz, London, 1978)

WINTER, P., *On the Trial of Jesus* (de Guyter, Berlin, 1961)

YADIN, Y., *Bar-Kokhba* (Weidenfeld & Nicolson, London, 1971)

'Epigraphy and Crucifixion' (*Israel Exploration Journal,* 23, 1973, pp.18-20)

(ed.), *Jerusalem Revealed: Archaeology in the Holy City, 1968-1974* (Yale University Press & Israel Exploration Society, 1976)

ZUGIBE, F., *The Cross and the Shroud* (Angelus Books, New York, 1982)

ACKNOWLEDGEMENTS

Cover: Royal Academy of Arts, London (detail)

Half title: National Gallery, London (detail); frontispiece: British Society for the Turin Shroud; National Gallery: El Greco: *Christ Driving Traders from the Temple*; imprint page: Barrie Schwortz; Contents page chapter headings: 1 John Rylands Library, University of Manchester; 2, Zev Radovan; 3 British Library; 4, 11 British Museum; 5, 6, 7, Weidenfeld & Nicolson Archives; 8 Garo Nalbaldian; 10 National Gallery, London; 9, 12 Israel Antiquities Authority.

Chapter 1: page 10 Werner Braun; pp11, 21 John Rylands Library, University of Manchester: *John Gospel Papyrus P52*; pp15, 18 Ekdotike Athenon, Athens; p20 British Library: *Egerton Papyrus 2*; p23 Magdalen College Oxford/Dr Christine Ferdinand: *Matthew Gospel Magdalen Greek Ms17*.

Chapter 2: pp24, 33 Sonia Halliday; pp25, 37 Zev Radovan; pp34-5 Werner Braun, p35tr Israel Antiquities Authority; p36 Art Resource, New York.

Chapter 3: pp40, 49 Weidenfeld & Nicolson Archives; pp41, 47 British Library *Papyrus 904*; p43 Ny Carlsberg Glyptotek.

Chapter 4: p50 Albatross; pp51, 58 British Museum; p53 Bad Kreuznach Museum; p54 Garo Nalbaldian; p56-7 Ira Block/National Geographic Society; p60t Leen Ritmeyer, b Leen Ritmeyer, after Ehud Netzer; p62 Martha Cooper/National Geographic Society.

Chapter 5: p64 Sonia Halliday; pp65, 69 Weidenfeld & Nicolson Archives; pp66, 74 Zev Radovan; p70 Erich Lessing.

Chapter 6: p76 David Harris; p77, 86 Weidenfeld & Nicolson; p79t Virgilio Corbo, b Garo Nalbaldian; pp 80, 81, 83 Danny Friedman; p82, 89 Zev Radovan; p84 Sonia Halliday; p85 Jo Moore.

Chapter 7: pp90, 91, 100 Weidenfeld & Nicolson Archives; p92 Sonia Halliday; p96 Dr A. A. Mason; p98 Victoria & Albert Museum, London; p99 Garo Nalbaldian.

Chapter 8: p102 Sonia Halliday; pp103, 108 Garo Nalbaldian; p105 Zev Radovan; p107t Israel Museum, b Leen Ritmeyer; p109b Israel Antiquities Authority; pp110-111, 112c Leen Ritmeyer; pp112t (?), b, 113t Zev Radovan; p114 Vatican Grottoes; p117-8 National Gallery, London (as title page).

Chapter 9: pp118, 129b Professor Umberto Fasola; pp119, 126 Israel Antiquities Authority; p128 Zev Radovan; pp120, 121 Weidenfeld & Nicolson Archives; p122 Leen Ritmeyer; p124 Garo Nalbaldian; p130b Israel Antiquities Authority; p131t Erich Lessing; p133 Oxford Research Laboratory; p134 British Society for the Turin Shroud; p135 Barrie Schwortz.

Chapter 10: p136 Silesian Publications; pp137, 147-8, 153 National Gallery, London: Orcagna: *Jesus Appearing to Mary Magdalen*; p138 Israel Antiquities Authority; p139 Sonia Halliday; p140t Carta Jerusalem; p141 Garo Nalbaldian; p144-5 Hershel Shanks; p.145 David Willis.

Chapter 11: pp154, 161, 162, Weidenfeld & Nicolson Archives; pp155, 169 British Museum; p163 Ian Wilson; p165 Zev Radovan; p166t Hershel Shanks, b Louis Hugues Vincent; p167 Joint Sepphoris Project, Duke University & Hebrew University.

Chapter 12: pp170, 177 Ian Wilson; pp171, 176 Israel Antiquities Authority; p172 Weidenfeld & Nicolson Archives.

INDEX

Page numbers in *italics* denote illustrations or charts

'*Abba*', 73

'Abd-al-Malik, Caliph, 103

Abraham, 52, 112

Acts, book of, 21, 26, 65, 72, 91, 97, 105, 126, 146, 152, 156-8, 162, 164, 166, 173-4

Aelia Capitolina, 167

Aenon, 66

Agapius, 44

Agrippa, Herod *see* Herod Agrippa

Ahab, King, 68

Akiba, Rabbi, 126

Albinus, Governor of Judaea, 161

Albright, William F., 38, 66

Alexander II, Tsar, 13-14

Alexander the Great, 58

Alexandria, 65

Alexandria text family, 21

Allegro, John: *The Sacred Mushroom and the Cross*, 41

Allenby, General Edmund Henry Hynman, 1st Viscount, 114

Ananias (disciple), 156

Ananus (high priest), 161

Andrew (disciple), 77

Angels, 146

Annas (high priest), 125

Antiochus IV Epiphanes, Seleucid King, 59, 114-15

Antipas *see* Herod Antipas

Antoninus Pius, Roman Emperor, 168

'Apocalypse of Paul', 19

'Apocalypse of Peter', 19

Aqsa mosque, Jerusalem, 102

Aramaic language, 31-5, 55, 62, 63

Arnold, Matthew, 93

Athos, Mount, 12

Augustus, Roman Emperor, 47, 173

Avigad, Nahman, 106-8, 126, 164, 177

Babylonians, 55, 105

Bagatti, Bellarmino, 53-4

Baigent, Michael and others: *The Holy Blood and the Holy Grail*, 87, 150

Bannos (hermit), 43

Baptism, 66-7
    of Jesus, 31, *64*, 65-7, 71

Bar-Kokhba, Simon, 126

Barabbas, 128

Barnabas, 173-4
    Epistle of, 14

Bassus, Junius, 114

Baur, Ferdinand Christian, 28, 156

Beatty, Alfred Chester, 20-1

Bell, Harold, 22

Bet Netofa Valley, Israel, 53

Bethesda (Beth-zatha), *92*, 93-4, 104

Bethlehem, 46, 48-9, 53

Bethsaida, 77

Blaiklock, E.M., 39

Blake, William, 72

Blatty, William: *The Exorcist*, 99

Boats, 79-83, *80*, *81*, *82-3*

Bodmer, Martin, 21

Bordeaux Pilgrim, 94

Brandon, S.G.F., 37, 71, 114

Breaking of legs (in crucifixion), *130*, 131-2

British Museum, 14, 20

Buddha, Gautama, 104

Bultmann, Rudolf, 30-2, 37, 73

Burial, 106

Burney, C.F., 34

Burnt House, Jerusalem, 107, 164-5

Byzantine text family, 21

Caesarea, *50*, 58, *61*, 104, 119, 151

Caesarean text family, 21

Caiaphas (high priest), 108-9, 119, 125-6, 138, 161, 176-7, 179

Cana, 101, 104

Capernaum, *76*, 77-9, *79*, 84, 168

Carmichael, Joel, 71

Carpocratians, 162

Case, Shirley Jackson, 61

Casson, Peter, 95

Celibacy, 88-9

Celsus, 52

Census, 47, *47*

Chester Beatty *see* Beatty, Alfred Chester

Chi-Rho monogram, 168, *169*

Christ
    as term, 42
    see also Jesus

Christmas, 46, 48

Chuza (Herod's steward), 87

Circumcision, 49, 51, 58, 156, 158

Clark, David, 48

Claudius, Roman Emperor, 42

Clement of Alexandria, 20

Cleopas (uncle of Jesus), 158, 166

Cohen, Orna, 80

Colosseum, Rome, *163*

Colossians, Paul's Epistle to, 67

Communal living, 72, 157, 160

Constantine the Great, Roman Emperor, 14, 79, 138, 140, 142, 168

Copperfield, David (magician), 101

Corinthians, Paul's Epistle to, 8, 87, 146, 151, 156-9

Covel, John, 12

Crassus (Roman consul), 129

Cremation, 140

Crucifixion, 129-32, *130*, *131*
    see also Jesus: death by crucifixion

Cupitt, Don, 32

Curzon, Robert, 12

Daniel, Book of, 171, 175-7

Dating of gospels *see* Gospels

Dating of manuscripts, 15, *16-17*

David, King of Israel, 52-3, 58, 68, 104
    tomb of, *166*, 166

Dead Sea Scrolls, 7, 23, 33-5, *35*, 73, 93, 126, *176*
    see also Qumran

Decapolis, 104

Decius, Roman Emperor, 168

Deicide: accusations against Jews, 36-7

Delphi, 146

Demons *see* Possession

Deuteronomy, Book of, 93
Dice, *128*
Didymos Judas Thomas *see*
　　Judas Thomas, Didymos
Diocletian, Roman Emperor,
　　168
Dionysius Exiguus, 47
Disciples
　dissensions after Jesus's
　　death, 155-62
　as followers, 77, 79-80,
　　83-4, 89, 103-4
　and Jesus's resurrection, 147
　life style, 72, 157, 160
　and Paul, 157
Disputed authorship, 27
Divinization (deification),
　　173-4
Divorce, 89
Docetists, 162
Dodd, Charles H., 32
Dome of the Rock,
　　Jerusalem, 102
Domitian, Roman Emperor,
　　53, 158, 168
Ebionites, gospel of, 20, 67
Egerton Papyrus 2, 20, *20*
Egypt, 15, 18, 20, 33
Egypt Exploration Fund, 18
Egyptians, gospel according
　　to, 20
Eisenman, Robert, 35
Elijah, 68, 178
Elisha, 44, 91
Empty tomb, 143, 146-7
Ephesus, 21, 29, 33
Ephraemi, Codex, 12
Epiphanius, Bishop, 20
Erasmus, Desiderius, 11-2
Essenes, 33-4, 72, 120, 123
Eucharist, 121
Eusebius of Caesarea, 53,
　　158-60
Eutychius, 166
Exorcism, 97-101
Feeding 'miracles', 69, 71,
　　78, 101
Festus (Governor of Judaea),

161
Fish and fishing, 54, 83-5,
　　84, 85
Fitzmyer, Joseph A., 63, 176
Francis of Assisi, St, 71
Futuh el Bahnasa, Egypt, 18
Gadara, 104
Galatians, Paul's Epistle to,
　　156-9
Galilee, 4, 44, 53-5, 59-60,
　　104
　Boat, 79-83
　Sea of, 28, *54*, 77-8, 80-4
Gallio (proconsul), 146
Gamaliel, 105
Gamla, Galilee, 73
Gandhi, Mohandas
　　Karamchand (Mahatma),
　　72, 127, 175
Garden Tomb, Jerusalem,
　　142, *144-5*
Gardens, 123
Garrard, Alec, 109, 122
Gentiles, 111, 113, 156-7,
　　168
Gerasa (Jerash), 28, 104
　demoniac of, 98, *99*, 100
Germanicus, 173
Gethsemane, garden of, 123,
　　124, 125
Giv'at ha-Mivtar, 131, 137-8
Gnosticism, 19, 162
God
　kingdom of, 71, 88-9, 103
　names of, 73
　see also Son of God
Goldstein, Rabbi Moritz, 53
Golgotha, 138, 140
Good Samaritan parable, 32
Goodman, Martin: *The
　　Ruling Class of Judaea*,
　　108
Gordon, General Charles
　　George, 142, 145
Gospels
　dating of, *17*, 19, 23, 28,
　　37-8, *38*
　discrepancies in, 26-7

disputed authorship of, 27
see also individual gospels
Greco, El, 117
Greek language, 62-3, 160
Gregory XVI, Pope, 13
Grenfell, Bernard Pyne,
　　18-19, 21-2
Griesbach, Johann, 27
Guilding, Aileen: *The Fourth
　　Gospel and Jewish
　　Worship*, 34
Haas, Nicu, 130-1
Hadrian, Roman Emperor,
　　168
Haematidrosis, 124
Halley, Edmund, 48
Handwriting: as aid to
　　manuscript dating, 12,
　　15, *16-17*, 18-19, 22-3,
　　26
Hanina ben Dosa, 91
Hannah, song of, 47
Hanotzri, 53
Harvey, Canon Anthony, 93,
　　114
Hasmonean dynasty, 59
Haward, Lionel, 97
Healings *see* Jesus: healings
Hebrews, gospel of the, 20,
　　159-60, 166
Hegel, G.W.F., 28, 93
Hegesippus, 53, 158-9, 161
Helena (mother of
　　Constantine), 140, 142
Hellenistic Jews, 155-6
Heracles, 173
Herculaneum, 23
Hermas, 'Shepherd' of,
　　14-15
Hermon, Mount, 104
Herod family, 109
Herod Agrippa, 140, 174
Herod Antipas (tetrarch),
　　60-1, 62, 67, 68-71, 78,
　　109
Herod the Great, King
　　Jerusalem rebuilding, 49,
　　58, 94, 102, 111-12

Palace, 50, 59, *60*
　rebuilds Temple, 49, 58,
　　102, 109, 111
　reign under Romans, 49, 59
　slaughters children, 46, 48-9
Herodias, 68
Herodotus, 93
Hillel, Rabbi, 30
Hinton St Mary, 169
Hippolytus, 67
Holy Sepulchre, Church of,
　　Jerusalem, *139*, 140,
　　141, 142, 145, 167
Honi the Circle Drawer, 73
Hosea, 115
Huleatt, Revd Charles
　　Bousfield, 22-3
Hunt, Arthur Surridge,
　　18-19, 21-2
Hypnosis, 94-5, *96*, 97,
　　100-1, 173
Hypocrite (word), 62
Hysteria, 94-5, 101
Ichthyosis, 95, *96*, 97
Images: Jewish prohibition
　　of, 58, 167
Isaac (son of Abraham), 112
Isaiah, 46, 53, 54, 155
　scroll of, *74*, 75
Iscariot, Judas *see* Judas
　　Iscariot
James the Righteous (brother
　　of Jesus), 43, 57, 77,
　　146, 151, 158-61, 164,
　　167, 177, 179
　killed, 161, 178
James (son of Zebedee), 81,
　　89
Jehonan (crucifixion victim),
　　130-2, *130, 131*, 135
Jeremiah, 52
Jeremias, Joachim, 94
Jerome, St, 20, 159
Jerusalem
　'Bishops' of, 167
　buildings and decorations,
　　34, *102*, 106-12, *106*,
　　107, 108, 112

described in gospels, 35
falls (70 AD), 7, 34, 36, 164-6, *164*
Jesus journeys to, 104, 106, 112, *114*
map, *140*
Moslems in, 94
see also individual buildings and sites
Jesus
agony in the garden, 124-5
ancestry and parentage, 52-3, 63, 104, 158
arrest and trial, 125-9
baptism, 31, 65-7, 71
birth, 30, 39, 46-9, 55, 119, 169, 179
blood, 122
brothers and sisters, 63, 158-9
burial and tomb, 133, 137, 140, 142-3, 167
as carpenter, 61-2
as countryman, 54
death by crucifixion, 8, 31, 37, 119-21, 129-30, 131-3, 135, 138, 143, 156, 177
and death of John the Baptist, 69-71
divinity (as 'God's Son'), 37, 156, 169, 173, 175-7, *177*
draws crowds, 89
entry into Jerusalem, 30, 114-15, *114*
existence questioned, 39, 42-3
faithfulness to Jewish religion and law, 89
followers and disciples, 77, 79-81, 83-4, 89, 103-4, 152-3, 155, 161-2
and forgiveness of sins, 30, 122
and Greek language, 62-3, 160
healings, 30, 78, 87, *90*, 91, 93-5, 97-8, *98*, *100*,

100-1, 104
importance and influence, 8-9
Jewish hostility to, 37
name, 45
pacifism, 72, 127
parables, 31-2, 42, 177
physical appearance, *frontis.*, 51, *170*, *172*, *177*
prophecies, 164-5, 177
relations with undesirables, 84, 89
relations with women and supposed marriage, 8, 84-5, 87-9, 112
resurrection appearances, 8, 43, 143, 146-7, *148-9*, 150-1, 156, 159
as Son of Man, 175-6, *177*
speech and accent, 55, 62
as supposed revolutionary (guerrilla), 27, 71, 114, 123, 128
teachings, 26-7, 29-31, 52, 62-3, 71-3, 89, 104
travels, 51
and Turin shroud, 15, 133-4, *133*, *134*, *135*, 150, 178
Jewish religion
abhorrence of human representation, 58, 167
and circumcision, 49, 51, 58, 156, 158
dietary requirements, 157
and execution, 126-7
feasts, 34
and kingdom of God, 88
and prophecies, 30, 38
worship, 73, 174
see also Synagogues
Jewish revolts
First (66-70 AD), 34-8, 43, 53, 110, 164
Second (Bar Kokhba, 132 AD), 121, 167-8
Jews
history, 57
responsibility for Jesus's

death, 36-7
and Romans, 58
Jezebel, Queen, 68
Joanna (wife of Chuza), 87, 146
John the Baptist, 47, 60, *64*, 65-7, 68-71, 84, 93, 115
John (disciple), 77, 81, 89
John, gospel of, 11, 15, 20-1, *21*, 27, 29, 33-4, 37, 46, 55, 65, 67, 71, 77-8, 81, 84, 87, 89, 93-4, 101, 104, 108-9, 111, 114-15, 120-3, 125-6, 129, 132-3, 135, 137-8, 140, 143, 146, 147, 150, 155, 158, 174
Joseph of Arimathea, 133-4, 137, 150
Joseph (father of Jesus), 46, 61-3, 167, 177
Joseph (son of Caiaphas), 108, *109*
Josephus, Flavius, author of *The Antiquities of the Jews* and *The Jewish War*, 43-5, *43*, 49, 51, 53-5, 66, 68, 72, 89, 93, 105-6, 108-9, 113, 119, 123, 127-8, 152, 159, 161, 164-5
Joset (brother of Jesus), 158
Judaea, *70*, 119
Judas Iscariot, 26, 105, 122-4, 126
Judas Thomas, Didymos (Jude; brother of Jesus), 19, 158
Kant, Immanuel, *28*, 93
Kathros family, 107-9, 125, 164
Keating, Fr Thomas: *The Mystery of Christ*, 178
Kenyon, Kathleen, 142
Kepler, John, 48
Kersten, Holger and Gruber, Elmar: *The Jesus Conspiracy*, 150
Kiddush, 120-2

Kingdom of God *see* God, kingdom of
Koester, Helmut, 31, 158, 175
Kümmel, Werner, 31, 37-8, 42
'L', gospel source, 31-2
Lachmann, Karl, 28
Last Supper, 119, *120*, 121, 123
Last Times: prediction of, 100
Law of Moses *see* Torah
Lawrence, D.H.: 'The Man Who Died', 150
Lazarus
name, 55
raising of, 93
Leonardo da Vinci, 134
'Letter of Peter to Philip', 19
Leviticus, 72
Lewis, Clive Staples, 39
Lucian, 93
Luke, gospel of, 11, 19-21, 26, 28, 31-2, 38, 46-9, 53-5, 61, 62, 69, 75, 77-8, 81-2, 87, 88, 93, 100, 101, 103-5, 109, 115, 119-25, 143, 146, 155, 162, 164-5, 167, 173, 175, 177-8
Luther, Martin, 160
Lystra, 173
'M', gospel source, 31-2
Maccabees, 59, 114
revolt of, 156
Maccoby, Hyam, 71, 114
Judas Iscariot and the Myth of Jewish Evil, 124
McIndoe, Sir Archibald, 95
Magdala (*now* Migdal), 82
Magdalen College, Oxford: Ms.Gr.17, 21-3
Magi (three wise men), *40*, *49*, 52
Magical Papyrus (Demotic), 97
'Manual of Discipline', 33-4
Marcionites, 162

Mark, gospel of, 11, 14, 20-1, 26, 28-32, 37-8, 46, 61, 62-3, 65, 67, 68-71, 77-8, 81, 83, 85, 89, 91, 98, 100, 101, 104-5, 115, 119-20, 123, 125-6, 128-9, 137, 143, 146-7, 158-9, 161, 164, 174, 176-85

Martha of Bethany, 87

Mary of Bethany, 87, 123

Mary Magdalen, 8, 83, 87, 146-7, *148*, 150

Mary (mother of Jesus), 46, 52, 54-6, 57, 146, 159, 179

Mary (wife of Cleopas), 158

Masada, 59, 87

Mason, Dr A.A., 95-7

Matthew
as disciple of Jesus, 84, 89
gospel of, 11, 19, 20-1, *22*, *23*, 26, 28-9, 31-2, 35-8, 41, 46-9, 54-5, 61, 62-3, 66, 68, 72, 77-8, 81, 84, 88, 89, 97, 101, 108-10, 115, 119-20, 122-3, 125, 127, 129, 137, 143, 147, 164-6, 173, 175, 177

Mazar, Benjamin, 103

Menorah (of Jerusalem Temple), 36, *38*

Messiah
concept of, 42, 46, 69, 155, 176
Jesus as, 29-30, 35, 43-4, 52, 67, 69, 126, 152, 176

Metzger, Bruce, 21

Meyers, Eric and Carol, 56

Midrash, 126

Migdal *see* Magdala

Millard, Alan, 73

Milligan, Billy, 99-100

Milvian Bridge, battle of (312 AD), 168

Miracles, 30, 42, 44-5, 69, 83, 91, 93-4, 97-101,

104, 173, 178

Mishnah, 45, 52, 55, 167

Møller-Christensen, V., 130, 131

money-changers, expulsion of, 111, 114-15, *116-17*

Montanists, 162

Mosaics, *106*

Moses (the lawgiver), 13, 58, 91, 93, 178

Moslems, 94, 143

'Multiple personality', 99-100

Mushrooms, sacred, 41

Musht ('St Peter's fish'), 82, *84*, 85

Nabi, nabi'im, 68, 72, 75

Nag Hammadi, 19-20, 35, 87, 158-9, 177

Nain, 104

Nathan, 68, 104

Nazareth, 46, 49, 53-5, *56-7*, 57, 61, 73, 75, 77-8, 100

Neil-Smith, Revd Christopher, 99

Nero, Roman Emperor, 37, 42, 162, 164

Nicaea, Council of (325 AD), 169, 173

Nicaean creed, 173

Nineham, Dennis, 31

Nudity, *58*

Nun, Mendel, 82-3

Oesterreich, T.K., 97-9

Olives, Mount of, 123

Olmstead, A.T., 34

Orcagna, 149

Origen, 20, 44, 52, 128

Oxyrhynchus, 18-22

Pacifism, 71, 127

Palatial Mansion, Jerusalem., 106-8, *107*, 126, 177

Pantera/Panthera, Tiberius Julius Abdas, 52, *53*

Papias, Bishop, 35

Parables of Jesus, 31-2, 42, 177

see also individual parables

Parallel passage technique, 27

Parkinson, John, 48

Passive resistance, 127-8

Passover, 119-23, 127

Paul (apostle), 20-1, 41-2, 46, 52, 67, 85, 146-7, 151, 155-60, 162, 173-4

see also individual Epistles

Peace Forest, Jerusalem, 108

Pella, 165-6

Peter (Simon Peter)
accent, 55
Capernaum house, 77, 79, 168
crucifixion, 131, 162, 178
as disciple of Jesus, 28, 37, 89, 103, *155*, *162*
fishing, 77, 82-4
and Gentile converts, 157-8
at Gethsemane, 123
grave, 169
and Jesus's arrest, 107, 126
and Jesus's miracles, 91
and Jesus's resurrection, 143, 146, 151
marriage, 88
in Rome, 162, 164
status in early Church, 159

Petrie, Flinders, 15

Pharisees, 32, 37, 72, 105, 161

'Philip, gospel of', 87-8

Pilate, Pontius, 34-7, 42-4, 63, *118*, 119, 126-8, 132-3, 142-3, 156, 161

Pixner, Bargil, 166

Pliny the Younger, 42

Pompeii, 23

Pompey the Great, 59

'Possession' (demonic), 97-100, 178

Post-hypnotic suggestion *see* Hypnosis

Pozzuoli, Italy, 129, 131

Prodigal Son, parable of, 32

Prostitutes: and Jesus, 84-5, 89, 112

Purbrook, Martin, 66

Purification, 67, 123

'Q', gospel source, 31-3

Quirinius, Governor of Syria, 47

Qumran, 23, *24*, 25, 33, *34-5*, 70, 75

see also Dead Sea Scrolls

Reimarus, Hermann Samuel, 27, 29

Resurrection
Jewish belief in, 105
see also Jesus: resurrection

Revelations, Book of, 21

Roberts, Colin H., 21-2, 33

Robinson, John A.T., 38, 69
Honest to God, 38, 88
Redating the New Testament, 38, 160

Rolling-stone tombs, *see* Tombs

Romans, Paul's Epistle to, 53

Rome and Romans
buildings, 78
destroy Jerusalem Temple, 34-7, *38*, 164-5
expel Jews from Jerusalem, 167
fire (64 AD), 162
and persecution of Christians, 162, 164, 168
and Saturnalia, 48

Royal Stoa, Jerusalem, 110-12

Russia (Soviet): and Jesus, 41

Rylands papyrus, 21, 21, 33

Sadducees, 37, 106-8, 114-15, 117, 125, 128-9, 155, 161, 167, 175-6

St Anne's church, Jerusalem, 94

St Catherine's monastery, Sinai, *10*, 11, 13

St Peter's House, Capernaum, 77, 79, 168

Salome (daughter of Herodias), 68

Salome (woman follower of Jesus), 146

Samuel, Book of, 47

Sanhedrin, 105, 111, 125-6

Santa Croce in Gerusalemme
     (church), Rome, 142

Schillebeeckx, Edward, 33

Schmidt, Karl Ludwig, 30

Schonfield, Hugh J.: *The
     Passover Plot*, 121, 124,
     150

Schweitzer, Albert: *The Quest
     for the Historical Jesus*, 29

'Secret Book of James, The',
     19

Seder, 120

Sepphoris, 45, *54*, 55-61, *62*,
     63, 71, 167

Septuagint, 46

'Sermon on the Mount', 26,
     32, 71, 160

Sharing of possessions *see*
     Communal living

Sheep Pool, Bethesda, *92*,
     93-5, 101

'*Shema Israel*', 174

Sherwin-White, Nicholas, 39

Shrine of the Book,
     Jerusalem, 75

Sidon, 28, 104

Siloam, Pool of, Jerusalem,
     34

Simeon (son of Cleopas),
     158, 167

Simon bar Giora, 36

Simon (brother of Jesus),
     158

Simon of Cyrene, 129

Simon Maccabeus, 114

Simon Peter *see* Peter

Simon the Zealot, 89, 105

Sinaiticus, codex, 11, 14, *15*,
     147

Sins, forgiveness of, 30, 65-7,

122

Sion, Convent, 35

Sizemore, Chris, 99

Skeat, T.C., 22

Slaughter of the innocents,
     46, 48-9

Smith, Morton, 67

Socrates Scholasticus, 142

Solomon, King of Israel, 58,
     103-4, 109-11

'Son of God', 37, 156, 169,
     173, 175-7

Spartacus, 129

Speaking with tongues, 162

Speirs, Sally, 23

Star of Bethlehem, 48

Stephen (martyr), 126, 152,
     155, 161

Stephenson, Richard, 48

Strange, James, 56, 61-2, *62*

Strauss, David Friedrich
     *The Life of Jesus Critically
          Examined*, 27-8, 39
     New Life of Jesus, 150-1

Streeter, Canon Burnett H.:
     The Four Gospels, 31-2,
     51

Susanna, 87

Synagogues, 73, 75

Tacitus, 23, 42, 119, 162

Talmud, 85, 105, 107, 125

Tax-collectors, 84, 89

Taylor, Joan, 123-4

Tel-Hum, 78

Temple (Jerusalem)
     desecrated, 59, 114-15
     destruction of, 34-8, 43,
          107, 109-10, 164-6
     money-changers expelled
          from, 111, 114-15,
          116-17
     organization and revenues,

108-9, 112, 115, 128
     place of sacrifice, 122
     rebuilt by Herod, 49, 58,
          103, 109, *110-11*, 111
     Stephen attacks materialism
          of, 152

tax, 37, 127

Teresa, Mother, 72

Tertullian, 158

Thiede, Carsten, 22-3

Thiering, Barbara: *Jesus the
     Man*, 87, 150

Thomas (disciple), 147

Thomas, gospel of, 19-20,
     35, 88, 146, 158-9, 177

Tiberius, Roman Emperor,
     42, 119, 121, 173-4

Timothy, Paul's letter to, 164

Tischendorf, Constantin,
     11-15

'Titulus' of Cross, 142

Titus, General, *36*, 37, 43,
     162

Tolstoy, Count Leo, 72

Tombs: and rolling stones,
     136, 137

Torah, 30, 34, 37

Trajan, Roman Emperor, 47

Transfiguration, 101, 178

Trinity, 8, 179

'True Cross', 142

Tübingen University, 27-8,
     97

Turin, Shroud of, 15, 133-4,
     133, *134*, *135*, 150, 178

Tyre, 28, 204

Uncial (form of
     handwriting), 12, *16-17*,
     18-19, 22, 26

Vaticanus, codex, 11, 13, 15,
     147

Vermes, Geza, 31, 35, 44,

55, 58

Vespasian, Roman Emperor,
     37, 166

Vibius Maximus, Gaius, 47

Vincent, Louis Hugues, 166

Virginity of Mary, 46, 159,
     179

Wachsmann, Shelley, 79

Walking on water (miracle),
     178, 204

Warner, Marina: *Alone of All
     Her Sex*, 46

Water into wine (miracle),
     101

Wells, G.A., 41-3, 143

West, Morris: *The Shoes of
     the Fisherman*, 88

Western text family, 21

Wilke, Christian, 28

Wilson, Charles, 78

Winter, Paul, 128

Women
     hair, *86*
     Jesus and, 8, 84-5, 87-9,
          112
     status of, 84-5, 87-9, 112,
          147

Wrede, Wilhelm: *The Secret
     of the Messiahship*, 29

Yadin, Yigael, 131

Yamauchi, Edwin M., 151

Yigal Allon Museum, Israel,
     80-1, 83

Yose, Rabbi, 85

Young, Frances, 179

Zealots, 89, 158

Zebedee, 82

Zechariah, 114

Zeus/Jupiter, 173

Zugibe, Frederick, 124

Traditional Japanese Small Motif

TEXTILE DESIGN I

PAGE ONE PUBLISHING

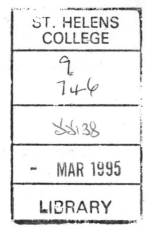
Original title "Textile Design in Japan: Japanese Small Motif"
© 1977 by Kamon Yoshimoto
First published in Japan by Graphic-sha Publishing Co., Ltd., Tokyo, Japan

© 1993 for this edition: Page One Publishing Pte Ltd., Singapore

Distributed worldwide (except Japan) by
Könemann Verlagsgesellschaft mbH, Bonner Str.126, D-50968 Köln
Edited by Kamon Yoshimoto
Owned by Research Association for Old Textiles

Printed in Singapore
ISBN 981 - 00 - 4776 - 2